MATCH OF THE DAY
BBC SPORT

GUIDE TO THE 2006 WORLD CUP

JUST HOW GOOD IS HE?

interact publishing

An Interact Publishing book

First published in 2006

© Interact Publishing Limited
All photographs © Getty Images
Data © Warner Leach Limited

Editor: Terry Pratt
Data interpretation: Tony Warner
Data management: Peter Watts
Production: Stephen Hall
Design: The Consult – www.theconsult.com
Programming: Jonathan Proud
Writing: Terry Pratt, Jeff Fletcher
Other contributions: Martin Jol, Stephen Beagrie

ISBN 0 95498 193 6

Printed and bound in Belgium by Proost.

By arrangement with the BBC
BBC logo © BBC 1996
Match of the Day logo © BBC 2004

Published by Interact Publishing, PO Box Football Yearbook 239, Ware, SG9 9WX
Web: www.footballyearbook.co.uk

CONTENTS

THE GROUPS

IN DEPTH ANALYSIS FOR EVERY GROUP AND EVERY TEAM. SPURS MANAGER MARTIN JOL WITH EXPERT OPINION ON THE STARS AND KEY GAMES.

TOP PLAYER FORM GUIDE

OUR UNIQUE 12-MONTH STATS RUNDOWN RANKS THE TOP PLAYERS BY FORM.

GERMANY 2006 ESSENTIALS

EVERYTHING YOU NEED TO KNOW TO STAY ON TOP OF THE TOURNAMENT AND ITS FINALISTS.

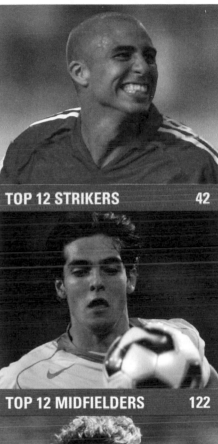

WHO'S IN OUR TOP 40?

THEY DIDN'T MAKE IT

1 HOW DOES LAMPARD'S FORM COMPARE TO VIEIRA?

2 WHICH NEW STRIKERS ARE SETTING SERIE A ALIGHT?

3 WHO'S CONCEDING FEWER GOALS THAN CASILLAS?

4 WHERE DO SHEVCHENKO'S UKRAINIAN TEAM-MATES PLAY?

5 AND ULTIMATELY… JUST HOW DO ENGLAND SHAPE-UP?*

This book starts with the belief that we can heighten your anticipation of this summer's World Cup and enhance your viewing pleasure after it's kicked off. We'll do it by increasing your knowledge of the teams and players appearing in Germany. This is our first World Cup book so we've put in all the things we wanted but could never find in other World Cup books…

- Our Form Guide – who's playing well and who's gone off the boil
- Expert analysis – Tottenham's Martin Jol adds professional insight
- Qualification groups – better analysis on the route to the finals
- Making predictions – we don't sit on the fence
- Top players – the best keepers, strikers, defenders and midfielders appearing in Germany
- World Rankings – we log league, international and cup performances on 4000 top players and rate them against each other
- The thrill of the draw – how other group results could impact England's chances.

As we focussed on the 32 finalists, we were drawn to their stories. We became excited by the prospect of a seemingly impregnable defence coming up against in-form strikers; intrigued by how team politics might affect performances; eager to see how legendary tacticians set up for vital matches.

If just some of our new-found enthusiasm for, say, the remoter fixtures of Group F rubs off on you, then you've got yourself a bargain.

INSIDE VIEW
Martin Jol has run his professional eye over each of the World Cup groups and all of the finalists. He gives his perceptive analysis of their strengths and weaknesses and ultimately picks his way through the entire tournament to a final winner.

Along the way, he reveals just how close an eye a Premiership manager keeps on the world football stage. We expected him to have forthright views on the Dutch, English and Germans; we were more surprised at how he challenged our views on Paraguay or enthused about the youngsters of the Ivory Coast.

He also gives an insight into the pressures that a forth-coming World Cup has on top players and how they in turn try to put pressure on clubs and managers.

Our in-house experts have also given their predictions on the ties but we don't always agree with Mr Jol. (see key right)

FORM GUIDE
We've tracked around 4,000 of the world's top players for the last 18 months and analysed their results for club and country. You'll find the results on every team page as we detail their appearances, non-appearances, goals scored or conceded and disciplinary records.

For their clubs we've focussed on league games over the last 12 months, for their international stats we've detailed all the qualifiers for this World Cup. (See panel)

THE WORLD RANKINGS
Most players will also have a World Ranking, by being awarded points for their domestic and competitive international records.

- They get points for appearances, staying fit, not being suspended and being selected. Top managers select their form players most of the time – ask Frank Lampard.
- They get points for scoring goals
- They get points in defence for clean sheets, or not conceding many goals (their Defensive rating) and how their record compares to their team colleagues.
- They get points in attack for team goals as well as those they've scored individually and again we add points for good averages compared to colleagues.

BUT THESE ALL DID!

- Midfielders are judged on both goals conceded and scored.
- They get points for the proportion of wins and draws they have against their records.
- Finally we add points based on the quality of opposition they are facing, especially in inter-league competitions such-as the Champions League.
- We don't include domestic cups where players are often rested, or international friendlies which have become increasingly meaningless.

The running total over 12 months we turn into a World Ranking simply by totting up the points and comparing them. It favours winning teams as ultimately that's the main objective standard of effectiveness but quality players in poorer teams usually stand out. It also finds out those players whose reputations are not matched by how well their teams defend or attack when they are playing.

Our World Ranking includes players who have not made it to this tournament but sadly, it doesn't extend to players whose domestic leagues we don't have reliable data for.

OUR TOP 40

The Rankings translate into the 40 Top Players likely to feature in the World Cup by simply leaving out those not attending. So, goodbye Samuel Eto'o (the second highest World Ranking for Strikers) and everyone else moves up one.

We've turned it into a Top 12 Strikers, Midfielders and Defenders and a Top Four keepers. There are a few surprise omissions and a few players selected on form, who may not even feature as first choice for their teams. But, just because their managers choose to ignore form, we didn't feel we could do the same.

Here, you'll see some of the famous faces who didn't make it into our Top Players and a few lesser known faces who did.

*ANSWERS

The answers to the questions posed at the start of this page are:
1) Exceedingly well 2) Iaquinta, Gilardino, Toni, to name a few 3) Two Spanish keepers for starters! 4) They play the ball to his feet every chance they get 5) Find out on page 22.

JUAN RIQUELME

Playing record	12 mths lge	wcq
Appearances:	32	9
Minutes played:	2797	723
Percentage played:	72.3%	44.6%
Goals scored:	16	3
Goals conceded:	32	7
Cards:	Y3, R0	Y0, R0
Power rating:	56mins	60mins
Power ranking:	69th	92nd

AGE 27 | **WORLD RANKING 12**

Juan Riquelme plays his league football for Villarreal in Spain. All our club stats go back a year from February 1st 2006, so it will also include four months from the 2004/5 season. In the first column headed '12 mths lge' we set out his club form.

His second column headed 'wcq' includes his record in all 18 of the World Cup qualifiers for Argentina.

Riquelme's played 32 league games, which translates into 2,797 minutes. However, he doesn't always play and has been on the pitch for 72% of Villarreal's league games.

He's scored 16 individual league goals (3 for Argentina) and Villarreal have let in 32 league goals while he's been playing.

His Power Rating is a measure of how regularly the club score when he's on the pitch. When Riquelme's directing the attack they score every 56 minutes on average. To show how that compares to other midfielders going to the World Cup, it ranks as the 69th best club record. All defenders get a Defensive Rating and strikers a Strike Rating.

His age is calculated as of 9th June, the start of the tournament. He has played more than 25% for his club so earns a World Ranking – his is 12.

TOTAL OF THE AVERAGE FIFA RANKINGS OF THE FOUR COUNTRIES 96

Position	1st	2nd	3rd	4th	5th	6th	7th	8th
Group	E	F	C	**A**	D	H	B	G
Total FIFA ranking	89	93	95	**96**	101	109	117	138

GERMANY V COSTA RICA
Munich, Friday 9th June 1700 BST

The pressure will be on Jurgen Klinsmann's team when they open the 2006 World Cup finals as hosts with this game against Costa Rica in Munich. The Germans have a reputation for being notoriously slow starters at major tournaments and the progress of the current side has been mixed. Costa Rica have caused major upsets in the past, but their defence is likely to be a weak link which may give emerging young German strikers such as Cologne's Lucas Podolski an early chance to shine in the tournament.

Costa Rica are always capable of scoring a goal though and Germany's defence is untried and went down heavily to Italy in their March friendly.

POLAND V ECUADOR
Gelsenkirchen, Friday 9th June 2000 BST

Poland would hope to get their 2006 World Cup campaign off to a winning start against an Ecuador side that has a superb home record but struggles when they play away from the country's high altitude capital Quito.

The Poles would expect to qualify for the Round of 16 stage from this group by finishing at least in the runners-up spot but they will need to secure maximum points against the South Americans.

GERMANY V POLAND
Dortmund, Wednesday 14th June 2000 BST

The winners of this match should finish first in the group, the reward for which will probably be a match against Sweden rather than much fancied England from group B. Germany will be favourites, but a very experienced Polish side will make them work hard for victory.

Klinsmann's tactic of playing all-out attacking football could face a stern test in this game. If Germany stick with it, it could be a high scoring game, but if they decide to play safe, it could just as easily end up being tactical and defensive. A word of warning for Germany though. Of the European sides, only Portugal and the Czech Republic scored more goals in qualifying than Poland so they are not shy in front of goal.

The Poles should have a good number of their supporters in the ground as they only need to make the relatively short trip across the border into Germany. The atmosphere could well be highly charged and add to the tempo of the game.

KEY MATCH

ECUADOR V COSTA RICA
Hamburg, Thursday 15th June 1400 BST

The battle for the third place will probably favour the more tournament-hardened Costa Ricans. The Central Americans have a habit of winning these third-place group games. Ecuador will be playing for pride but if Augustin Delgado and Ulises de la Cruz are both short of match practice then they will struggle. The leggy Paulo Wanchope should prove a handful for the Ecuador defence but there are plenty of other Ticos who can find the net.

ECUADOR V GERMANY
Berlin, Tuesday 20th June 1500 BST

Depending on how results have gone so far, Germany may still need to beat Ecuador comfortably to ensure they finish as winners of the group. Michael Ballack and his fellow midfielders will be expected to create chances against a suspect Ecuador defence and if the German strikers are patient they should be among the goals.

COSTA RICA V POLAND
Hanover, Tuesday 20th June 1500 BST

Poland proved during the qualifying matches for the World Cup finals that they know how to score goals, and their final Group A match against an attack-minded Costa Rica side should be one full of chances and goals.
The Poles could win the group if Germany have slipped up in any of their matches.

Ecuador's Augustin Delgado

MARTIN JOL'S VIEW

Host nation Germany may play down their billing as one of the leading contenders for the 2006 World Cup but besides having the huge advantage of playing at home, the draw has placed them in, what on paper at least, looks to be one of the easiest groups.

Their star player is of course Michael Ballack. Although I think his tempo of playing could be a little higher at times, he is often unstoppable when arriving late in the box to meet crosses from the flanks. There is hardly a midfield player in the world who does this better than Ballack. Emerging young German players who could enhance their reputations during the tournament are Robert Huth, Bastian Schweinsteiger and - hopefully, since I think he is a great player - Lucas Podolski. I hope Jurgen Klinsmann - who was of course a firm favourite with the Tottenham fans - has a good World Cup. It would be great for him to have the last laugh over those who have criticized his unorthodox way of working.

"I hope Jurgen Klinsmann – who was of course a firm favourite with the Tottenham fans – has a good World Cup."

I will also be interested to find out who will be first-choice goalkeeper for Germany when the tournament gets underway. During the build-up to the World Cup, Klinsmann could not make up his mind between Oliver Kahn of Bayern Munich and Arsenal's Jens Lehmann. It would not surprise me, however, if against all the odds Lehmann gets the nod over his long-term rival.

Costa Rica will be Germany's opponents in the opening game of the tournament in Munich and I can't see the Ticos winning this one, although World Cup history has shown that it is not always easy for a host nation to win its first game of the tournament.

I expect the third game of the group, Costa Rica against Poland in Hanover to be the decisive match.

Ecuador may have had a successful qualifying campaign, finishing third in the South America group and reaching the World Cup finals for the second time in a row, but they won most of their points at home in Quito, where the high altitude often left their opponents fighting for their breath. They struggle away from home and that is the reason I do not expect much of them.

Their biggest stars are Agustin Delgado, who I know from his spell at St Mary's and strikers Roberto Mina and 'wizard' Franklin Salas who is only 1.65m tall.

I have good connections with the Poland squad and I sincerely hope that their striker Grzegorz Rasiak – who was with Spurs in the summer – will do the trick for them even though he has since moved on loan to Southampton. One of Poland's stars this summer could well be Celtic striker Maciej Zurawski, who finished top scorer with seven goals in a qualification group that included England. Another very good young Poland player is Ebi Smolarek, a former Feyenoord striker, who has subsequently became top-scorer of the Bundesliga. One disadvantage for Poland is that most of their players are 30 or over and that could cost them dear if they reach the later stages of the tournament. I think Poland and Germany are the favourites to reach the knockout stages. Ecuador will do well to beat Costa Rica, who have former West Ham and Manchester City striker Paolo Wanchope, now playing in Qatar, as their best player. Wanchope's partner in attack is likely to be the veteran Rolando Fonseca, who has more than 100 international caps, despite the fact that he does not score as often now.

> "Schweinsteiger and Podolski, who I think is a great player, can enhance their reputations."

MARTIN JOL'S PREDICTIONS FOR THE TOP TWO TEAMS FROM THIS GROUP

Schedule of play is on page 80

GROUP STAGE
FIRST GROUP A

| GERMANY |

LAST SIXTEEN
v SECOND GROUP B

| GERMANY v SWEDEN |

QUARTER-FINALS
v FIRST GROUP C or SECOND GROUP D

| GERMANY v ARGENTINA |

SECOND GROUP A

| POLAND |

v FIRST GROUP B

| POLAND v ENGLAND |

v FIRST GROUP D or SECOND GROUP C

| ENGLAND v PORTUGAL |

GROUP A
GERMANY, COSTA RICA, POLAND, ECUADOR

GROUP B
ENGLAND, PARAGUAY, TRINIDAD & TOBAGO, SWEDEN

GROUP C
ARGENTINA, IVORY COAST, SERB & MONT, HOLLAND
GROUP D
MEXICO, IRAN, ANGOLA, PORTUGAL

If Germany win this group and England finish narrow runners-up in Group B this gives a mouth-watering last 16 game. If so, what price penalties?

GERMANY

SEEDED 4 FIFA RANKING 16

ROUTE TO THE FINALS

Germany used the Confederation Cup as their competitive measure for the World Cup and were encouraged to finish as the tournament's top scorers with 15 goals in five games.

This backed Jurgen Klinsmann's promise to build a more attacking side. However, the bulk of the goals came from midfield and defence. The defending, with 11 goals conceded over the five games, shows where the coach has more work to do. More recent friendlies against Holland 2-2 and a 2-0 defeat to the Marek Mintal-inspired Slovakia, saw Klinsmann ringing the defensive changes. Chelsea's young centre half Robert Huth did well in November's clean sheet against France but will lack games going into the finals.

Lukas Podolski's hat-trick against South Africa saw him nudge ahead of Kevin Kuranyi for a June start.

#	Date	Venue	Opponent	FIFA ranking	Result	Score	Scorers
1	16 Dec 04	Away	Japan	16	W	0 3	Klose 54, 90, Ballack 69
2	19 Dec 04	Away	South Korea	89	L	3 1	Ballack 26
3	21 Dec 04	Away	Thailand	91	W	1 5	
4	09 Feb 05	Home	Argentina	3	D	2 2	Frings 28pen, Kuranyi 45
5	26 Mar 05	Away	Slovenia	50	W	0 1	Podolski 27
6	04 Jun 05	Away	N Ireland	109	W	1 4	Asamoah 17, Ballack 62, 66pen, Podolski 81
7	08 Jun 05	Home	Russia	31	D	2 2	Schweinsteiger 30, 68
8	15 Jun 05	Home	Australia	55	W	4 3	Kuranyi 17, Mertesacker 23, Ballack 60pen, Podolski 88
9	18 Jun 05	Away	Tunisia	32	W	0 3	Ballack 74pen, Schweinsteiger 80, Hanke 88
10	21 Jun 05	Away	Argentina	3	D	2 2	Kuranyi 29, Asamoah 51
11	25 Jun 05	Home	Brazil	1	L	2 3	Podolski 23, Ballack 48pen
12	29 Jun 05	Home	Mexico	6	W	4 3	Podolski 37, Schweinsteiger 41, Huth 79, Ballack 97
13	17 Aug 05	Away	Holland	4	D	2 2	Ballack 50, Asamoah 81
14	03 Sep 05	Away	Slovakia	47	L	2 0	
15	07 Sep 05	Home	South Africa	41	W	4 2	Podolski 12, 48, 55, Borowski 47
16	08 Oct 05	Away	Turkey	12	L	2 1	Neuville 90
17	12 Oct 05	Home	China PR	59	W	1 0	Frings 52pen
18	12 Nov 05	Away	France	4	D	0 0	
Average FIFA ranking of opposition				**36**			

MAIN PLAYER PERFORMANCES IN QUALIFICATION

Match	1 2 3 4 5 6 7 8 9 10 11 12 13 14 15 16 17 18	Appearances	Started	Subbed on	Subbed off	Mins played	% played	Goals	Yellow	Red
Venue	A A A H A A H H A A H H A A H A H A									
Result	W L W D W W D W W D L W D L W L W D									
Goalkeepers										
Oliver Kahn		9	9	0	0	840	50.9	0	0	0
Jens Lehmann		7	7	0	0	630	38.2	0	0	0
Defenders										
Tim Borowski		9	3	6	1	332	20.1	1	0	0
Arne Friedrich		9	9	0	1	793	48.1	0	3	0
Andreas Hinkel		7	5	2	3	405	24.5	0	1	0
Robert Huth		10	8	2	0	744	45.1	1	2	1
Marcell Jansen		4	3	1	0	315	19.1	0	0	0
Per Mertesacker		15	15	0	2	1310	79.4	1	0	0
Patrick Owomoyela		8	6	2	1	587	35.6	0	0	0
Christian Worns		5	5	0	2	403	24.4	0	0	0
Midfielders										
Michael Ballack		13	13	0	1	1182	71.6	9	1	0
Sebastian Deisler		13	8	5	4	793	48.1	0	2	0
Marco Engelhardt		2	0	2	0	35	2.1	0	1	0
Fabian Ernst		12	8	4	4	688	41.7	0	1	0
Torsten Frings		13	12	1	2	1085	65.8	2	1	0
Tomas Hitzlsperger		11	8	3	2	689	41.8	0	0	0
Bernd Schneider		16	14	2	6	1211	73.4	0	0	0
Christian Schulz		1	1	0	0	90	5.5	0	0	0
Bastian Schweinsteiger		15	10	5	8	988	59.9	4	2	0
Lukas Sinkiewicz		3	2	1	0	225	13.6	0	0	0
Forwards										
Gerald Asamoah		13	7	6	5	628	38.1	3	1	0
Miroslav Klose		7	7	0	3	554	33.6	2	0	0
Kevin Kuranyi		16	8	8	5	751	45.5	3	1	0
Oliver Neuville		3	2	1	1	217	13.2	1	0	0
Lukas Podolski		14	11	3	7	974	59.0	8	0	0

FINAL PROSPECTS

The Germans have a great World Cup pedigree and, despite a dearth of world-class players in their squad, the host nation will expect to make a big impact at their 2006 finals.

Captain Michael Ballack is singled out as Germany's one genuine star, but he can't win the World Cup on his own.

Having said that, Ballack was the main reason why a functional Germany side surprised everybody by reaching the 2002 World Cup final only to be beaten 2-0 by Brazil. Ballack scored the 75th-minute winner in the 1-0 semi-final win over South Korea only five minutes after picking up a booking that meant he would be banned from the final.

Germany head coach Jurgen Klinsmann has recently introduced a more attacking style of play to the German team and Ballack now has good players around him, with his Bayern Munich team-mates Sebastian Deisler and Bastian Schweinsteiger, together with Werder Bremen's Torsten Frings forming a powerful midfield combination.

> **"During the build up to the World Cup Klinsmann could not make up his mind between Oliver Khan and Jens Lehmann."**
> Martin Jol

Bayern's Oliver Kahn and Jens Lehmann of Arsenal are still waging an ill-mannered personal battle against each other for the right to wear the goalkeeper's jersey, although the much younger Timo Hildebrand of Stuttgart could sneak up on the blind side.

Cologne's young striker Lukas Podolski has emerged as a player of real promise and the Polish-born forward is likely to start alongside Bremen's Miroslav Klose, with Kevin Kuranyi offering support from the bench.

The defence has an inexperienced look with the reliable Christian Worns being left out in the autumn for the 21-year-old Huth, partnering even younger Per Mertesacker. Marcell Jansen replaced the injured Phillip Lahm for the friendly against France and Arne Friedrich will be on the right flank.

Still, they look stronger than in 2002 and this time they have home support.

GROUP FIXTURES

COSTA RICA	Fri 9 June 1700 BST
POLAND	Wed 14 June 2000 BST
ECUADOR	Tue 20 June 1500 BST

KEY PLAYER

MICHAEL BALLACK BAYERN MUNICH

German hopes are pinned on the creative skills and goal-scoring instincts of Michael Ballack.

The attacking midfielder is one of only two world-class talents the hosts have been able to call on over the last five years. However, Ballack and Oliver Kahn were enough to scrape the country a World Cup final place in 2002. That was on the back of a golden season for Ballack, who hit 29 goals from midfield for Leverkusen and Germany.

His instinct for goal and the variety of threats he causes – from range, in the box and with his head – make him an extra special talent.

Ballack is a Top 12 Midfielder.

Other German Top Players are Kahn and Klose.

AGE 29 | **MIDFIELDER** | **WORLD RANKING 15**

Berlin

Zone	Europe
Population	82,000,000
Capital	Berlin
Language	German
Top league	Bundesliga
Major clubs	**Capacities**
B. Munich	70,000
Hamburg	55,000
W. Bremen	42,000

Where likely squad players play:

In Germany	21	In Premiership	2
In Italy	0	In France	0
In Spain	0	In Holland	0

Number of German players playing:

In Germany	339	In Premiership	5
In Italy	0	In France	1
In Spain	0	In Holland	3

World Cup record (1930-1990 West Germany)

1930 -	Did not enter	1974 -	Champions
1934 -	Third place	1978 -	Round 2
1938 -	Round 1	1982 -	Runners-up
1950 -	Did not enter	1986 -	Runners-up
1954 -	Champions	1990 -	Champions
1958 -	Fourth place	1994 -	Quarter-finals
1962 -	Quarter-finals	1998 -	Quarter-finals
1966 -	Runners-up	2002 -	Runners-up
1970 -	Third place		

THE SQUAD

Goalkeepers	Club side	Age	QG
Timo Hildebrand	Stuttgart	27	1
Oliver Kahn	Bayern Munich	36	9
Jens Lehmann	Arsenal	36	7
Defenders			
Frank Baumann	W Bremen	30	1
Tim Borowski	W Bremen	26	9
Arne Friedrich	Hertha Berlin	27	9
Andreas Hinkel	Stuttgart	24	7
Robert Huth	Chelsea	21	10
Marcell Jansen	B M'gladbach	20	4
Philip Lahm	Bayern Munich	22	1
Per Mertesacker	Hannover 96	21	15
Christophe Metzelder	B Dortmund	25	1
Patrick Owomoyela	W Bremen	26	8
Christian Worns	B Dortmund	34	5
Midfielders			
Michael Ballack	Bayern Munich	29	13
Sebastian Deisler	Bayern Munich	26	13
Marco Engelhardt	Kaiserslautern	25	2
Fabian Ernst	Schalke	27	12
Torsten Frings	W Bremen	29	13
Dietmar Hamann	Liverpool	32	1
Mike Hanke	Wolfsburg	22	6
Tomas Hitzlsperger	Stuttgart	24	11
Bernd Schneider	B Leverkusen	32	16
Christian Schulz	W Bremen	23	1
Bastian Schweinsteiger	Bayern Munich	21	15
Lukas Sinkiewicz	Cologne	20	3
Forwards			
Gerald Asamoah	Schalke	27	13
Thomas Brdaric	Hannover 96	31	1
Miroslav Klose	W Bremen	28	7
Kevin Kuranyi	Schalke	24	16
Oliver Neuville	B M'gladbach	33	3
Lukas Podolski	Cologne	21	14

■ Probable ■ Possible **QG** Qualification Games

KEY GOALKEEPER

JENS LEHMANN
ARSENAL

Germany's coach Jurgen Klinsmann put the cat among the goalkeeping pigeons. He told former team captain and national institution Oliver Kahn that he has to fight for his World Cup place.

In the blue corner is the Bayern jersey of Kahn and in the red corner is Jens Lehmann of Arsenal. The two are bitter rivals but Kahn has three previous finals behind him and is still in imperious form for Bayern. He's a Top Four goalkeeper.

The prickly Lehmann replaced David Seaman in 2003/4 and went on a remarkable run. He lost only three of his first 66 games.

Playing record	12 mths lge	int
Appearances:	39	7
Minutes played:	3510	630
Percentage played:	97.5%	38.2%
Goals conceded:	28	10
Clean sheets:	19	2
Cards:	0, 0	0, 0
Defensive rating:	125mins	63mins
Defensive ranking:	3rd	18th

AGE 36	WORLD RANKING 94

KEY DEFENDERS

ROBERT HUTH
CHELSEA

Chelsea defender Robert Huth has taken advantage of an injury to Borussia Dortmund's Christoph Metzelder to stake a claim to be Germany's centre back.

In his favour will be a robust perfromance and a clean sheet in the November friendly against France. Against him will be a lack of games at club level and his age – especially given that the other centre half, Mertesacker, is also only 21.

Playing record	12 mths lge	int
Appearances:	15	10
Minutes played:	783	744
Percentage played:	20.7%	45.1%
Goals conceded:	8	11
Clean sheets:	8	6
Cards:	Y1, R0	Y2, R1
Defensive rating:	-	68mins
Defensive ranking:	-	82nd

AGE 21	WORLD RANKING –

CHRISTIAN WORNS
B DORTMUND

Playing record	12 mths lge	int
Appearances:	31	5
Minutes played:	2705	403
Percentage played:	81.2%	24.4%
Goals conceded:	37	9
Clean sheets:	8	1
Cards:	Y5, R1	Y0, R0
Defensive rating:	73mins	-
Defensive ranking:	85th	-

AGE 34	WORLD RANKING 596

CHRISTOPH METZELDER
B DORTMUND

If Metzelder is fit and playing, he's certain to be in Klinsmann's squad.

Playing record	12 mths lge	int
Appearances:	28	1
Minutes played:	2338	90
Percentage played:	68.4%	5.5%
Goals conceded:	37	0
Clean sheets:	8	1
Cards:	Y3, R0	Y0, R0
Defensive rating:	63mins	-
Defensive ranking:	97th	-

AGE 25	WORLD RANKING 673

ARNE FRIEDRICH
HERTHA BERLIN

Germany's form defender is Arne Friedrich the right wing back and Hertha Berlin captain.

He's played every game bar one for Hertha this season and was in good form in three Confederations Cup appearances. His strengths lie in tackling and heading.

Playing record	12 mths lge	int
Appearances:	36	9
Minutes played:	3217	793
Percentage played:	94.1%	48.1%
Goals conceded:	42	13
Clean sheets:	11	4
Cards:	Y5, R1	Y3, R0
Defensive rating:	77mins	61mins
Defensive ranking:	76th	83rd

AGE 27	WORLD RANKING 314

PHILIPP LAHM
BAYERN MUNICH

Philipp Lahm suffered a cruciate ligament injury and only returned to Munich's playing squad in December.

He played for his country in Euro 2004.

AGE 22	WORLD RANKING –

ONE TO WATCH

PER MERTESACKER HANNOVER 96

Young Per Mertesacker came of age in the Confederations Cup last summer. He didn't just play himself into contention for the 2006 finals, he made himself the key defender.

His 31 appearances for Hannover 96 last season gave him the best record among their defenders He only conceding a goal every 90 minutes in the third best defence in the Bundesliga.

Playing record	12 mths lge	int
Appearances:	30	15
Minutes played:	2692	1310
Percentage played:	80.8%	79.4%
Goals conceded:	36	24
Clean sheets:	7	4
Cards:	Y0, R0	Y0, R0
Defensive rating:	75mins	55mins
Defensive ranking:	79th	86th

AGE 21   **DEFENDER**   **WORLD RANKING 543**

KEY MIDFIELDERS

BERND SCHNEIDER
B LEVERKUSEN

Bernd Schneider will be pumping energy into German attacks this summer.

The right midfielder only knows one way to play and his up and down style, pugnacity and crisp passing has inspired Germany in past World Cups. It was Schneider who took the game to Brazil in the 2002 World Cup final when all the pundits expected Germany to shrink back on defence.

Playing record	12 mths lge	int
Appearances:	31	16
Minutes played:	2775	1211
Percentage played:	83.3%	73.4%
Goals scored:	4	0
Goals conceded:	48	24
Cards:	Y4, R0	Y0, R0
Power rating:	48mins	43mins
Power ranking:	37th	45th

AGE 32	WORLD RANKING 166

SEBASTIAN DEISLER
BAYERN MUNICH

Playing record	12 mths lge	int
Appearances:	30	13
Minutes played:	1512	793
Percentage played:	43.1%	48.1%
Goals scored:	3	0
Goals conceded:	15	14
Cards:	Y4, R1	Y2, R0
Power rating:	34mins	42mins
Power ranking:	3rd	32nd

AGE 26	WORLD RANKING 117

BASTIAN SCHWEINSTEIGER
BAYERN MUNICH

A great young German talent, Bastian Schweinsteiger is having a breakthrough season for Bayern and the national side.

The Munich younster is now playing in the champions' first XI after a spell out last season.

Klinsmann looks likely to start with him. He can play as an attacking wing or in the centre, is difficult to shake off the ball and has a good goals and assists record.

Playing record	12 mths lge	int
Appearances:	30	15
Minutes played:	1923	988
Percentage played:	57.7%	59.9%
Goals scored:	2	4
Goals conceded:	13	12
Cards:	Y4, R0	Y2, R0
Power rating:	52mins	38mins
Power ranking:	50th	23rd

AGE 21	WORLD RANKING 61

TORSTEN FRINGS
W BREMEN

Playing record	12 mths lge	int
Appearances:	32	13
Minutes played:	2476	1085
Percentage played:	74.4%	65.8%
Goals scored:	3	2
Goals conceded:	29	18
Cards:	Y5, R1	Y1, R0
Power rating:	41mins	43mins
Power ranking:	10th	46th

AGE 29	WORLD RANKING 69

KEY STRIKERS

MIROSLAV KLOSE
W BREMEN

Miroslav Klose is having a great season at Werder Bremen with 21 goals in just 22 games so far.

Bremen won through the group stages of the Champions League with Klose hitting the target. He's fast, good in the air and has a good touch. At his best when his side are bossing the game though.

He is a Top 12 Striker.

AGE 28	WORLD RANKING 41

KEVIN KURANYI
SCHALKE

Brazilian-born Kevin Kuranyi is Germany's most prolific centre forward since Jurgen Klinsmann.

His first 27 caps brought 14 goals and a place in the Euro 2004 squad.

First choice in the pre-Klinsmann era, the new manager has moved him onto the sub's bench. A lack of international goals has coincided with a tough first season for Kuranyi at Schalke 04.

Playing record	12 mths lge	int
Appearances:	34	16
Minutes played:	2782	751
Percentage played:	83.5%	45.5%
Goals scored:	12	3
Percentage share:	20.34	8.33
Cards:	Y9, R0	Y1, R0
Strike rate:	232mins	250mins
Power ranking:	56th	45th

AGE 24	WORLD RANKING 175

THE MANAGER

Jurgen Klinsmann was the surprise choice as German head coach just over two years ago. He replaced Rudi Voeller, who resigned after the team's poor performance at Euro 2004.

Klinsmann, who won the World Cup as a player with Germany in 1990, had no previous experience as a coach.

During an illustrious playing career he won 108 caps and scored 47 goals for his country and earned the nickname 'Golden Bomber'. He also captained Germany in the final of Euro 96 at Wembley.

He started his playing career at Stuttgart, before moving to Bayern Munich, Monaco, Inter Milan, Sampdoria and Tottenham, where he had two spells.

Hosts Germany did not have to qualify for the finals, so Klinsmann has not been tested in a competitive match environment. He has been criticised for continuing to live in the US and for setting off his two top keepers, Khan and Lehmann, against each other.

KEY STRIKER

LUKAS PODOLSKI COLOGNE

Polish-born Lukas Podolski is the most natural striker Germany has produced for years. Fast and strong on his left, he seems likely to play alongside Klose. Podolski hit 24 goals for Cologne as they were promoted last season but has found it harder to continue that streak in the top league. However, he impressed for Germany with a hat-trick against South Africa.

Playing record	12 mths lge	int
Appearances:	20	14
Minutes played:	1727	974
Percentage played:	83.4%	59.0%
Goals scored:	4	8
Percentage share:	11.43	25.00
Cards:	Y5, R0	Y0, R0
Strike rate:	432mins	122mins
Power ranking:	80th	16th

AGE 21 | STRIKER | WORLD RANKING 1439

ROUTE TO THE FINALS

Costa Rica made hard work of booking their trip to Germany. They scraped past Cuba only on the away goals rule after two score draws in the first qualifying round and were then beaten by Honduras and Guatemala in early CONCACAF Group stage matches.

The Costa Rican Football Federation took the drastic step in April 2005 of sacking national coach Jorge Luis Pinto and re-instating Alexandre Guimaraes, who was in charge of the side at the 2002 World Cup finals.

Brazilian-born Guimaraes steadied the ship and successfully guided the Ticos to third place in the standings behind the United States and Mexico after the final round of qualifying

matches. That was good enough for Costa Rica to secure a place at the World Cup finals for only the third time in their history.

Their best performance was probably the 3-0 home victory over a powerful United States side on 8th October 2005, which saw them qualify with a game still to play.

FINAL QUALIFYING TABLE
N/C AMERICA & CAR STAGE 3

USA	10	7	1	2	16	6	22
Mexico	10	7	1	2	22	9	22
Costa Rica	10	5	1	4	15	14	16
Trinidad & Tobago	10	4	1	5	10	15	13
Guatemala	10	3	2	5	16	18	11
Panama	10	0	2	8	4	21	2

					FIFA ranking			
1	18 Aug 04	Home	Honduras	46	L	**2 5**	Herron 20, 36
2	05 Sep 04	Away	Guatemala	60	L	**2 1**	A.Solis 24
3	08 Sep 04	Home	Canada	85	W	**1 0**	Wanchope 46
4	09 Oct 04	Home	Guatemala	60	W	**5 0**	Hernandez 19, Wanchope 36, 62, 69, R.Fonseca 83
5	13 Oct 04	Away	Canada	85	W	**1 3**	Wanchope 49, Sunsing 81, Hernandez 87
6	17 Nov 04	Away	Honduras	46	D	**0 0**	
7	09 Feb 05	Home	Mexico	6	L	**1 2**	Wanchope 38
8	26 Mar 05	Home	Panama	88	W	**2 1**	Wright 40pen, Myre 90
9	30 Mar 05	Away	Trinidad & Tobago	57	D	**0 0**	
10	04 Jun 05	Away	United States	8	L	**3 0**	
11	08 Jun 05	Home	Guatemala	60	W	**3 2**	Hernandez 34, Gomez 65, Wanchope 90
12	17 Aug 05	Away	Mexico	6	L	**2 0**	
13	03 Sep 05	Away	Panama	88	W	**1 3**	Saborio 44, Centeno 51, Gomez 73
14	07 Sep 05	Home	Trinidad & Tobago	57	W	**2 0**	Saborio 15, Centeno 50
15	08 Oct 05	Home	United States	8	W	**3 0**	Wanchope 34, Hernandez 60, 88
16	12 Oct 05	Away	Guatemala	60	L	**3 1**	Myre 60
	Average FIFA ranking of opposition			51			

MAIN PLAYER PERFORMANCES IN QUALIFICATION

Match	1 2 3 4 5 6 7 8 9 10 11 12 13 14 15 16	Appearances	Started	Subbed on	Subbed off	Mins played	% played	Goals	Yellow	Red
Venue	H A H H A A H H A A H A A H H A									
Result	L L W W W D L W D L W L W W W L									
Goalkeepers										
Alvaro Mesen		8	8	0	0	720	50.0	0	0	0
Jose Porras		7	7	0	0	630	43.8	0	2	0
Defenders										
Jervis Drummond		6	6	0	0	540	37.5	0	0	0
Leonardo Gonzalez		11	11	0	1	938	65.1	0	1	0
Luis Antonio Marin		14	14	0	1	1215	84.4	0	1	0
Gilberto Martinez		14	13	1	1	1162	80.7	0	1	0
Douglas Sequeira		6	4	2	0	419	29.1	0	0	1
Michael Umana		4	2	2	0	251	17.4	0	0	0
Harold Wallace		6	6	0	0	540	37.5	0	1	0
Midfielders										
Cristian Badilla		6	6	0	2	487	33.8	0	2	0
Walter Centeno		13	8	5	1	865	60.1	2	4	0
Daniel Fonseca		4	2	2	0	219	15.2	0	0	0
Carlos Hernandez		9	4	5	1	485	33.7	5	1	0
Jose Luis Lopez		4	4	0	0	316	21.9	0	1	1
Roy Myre		2	1	1	0	120	8.3	2	0	0
Alonso Solis		12	8	4	7	578	40.1	1	1	0
Mauricio Solis		5	5	0	2	407	28.3	0	3	0
Jaffet Soto		7	5	2	3	381	26.5	0	0	0
Forwards										
Stevens Bryce		7	6	1	3	531	36.9	0	2	0
Ronald Gomez		8	6	2	1	576	40.0	2	1	0
Andy Herron		6	5	1	4	279	19.4	2	2	1
Ivaro Saborio		5	5	0	5	302	21.0	2	0	0
Paulo Wanchope		14	10	4	2	1023	71.0	8	3	0

FINAL PROSPECTS

Costa Rica are in a tough group, along with hosts Germany, Poland and the unpredictable Ecuador.
They are always likely to score goals, with such good attacking players as Paulo Wanchope, Winston Parks and Walter Centeno in the side but their major problem is likely to be in defence. Germany, Poland and even Ecuador all have strikers capable of getting in behind defenders, so Costa Rica's hopes of qualifying for the knockout stages will probably depend on how well their own strikers start the tournament, particularly in their opening game against the hosts Germany.

THE MANAGER

Brazilian-born Alexandre Guimaraes was a player in Costa Rica's Italia 90 squad and is now in his second spell as the team's head coach.
He played in the Ticos side that beat both Scotland and Sweden and they surprised everyone by reaching the last 16. He was also coach 12 years later when they failed to reach the second stage only on goal difference behind Turkey, who went on to reach the semi-finals.
The Ticos were having a dismal time in the early qualifying matches for the World Cup finals until Guimaraes was brought in for the sacked Jorge Luis Pinto.
The 45-year-old is confident about their chances of reaching the knockout stages, and insisted after the draw last December that his team was 'neither bigger nor smaller' than Poland and Ecuador. Guimaraes is well respected as a sound tactician but he may struggle in Germany to emulate his previous achievements.

Alexandre Guimaraes

GROUP FIXTURES

GERMANY	Fri 9 June 1700 BST
ECUADOR	Thu 15 June 1400 BST
POLAND	Tue 20 June 1500 BST

San José

Zone	North, Central & Caribbean
Population	4,054,227
Capital	San Jose
Language	Spanish/English
Top league	Primera Division
Major clubs	**Capacities**
Dep Saprissa	23,000
L. D. Alajuelens	17,800
CS Herediano	7,800

Where likely squad players play:

In Premiership	0
In other major five European Leagues	1
Outside Major European Leagues	22

Number of Costa Rican players playing:

In Premiership	0
In other major five European Leagues	1

World Cup record

1930 -	Did not enter	1974 -	Did not qualify
1934 -	Did not enter	1978 -	Did not qualify
1938 -	Withdrew	1982 -	Did not qualify
1950 -	Did not enter	1986 -	Did not qualify
1954 -	Did not enter	1990 -	Last 16
1958 -	Did not qualify	1994 -	Did not qualify
1962 -	Did not qualify	1998 -	Did not qualify
1966 -	Did not qualify	2002 -	Group 3rd
1970 -	Did not qualify		

THE SQUAD

Goalkeepers	Club side	Age	QG
Ricardo Gonzalez	CO Guatemala	32	1
Alvaro Mesen	Herediano	33	8
Jose Porras	Saprissa	35	7
Defenders			
Try Bennett	Saprissa	30	2
Alexander Castro	Alajeulense	27	2
Carlos Castro	Alajuela	27	1
Pablo Chinchilla	LA Galaxy	27	4
Jervis Drummond	Saprissa	29	6
Leonardo Gonzalez	Herediano	25	11
Luis Antonio Marin	Alajuelense	31	14
Gilberto Martinez	Brescia	27	14
Douglas Sequeira	CD Chivas	28	6
Michael Umana	LA Galaxy	23	4
Harold Wallace	Alajuelense	30	6
Midfielders			
Cristian Badilla	Herediano	27	6
Christian Bolanos	Saprissa	22	4
Walter Centeno	Saprissa	31	13
Rodrigo Cordero	Cartagines	32	2
Daniel Fonseca	Cartagines	26	4
Carlos Hernandez	Alajuelense	24	9
Jose Luis Lopez	Saprissa	25	4
Wilmer Lopez	Saprissa	34	3
Alonso Solis	Saprissa	27	12
Mauricio Solis	Alajuelense	33	5
Jaffet Soto	Herediano	30	7
Forwards			
Stevens Bryce	A Ammochostos	28	7
Minor Diaz	Herediano	25	1
Ronald Gomez	Saprissa	31	8
Andy Herron	Chicargo Fire	28	6
Winston Parks	Lokomotiv Moscow	24	3
Oscar Rojas	Veracruz	27	3
Alvaro Saborio	Saprissa	24	5
Erick Scott	Columbus Crew	25	3
Paulo Wanchope	Herediano	29	14

■ Probable ■ Possible **QG** Qualification Games

KEY PLAYER

PAULO WANCHOPE AL-GARAFAH

Now 30 and playing for Al-Garafah In Qatar, Paulo Wanchope is famous for being so unpredictable that his own side don't know what to expect, let alone the opposition. He also has a proven goal scoring record; for Derby and Manchester City during his time in the Premiership and with 43 goals in 67 internationals for Costa Rica. Knee injuries have been a problem for Wanchope in his latter career and he only just made the the 2002 World Cup where Costa Rica came third in their group. He became the all-time leading goal scorer with 43 goals when scoring in the opening qualifier against the USA. He will be used up front in a 4-4-2 formation with Alvaro Saborio or Ronald Gomez as his strike partner.

AGE 30 | **STRIKER** | **WORLD RANKING** –

ROUTE TO THE FINALS

Poland qualified comfortably after finishing second to England in European Group 6, just one point behind Sven-Goran Eriksson's side (but having scored ten more goals) and nine points ahead of Austria.

The Poles averaged 2.7 goals per game in ten qualifiers and wracked up eight wins, four at home and an impressive four on their travels. Their biggest win was an 8-0 drubbing of Azerbaijan.

Strikers Maciej Zurawski and Tomas Frankowski scored 14 goals between them in the qualifiers, while Celtic's Artur Boruc emerged as a goalkeeper with real potential.

England were the only team to beat Poland, recording a 2-1 victory in Chorzow and repeating the score-line at Old Trafford last October, a result that decided the top two places in the group.

Poland have a reasonable World Cup record, having finished third in 1974 and (inspired by the brilliant Zbigniew Boniek) doing so again in 1982.

FINAL QUALIFYING TABLE
EUROPE GROUP 6

	P	W	D	L	GF	GA	Pts
England	10	8	1	1	17	5	25
Poland	10	8	0	2	27	9	24
Austria	10	4	3	3	15	12	15
N Ireland	10	2	3	5	10	18	9
Wales	10	2	2	6	10	15	8
Azerbaijan	10	0	3	7	1	21	3

				FIFA ranking			
1	04 Sep 04	Away	N Ireland	109	W	**0 3**	Zurawski 4, Wlodarczyk 37, Krzynowek 57
2	08 Sep 04	Home	England	8	L	**1 2**	Zurawski 48
3	09 Oct 04	Away	Austria	74	W	**1 3**	Kaluzny 10, Krzynowek 78, Frankowski 90
4	13 Oct 04	Away	Wales	74	W	**2 3**	Frankowski 72, Zurawski 81, Krzynowek 85
5	26 Mar 05	Home	Azerbaijan	115	W	**8 0**	Frankowski 12, 62, 66, Hadzhiev 16, Kosowski 40, Krzynowek 72, Saganowski 85, 89
6	30 Mar 05	Home	N Ireland	109	W	**1 0**	Zurawski 86
7	04 Jun 05	Away	Azerbaijan	115	W	**0 3**	Frankowski 28, Klos 57, Zurawski 79
8	03 Sep 05	Home	Austria	74	W	**3 2**	Smolarek 13, Kosowski 22, Zurawski 68
9	07 Sep 05	Home	Wales	74	W	**1 0**	Zurawski 53pen
10	12 Oct 05	Away	England	8	L	**2 1**	Frankowski 45
Average FIFA ranking of opposition				67			

MAIN PLAYER PERFORMANCES IN QUALIFICATION

Match	1 2 3 4 5 6 7 8 9 10	Appearances	Started	Subbed on	Subbed off	Mins played	% played	Goals	Yellow	Red
Venue	A H A A H H A H H A									
Result	W L W W W W W W W L									
Goalkeepers										
Artur Boruc		3	3	0	0	270	30.0	0	0	0
Jerzy Dudek		5	5	0	0	450	50.0	0	0	0
Defenders										
Jacek Bak		6	6	0	0	540	60.0	0	0	0
Marcin Baszczynski		7	7	0	0	630	70.0	0	1	0
Arkadiusz Glowacki		1	1	0	0	90	10.0	0	1	0
Tomasz Hajto		1	1	0	0	90	10.0	0	0	0
Mariusz Jop		2	2	0	0	180	20.0	0	0	0
Tomasz Klos		4	4	0	0	360	40.0	1	0	0
Michal Zewlakow		4	2	2	0	189	21.0	0	0	0
Midfielders										
Radoslaw Kaluzny		2	2	0	1	160	17.8	1	0	0
Kamil Kosowski		7	6	1	4	513	57.0	2	1	0
Jacek Krzynowek		4	4	0	0	360	40.0	2	1	0
Mariusz Lewandowski		2	2	0	0	180	20.0	0	0	0
Sebastian Mila		4	3	1	2	256	28.4	0	0	0
Arek Radomski		5	0	5	0	44	4.9	0	1	1
Tomasz Rzasa		7	7	0	0	630	70.0	0	0	0
Ebi Smolarek		4	3	1	3	243	27.0	1	1	0
Radoslaw Sobelewski		5	5	0	1	444	49.3	0	1	0
Miroslaw Szymkowiak		5	5	0	2	441	49.0	0	0	0
Forwards										
Tomasz Frankowski		6	3	3	2	315	35.0	6	0	0
Andrzej Niedzielan		3	0	3	0	81	9.0	0	0	0
Grzegorz Rasiak		5	5	0	3	377	41.9	0	0	0
Marek Saganowski		1	1	0	1	18	2.0	2	0	0
Maciej Zurawski		8	8	0	2	649	72.1	5	0	0

FINAL PROSPECTS

Poland showed during the qualifiers they are capable of taking apart teams of moderate ability and have players who can put the ball in the net.

However, they struggle to get a result against stronger opposition, as their two defeats by England proved.

The Poles are good enough to make it through to the knockout stage from Group A, and are capable of beating Costa Rica and Ecuador with enough goals to spare that Germany won't want to risk a draw against them in the second game.

Several Poland stars play their club football in the Bundesliga and are used to the conditions in Germany.

This could be the last major tournament for a number of the squad's thirty-something players but they are unlikely to progress to the last eight this time around.

THE MANAGER

Pawel Janas has been Poland head coach since taking over from Jerzy Engel after the 2002 World Cup finals.

During his playing days Janas was a solid defender and featured in all Poland's games at the 1982 World Cup finals in Spain, when they finished in third place. He won a total of 53 caps.

The 53-year-old Janas is popular with the fans, although being criticised initially, and he goes about his business in a quiet but professional manner. He is also a realist and said after the draw in Leipzig that a last 16 finish would not be a disaster for his side.

Only dropping points to England in a group with some tricky away fixtures shows the discipline he has installed in the side.

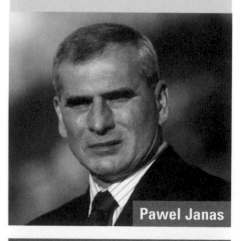

Pawel Janas

GROUP FIXTURES

ECUADOR	Fri 9 June 2000 BST
GERMANY	Wed 14 June 2000 BST
COSTA RICA	Tue 20 June 1500 BST

KEY PLAYER

MACIEJ ZURAWSKI CELTIC

The Polish striker Maciej Zurawski is in devastating form for Celtic. He's hit 15 goals from 17 games including a goal-a-game spree of ten in seven appearances in January and February.

The former Wisla Krakow striker joined Celtic last July and after a spell out of the team came back strongly early this year. Watch out Germany.

Playing record	12 mths lge	wcq
Appearances:	15	8
Minutes played:	1111	649
Percentage played:	29.4%	72.1%
Goals scored:	12	5
Percentage share:	14.81	29.41
Cards:	Y0, R0	Y0, R0
Strike rate:	93mins	130mins
Strike rate ranking:	2nd	19th

AGE 29   **STRIKER**   **WORLD RANKING** –

Zone	Europe
Population	38,558,000
Capital	Warsaw
Language	Polish
Top league	Ekstraklasa
Major clubs	**Capacities**
Wisla Krakow	30,000
Legia Warsaw	13,700
Lech	26,500

Where likely squad players play:

In Premiership	4
In other major five European Leagues	6
Outside major European Leagues	13

Number of Polish players playing:

In Premiership	4
In other major five European Leagues	17

World Cup record

1930 -	Did not enter	1974 -	Third place
1934 -	Withdrew	1978 -	Round 2
1938 -	Round 1	1982 -	Third place
1950 -	Did not enter	1986 -	Last 16
1954 -	Withdrew	1990 -	Did not qualify
1958 -	Did not qualify	1994 -	Did not qualify
1962 -	Did not qualify	1998 -	Did not qualify
1966 -	Did not qualify	2002 -	Group 4th
1970 -	Did not qualify		

THE SQUAD

	Club side	Age	QG
Goalkeepers			
Artur Boruc	Celtic	26	3
Jerzy Dudek	Liverpool	33	5
Tomasz Kuszczak	WBA	24	0
Defenders			
Jacek Bak	Al-Rayyan	33	7
Marcin Baszczynski	Wisla Krakow	29	7
Bartosz Bosacki	Lech Poznan	30	1
Arkadiusz Glowacki	Wisla Krakow	27	1
Tomasz Hajto	Derby	33	1
Mariusz Jop	FK Moscow	27	2
Tomasz Klos	Wisla Krakow	33	4
Mariusz Kukielka	Dynamo Dresden	29	1
Michal Zewlakow	Anderlecht	30	4
Midfielders			
Arkadiusz Bak	Polonia Warsaw	31	1
Damian Gorawski	FK Moskva	27	1
Radoslaw Kaluzny	LR Ahlen	32	2
Bartosz Karwan	Legia Warsaw	30	1
Kamil Kosowski	Southampton	28	7
Jacek Krzynowek	B Leverkusen	30	4
Mariusz Lewandowski	Shakhtar Donetsk	27	2
Sebastian Mila	Austria Vienna	23	4
Arek Radomski	Austria Vienna	28	5
Tomasz Rzasa	Den Haag	33	7
Radoslaw Sobelewski	Wisla Krakow	29	5
Miroslaw Szymkowiak	Trabzonspor	29	5
Marcin Zajac	DGW	31	1
Marek Zienczuk	Wisla Krakow	27	1
Forwards			
Tomasz Frankowski	Wolverhampton	31	6
Andrzej Niedzielan	NEC Nijmegen	27	3
Grzegorz Rasiak	Tottenham	27	5
Marek Saganowski	Vitoria Guimaraes	27	1
Ebi Smolarek	B Dortmund	25	4
Maciej Zurawski	Celtic	29	8

■ Probable ■ Possible **QG** Qualification Games

ROUTE TO THE FINALS

Ecuador finished third in the South America Group and secured their place in Germany with a game in hand after a hard-fought draw at home to Uruguay in October.

They had an astonishing home record, winning seven out of nine qualifiers played in the high altitude of their capital city Quito. Colombia-born coach Luis Fernando Suarez succeeded his fellow countryman Hernan Dario Gomez midway through the qualification campaign in June 2004 and set about reviving the spirits of the side.

Centre back Giovany Espinoza was the only player in the South America group to play in all 18 qualifiers and formed a reliable partnership at the back with captain Ivan Hurtado. Ecuador accumulated just five points from nine matches on their travels but finished ahead of far bigger countries.

Ecuador's two best performances were home wins over Brazil and Argentina.

	Date	Venue	Opposition	FIFA ranking	Result		Scorers
1	06 Sep 03	Home	Venezuela	66	W	2 0	G.Espinoza 5, C.Tenorio 72
2	10 Sep 03	Away	Brazil	1	L	1 0	
3	15 Nov 03	Away	Paraguay	30	L	2 1	Mendez 58
4	19 Nov 03	Home	Peru	68	D	0 0	
5	30 Mar 04	Away	Argentina	3	L	1 0	
6	02 Jun 04	Home	Colombia	25	W	2 1	Delgado 3, Salas 66
7	05 Jun 04	Home	Bolivia	96	W	3 2	Soliz 27og, Delgado 32, De La Cruz 38
8	05 Sep 04	Away	Uruguay	18	L	1 0	
9	10 Oct 04	Home	Chile	72	W	2 0	Kaviedes 49, Mendez 64
10	14 Oct 04	Away	Venezuela	66	L	3 1	M.Ayovi 41pen
11	17 Nov 04	Home	Brazil	1	W	1 0	Mendez 77
12	27 Mar 05	Home	Paraguay	30	W	5 2	Valencia 32, 49, Mendez 45, 47, M.Ayovi 77pen
13	30 Mar 05	Away	Peru	68	D	2 2	De La Cruz 4, Valencia 45
14	04 Jun 05	Home	Argentina	3	W	2 0	Lara 53, Delgado 89
15	08 Jun 05	Away	Colombia	25	L	3 0	
16	03 Sep 05	Away	Bolivia	96	W	1 2	Delgado 8, 49
17	08 Oct 05	Home	Uruguay	18	D	0 0	
18	12 Oct 05	Away	Chile	72	D	0 0	
	Average FIFA ranking of opposition			42			

MAIN PLAYER PERFORMANCES IN QUALIFICATION

Match	Venue	Appearances	Started	Subbed on	Subbed off	Mins played	% played	Goals	Yellow	Red
Goalkeepers										
Jose Francisco Cevallos		5	5	0	0	450	27.8	0	1	0
Jacinto Espinoza		2	2	0	0	180	11.1	0	0	0
Christian Mora		2	2	0	0	180	11.1	0	1	0
Edwin Villafuerte		9	9	0	0	810	50.0	0	0	0
Defenders										
Ulises De La Cruz		17	16	1	0	1474	91.0	2	0	0
Geovanny Espinoza		18	18	0	0	1620	100.0	1	1	0
Jorge Guagua		1	1	0	0	90	5.6	0	1	0
Ivan Angulo Hurtado		17	17	0	0	1530	94.4	0	1	0
Neicer Reasco		12	11	1	2	947	58.5	0	4	0
Midfielders										
Vicente Paul Ambrosi		13	11	2	4	965	59.6	0	1	0
Marlon Ayovi		16	15	1	4	1289	79.6	2	1	0
Walter Ayovi		5	2	3	2	185	11.4	0	0	0
Cleber Chala		7	7	0	3	564	34.8	0	0	0
Luis Gomez		2	2	0	1	135	8.3	0	1	0
Edison Mendez		15	14	1	2	1254	77.4	5	1	0
Alfonso Obregon		5	5	0	2	404	24.9	0	2	0
Luis Saritama		1	1	0	0	90	5.6	0	1	0
Edwin Tenorio		13	13	0	3	1125	69.4	0	3	0
Luis Valencia		7	6	1	4	424	26.2	3	0	0
Forwards										
Johnny Baldeon		3	2	1	2	124	7.7	0	0	0
Felix Borja		2	2	0	2	163	10.1	0	2	0
Augustin Delgado		11	9	2	2	856	52.8	5	2	0
Ivan Kaviedes		5	3	2	2	289	17.8	1	1	0
Christian Lara		5	1	4	1	208	12.8	1	0	0
Franklin Salas		11	2	9	1	495	30.6	1	0	0
Carlos Tenorio		8	7	1	2	611	37.7	1	1	0

Match venues: H A A H A H H H A H A H H H A A H A
Results: W L L D L W W L W L W W D W L W D D

FINAL PROSPECTS

Ecuador's moderate record away from home and the fact that they have only ever played three games in Europe suggests they will struggle to win a match, yet alone make it through the group stage in Germany.

A lot will depend on the form and fitness of midfielder Edison Mendez, a technically gifted playmaker who packs a powerful shot and hit five goals in qualifying. And younger players, such as the promising Luis Valencia and Christian Lara, must learn to cope with the pressure of World Cup football.

Striker Augustin Delgado is his country's joint top-scorer with 29 goals in 67 games but he was suspended in February by his Ecuadorian club Barcelona for being seen at a disco. He had a troubled spell at Southampton but his Premiership experience, along with the Villa wing back Ulises De La Cruz, could be vital.

THE MANAGER

Luis Fernando Suarez is a popular figure in Ecuador having turned the fortunes of the side around after being appointed coach midway through the qualifying campaign.

The Colombian-born Suarez took over from compatriot Hernan Dario Gomez after Ecuador's poor showing at the 2004 Copa America.

At the time of his appointment Ecuador were struggling in fifth place in the South American World Cup qualifying group on ten points from seven matches. The 46-year-old coach started former Saints' striker, Delgado, regularly and was rewarded with five goals. His defence is settled and looks to be a major strength.

Luis Fernando Suarez

GROUP FIXTURES

POLAND	Fri 9 June 2000 BST
COSTA RICA	Thu 15 June 1400 BST
GERMANY	Tue 20 June 1500 BST

KEY PLAYER

ULISES DE LA CRUZ ASTON VILLA

Ulises De La Cruz is desperate to leave Villa to get in some match practice before the World Cup. He was a regular on the right flank last season, making 31 appearances at full back or in midfield. This season he has played just two games. He has made 107 appearances for Ecuador but fears for his World Cup place if he is unable to become a regular first team player at Villa.

Playing record	12 mths lge	wcq
Appearances:	15	17
Minutes played:	1187	1474
Percentage played:	33.0%	91.0%
Goals conceded:	21	16
Clean sheets:	2	7
Cards:	Y1, R0	Y0, R0
Defensive rating:	57mins	92mins
Defensive ranking:	106th	70th

AGE 31   **DEFENDER**   **WORLD RANKING –**

Quito

Zone	South America
Population	13,525,128
Capital	Quito
Language	Spanish
Top league	Campeonato Nacional
Major clubs	**Capacities**
Barcelona SC	90,000
El Nacional	40,000
CS Elomeo	20,000

Where likely squad players play:

In Premiership	1
In other major five European Leagues	0
Outside major European Leagues	22

Number of Ecuadorians players playing:

In Premiership	1
In other major five European Leagues	2

World Cup record

1930 -	Did not enter	1974 -	Did not qualify
1934 -	Did not enter	1978 -	Did not qualify
1938 -	Did not enter	1982 -	Did not qualify
1950 -	Withdrew	1986 -	Did not qualify
1954 -	Did not enter	1990 -	Did not qualify
1958 -	Did not enter	1994 -	Did not qualify
1962 -	Did not qualify	1998 -	Did not qualify
1966 -	Did not qualify	2002 -	Group 4th
1970 -	Did not qualify		

THE SQUAD

Goalkeepers	Club side	Age	QG
Jose Cevallos	Onou Culdao	05	9
Christian Mora	Macara Ambato	26	2
Edwin Villafuerte	Barce De Guayaquil	27	9
Defenders			
Banner Caicedo	Barce De Guayaquil	25	1
Jose Cortez	Aucas Quito	26	1
Ulises De La Cruz	Aston Villa	31	17
Geovanny Espinoza	LDU Quito	29	18
Raul Guerron	Deportivo Quito	29	2
Ivan Angulo Hurtado	Al-Arabia Doha	31	17
Midfielders			
Alex Aguinaga	LDU Quito	37	4
Vicente Paul Ambrosi	LDU Quito	25	13
Marlon Ayovi	Deportivo Quito	34	16
Walter Ayovi	Barce De Guayaquil	26	5
Luis Caicedo	Olmedo	27	3
Segundo Castillo	El Nacional Quito	24	2
Cleber Chala	Deportivo Quito	34	7
Jacinto Espinoza	LDU Quito	-	2
Luis Gomez	Barce De Guayaquil	34	2
Edison Mendez	LDU Quito	27	15
Alfonso Obregon	LDU Quito	34	5
Mario Quiroz	El Nacional Quito	23	2
Yano Neicer Reasco	LDU Quito	-	12
Franklin Salas	LDU Quito	-	11
Edwin Tenorio	Barce De Guayaquil	29	13
Luis Valencia	Recreativo Huelva	20	7
Forwards			
Johnny Baldeon	Deportivo Quito	24	3
Felix Borja	El Nacional Quito	23	2
Augustin Delgado	Barce De Guayaquil	31	11
Ivan Kaviedes	Argentinos Juniors	28	5
Christian Lara	El Nacional Quito	26	5
Ebelio Ordonez	Shanghai Jiucheng	32	4
Carlos Quinonez	Emelec Guayaquil	30	1
Carlos Tenorio	Al-Sadd Doha	27	8

■ Probable ■ Possible **QG** Qualification Games

B

Position	1st	2nd	3rd	4th	5th	6th	7th	8th
Group	E	F	C	A	D	H	B	G
Total FIFA ranking	89	93	95	96	101	109	117	138

ENGLAND V PARAGUAY
Frankfurt, Saturday 10th June 1400 BST

Roque Santa Cruz's chances of recovering from his long-term knee injury for this game are starting to look slim. The tall young striker doesn't get much match practice in the Bayern Munich first team even when he is fit, but he does offer something different in their attack. Paraguay have Nelson Valdez coming through at Werder Bremen but Cruz is the kind of player who can steal an unlikely goal as he showed against Argentina in qualifying. Frank Lampard is Mr Consistency for Chelsea and England, rarely putting a pass astray, tackling back to protect the defence and could be key if England are to open with a win.

TRINIDAD & TOBAGO V SWEDEN
Dortmund, Saturday 10th June 1700 BST

Trinidad & Tobago's dream fixture comes in the next game so it's hard to know how they will react to this one. Larsson and Ibrahimovic represent the kind of consistent high-class goal-machines Wrexham's Dennis Lawrence just isn't used to. He would probably have preferred to meet England first.

While for Sweden, Henrik Larsson responded to public demands to return for Euro 2004 and proved he's still a top scorer with one of the goals of the tournament. He's stayed on and Trinidad & Tobago represent the standard of opposition that he used to hammer goals against whilst at Celtic.

ENGLAND V TRINIDAD & T
Nuremberg, Thursday 15th June 1700 BST

Don't mention Northern Ireland. A brilliant day in the sun for Trinidad & Tobago's players and supporters as the tiny Caribbean country with a population of just five million sets about England's finest.

A team of fired-up players from England's lower leagues who will be playing for pride and a place in history – we said not to mention Northern Ireland!

SWEDEN V PARAGUAY
Berlin, Thursday 15th June 2000 BST

It was only the exceptionally dogged defence of Croatia that could withstand Sweden in qualifying.

Hungary and Bulgaria would both expect to give Paraguay a good game and the Swedes hit 11 goals in four games against them. While all eyes are on Ibrahimovic watch out for Ljungberg.

Paraguay's Roque Santa Cruz

KEY MATCH

SWEDEN V ENGLAND
Cologne, Tuesday 20th June 2000 BST

Expect to hear a lot of Sweden's unbeaten record against England leading into this fixture. Somehow, a final group game when both sides have already qualified doesn't seem like the time that the record is going to be upset. Rooney, Gerrard and Owen have the fire-power to undo Sweden but will they have the motivation and might Sven even think about resting them. The argument about needing to avoid Germany presumes that the hosts finish top of Group A. After all, Poland gave England two tough games in qualifying, nearly sending Sven to the play-offs in the final game.

PARAGUAY V TRINIDAD & T
Kaiserslauten, Tuesday 20th June 2000 BST

Paraguay will want to finish on a high note and this is their chance. They will catch Trinidad & Tobago coming down from the England game and have the players to take advantage. Although this game may not mean much in the context of the group it will be a huge fixture for the two countries involved.

The lower league players and former stars from Trinidad & Tobago will want to have a heroic end to their adventure but Paraguay may have too much fire power. Even if Roque Santa Cruz is not fit, Nelsen Valdez and Jose Cardoza are both in form and should secure a win for the South Americans.

MARTIN JOL'S VIEW

Although they had to fight for their lives in qualification – Poland were the group leaders until the last week of qualification - England still managed to finish top.

They had some bad results, like losing to Northern Ireland, but I expect England to do well in Germany because they have so much quality and, in Wayne Rooney, possibly one of the stars of the tournament.

They need to play 4-4-2 and focus on their own strength. That means dropping Rooney into midfield with a small striker (either Owen or Defoe) and a big front man such as a Shearer, in front of him. It is a pity that England have not found a successor to the Newcastle striker.

If they play that way I am sure they will qualify but they will have to win their first game, in Frankfurt against Paraguay, to finish top of the group and to have an easy ride into the last 16.

England's second qualification game against Trinidad & Tobago - with my Dutch colleague Leo Beenhakker as coach - will be a walkover against a team with many players from the lower divisions.

Even if England do not win against Paraguay, I expect them to qualify but the last game against Sweden could be a big one. I think it will be a game England only have to draw but Sweden need to win. One good thing for England is the fact that Sweden play the same system as

> **"I expect England to do well because they have so much quality and, in Wayne Rooney, possibly, one of the stars of the tournament"**

England – it's Sweden's biggest disadvantage when coming up against a stronger opponent.

I believe that all five of my internationals at Tottenham will go to the World Cup: Paul Robinson, Michael Carrick, Jermain Defoe, Jermaine Jenas and Ledley King.

If England have a good World Cup tournament, Paul Robinson may be regarded as the best keeper of the tournament, even though he is still quite young. Moreover, my playmaker Michael Carrick - if given the chance - could be a revelation.

Paraguay are not to be underestimated

I regard them – after Brazil and Argentina – as the third strongest South American country. They finished second during the last Olympic Games, so nobody should take them lightly.

It's a pity for Paraguay that they have to start against England and play Trinidad & Tobago as their last game. Their game against Sweden will be decisive, and they will probably have to win.

They have a strong team with some fine players. Carlos Paredes for example is having a great season with Reggina and I know midfielder Edgar Barreto from NEC Nijmegen in Holland.

One crucial fact will be whether Bayern Munich striker Roque Santa Cruz is fit. The 1.91m tall forward was brought to Europe when only 18-years-old with Bayern prepared to pay £5m for him; however, he is injury prone.

Sweden are lucky to start against Trinidad and it may be that the final group game against England turns out not to be crucial for the English. Their best-known players are Arsenal's Freddie Ljungberg and their biggest star Zlatan Ibrahimovic from Juventus, who could be the player of the tournament. And Henrik Larsson is in the squad.

I expect a lot from Kim Kallstrom of Rennes and from Anderlecht's Christian Wilhelmsson, who is usually able to get past his man.

Sweden play the English 4-4-2 and always are strong but also predictable.

I hope my former player Eric Edman – a solid defender at Spurs – makes the team and the second round.

Trinidad & Tobago's qualification is a wonder and the highlight of their football history.

Dwight Yorke is the star and West Ham's Shaka Hislop is a well-respected keeper, but the rest of their players are not used to playing games against quality opposition. However, they will have some colourful support.

In Wayne Rooney, England possibly have one of the stars of the tournament

MARTIN JOL'S PREDICTIONS FOR THE TOP TWO TEAMS FROM THE GROUP
For the full draw please see page 80

GROUP STAGE	LAST SIXTEEN	QUARTER-FINALS
FIRST GROUP B	v SECOND GROUP A	v FIRST GROUP C or SECOND GROUP D
ENGLAND	ENGLAND v POLAND	ENGLAND v PORTUGAL
SECOND GROUP B	v FIRST GROUP A	v FIRST GROUP D or SECOND GROUP C
SWEDEN	SWEDEN v GERMANY	GERMANY v ARGENTINA

GROUP B	GROUP A	GROUP D
ENGLAND, PARAGUAY, TRINIDAD & TOBAGO, SWEDEN	GERMANY, COSTA RICA, POLAND, ECUADOR	MEXICO, IRAN, ANGOLA, PORTUGAL
		GROUP C
		ARGENTINA, IVORY COAST, SERBIA & MONT, HOLLAND

Looking ahead to the semi-finals, the Group winners would get through to meet Brazil, while the runners-up couldn't meet the favourites until the final.

ROUTE TO THE FINALS

England qualified for the World Cup finals with a game in hand before Frank Lampard's late winner in the 2-1 win over Poland.

That final game determined who would go to Germany as winners of European Group Six and England squeezed through without looking completely convincing.

Lampard, who played in all ten qualifiers, finished as England's top scorer with five goals. The Chelsea midfielder also stroked home the penalty that gave the Three Lions a 1-0 win over Austria in October. That victory, combined with results elsewhere, secured England's trip to the finals.

In one of the easier European qualifying groups, Poland and England quickly emerged as the only two contenders. Joe Cole renewed his claim to the left midfield slot and Rooney failed to score.

The qualifying campaign was not plain sailing, with the embarrassing 1-0 defeat against Northern Ireland and skipper David Beckham's sending-off against Austria, two of the low points. However, the November friendly against Argentina showed England's hidden potential.

FINAL QUALIFYING TABLE
EUROPE GROUP 6

	P	W	D	L	GF	GA	Pts
England	10	8	1	1	17	5	25
Poland	10	8	0	2	27	9	24
Austria	10	4	3	3	15	12	15
N Ireland	10	2	3	5	10	18	9
Wales	10	2	2	6	10	15	8
Azerbaijan	10	0	3	7	1	21	3

					FIFA ranking			
1	04 Sep 04	Away	Austria	74	D	2 2	Lampard 24, Gerrard 65
2	08 Sep 04	Away	Poland	23	W	1 2	Defoe 37, Glowacki 58og
3	09 Oct 04	Home	Wales	74	W	2 0	Lampard 4, Beckham 76
4	13 Oct 04	Away	Azerbaijan	115	W	0 1	Owen 22
5	26 Mar 05	Home	N Ireland	109	W	4 0	J.Cole 47, Owen 52, Baird 54og Lampard 62
6	30 Mar 05	Home	Azerbaijan	115	W	2 0	Gerrard 51, Beckham 62
7	03 Sep 05	Away	Wales	74	W	0 1	J.Cole 54
8	07 Sep 05	Away	N Ireland	109	L	1 0	
9	08 Oct 05	Home	Austria	74	W	1 0	Lampard 25pen
10	12 Oct 05	Home	Poland	23	W	2 1	Owen 43, Lampard 81
	Average FIFA ranking of opposition			67			

MAIN PLAYER PERFORMANCES IN QUALIFICATION

Match	1 2 3 4 5 6 7 8 9 10	Appearances	Started	Subbed on	Subbed off	Mins played	% played	Goals	Yellow	Red
Venue	A A H A H H A A H H									
Result	D W W W W W W L W W									
Goalkeepers										
David James		1	1	0	0	90	10.0	0	0	0
Paul Robinson		9	9	0	0	810	90.0	0	0	0
Defenders										
Wayne Bridge		2	2	0	0	180	20.0	0	0	0
Sol Campbell		3	3	0	1	243	27.0	0	0	0
Jamie Carragher		5	4	1	0	419	46.6	0	0	0
Ashley Cole		8	8	0	0	720	80.0	0	0	0
Rio Ferdinand		8	7	1	0	657	73.0	0	0	0
Ledley King		4	3	1	0	300	33.3	0	0	0
Gary Neville		6	6	0	1	481	53.4	0	0	0
John Terry		6	6	0	0	540	60.0	0	0	0
Luke Young		4	4	0	0	360	40.0	0	0	0
Midfielders										
David Beckham		8	8	0	2	668	74.2	2	1	1
Nicky Butt		2	2	0	0	180	20.0	0	1	0
Joe Cole		7	5	2	3	443	49.2	2	1	0
Kieron Dyer		2	0	2	0	23	2.6	0	0	0
Steven Gerrard		7	7	0	3	588	65.3	2	0	0
Owen Hargreaves		4	0	4	0	46	5.1	0	0	0
Jermaine Jenas		2	1	1	1	79	8.8	0	0	0
Frank Lampard		10	10	0	1	889	98.8	5	0	0
Kieran Richardson		2	0	2	0	18	2.0	0	0	0
Shaun Wright-Phillips		3	3	0	3	184	20.4	0	0	0
Forwards										
Peter Crouch		2	1	1	0	115	12.8	0	0	0
Jermain Defoe		6	3	3	2	281	31.2	1	0	0
Michael Owen		9	9	0	2	791	87.9	3	1	0
Wayne Rooney		7	7	0	2	613	68.1	0	2	0
Alan Smith		3	1	2	0	131	14.6	0	0	0

FINAL PROSPECTS

This is England's best chance of winning a World Cup since 1966 is the popular view.

The competitive record is impressive and Sven inherited a brilliant set of performers.

One prime reason is that the Premiership is now every bit as tough a proving ground as Spain's Primera Liga and Italy's Serie A. English players are fulfilling their ambitions in the Premiership and developing their talents against the best in the world.

So just how good is this England side?

The midfield looks to be the best in Germany. Our World Rankings are a function of playing and winning against top opposition, but England have six players in the top 35 midfield places and none of them are bit-part players. Frank Lampard, Steven Gerrard and Joe Cole are all among the best at their clubs. And, while David Beckham has disappointed in an England shirt recently, he remains the pick of Madrid's aging midfield and consistently one of the better performers in Spain.

Defensively, England has quantity plus a bit of quality. John Terry has emerged as the leader of the best defensive unit in Europe. While Rio Ferdinand has had a poor spell, he is still the pick of a shifting United back line and in our top 30 world defenders. Jamie Carragher is rocketing up that list and a fit Ashley Cole would be in the top 50. We base our rankings on the last year but run the data over three years and Wayne Bridge would be a top 12 player. In goal, Paul Robinson and David James are both ranked in the top 40. France has the best defensive line-up on paper but don't always play them.

Up front, we have the perfect combination. When Michael Owen is fit, he scores – even 'failing' at Madrid, he had a Strike Rate of a goal every 145 minutes. Wayne Rooney plays deeper and while his goals have slowed, his performances and build up play haven't been affected. Keeping these two fit is crucial because they are the only two top-class strikers we have. France and Holland both have a better pairing and Brazil have strength in depth.

Argentina saw England's best attacking display for four years and on paper, England's first XI is behind only Brazil and France with the Italian team about level. That says semi-finals and from there... we could win it.

GROUP FIXTURES

PARAGUAY	Sat 10 June 1400 BST
TRINIDAD & T.	Thu 15 June 1700 BST
SWEDEN	Tue 20 June 2000 BST

London

Zone	Europe
Population	60,500,000
Capital	London
Language	English

Where likely squad players play:

In Premiership	21	In Spain	1
In Holland	0	In France	0
In Italy	0	In Germany	0

Number of English players playing:

In Premiership	243
In Spain	2
In Holland	2
In France	0
In Italy	0
In Germany	1

World Cup record

1930 -	Did not enter	1974 -	Did not qualify
1934 -	Did not enter	1978 -	Did not qualify
1938 -	Did not enter	1982 -	Round 2
1950 -	Group 2nd	1986 -	Quarter-finals
1954 -	Quarter-finals	1990 -	Fourth place
1958 -	Group 3rd	1994 -	Did not qualify
1962 -	Quarter-finals	1998 -	Last 16
1966 -	Champions	2002 -	Quarter-finals
1970 -	Quarter-finals		

KEY PLAYER

WAYNE ROONEY MAN UTD.

Wayne Rooney became a worldwide phenomenon at Euro 2004. His performances in the group games brought four goals and promised much more. He packs a fearsome shot and can accelerate past defenders but its vision and his ability to spot the killer pass or the perfect touch in a tight situation that set him apart.

Only 20, he's surprisingly strong and his approach to the game is more mature and effective than his club-mate, Cristiano Ronaldo. Certainly United's best player in an average season but he isn't always able to inspire his colleagues. If he's fit and on form England will always have a chance of scoring.
Rooney is one of our Top 12 Players; as are Terry, Lampard and Gerrard.

AGE 20   **STRIKER**   **WORLD RANKING** 31

THE SQUAD

Goalkeepers	Club side	Age	QG
Robert Green	Norwich	26	0
David James	Man City	35	1
Paul Robinson	Tottenham	26	9
Defenders			
Wayne Bridge	Fulham	25	2
Wes Brown	Man Utd	26	0
Sol Campbell	Arsenal	31	3
Jamie Carragher	Liverpool	28	5
Ashley Cole	Arsenal	25	8
Rio Ferdinand	Man Utd	27	8
Ledley King	Tottenham	25	4
Gary Neville	Man Utd	31	6
John Terry	Chelsea	25	6
Jonathan Woodgate	Real Madrid	26	0
Luke Young	Charlton	26	4
Midfielders			
David Beckham	Real Madrid	31	8
Michael Carrick	Tottenham	24	0
Joe Cole	Chelsea	24	7
Stewart Downing	Middlesbrough	21	0
Kieron Dyer	Newcastle	27	2
Steven Gerrard	Liverpool	26	7
Owen Hargreaves	Bayern Munich	25	4
Jermaine Jenas	Tottenham	23	2
Frank Lampard	Chelsea	27	10
Kieran Richardson	Man Utd	21	2
Shaun Wright-Phillips	Chelsea	24	3
Forwards			
Darren Bent	Charlton	22	0
Peter Crouch	Liverpool	25	2
Jermain Defoe	Tottenham	23	6
Michael Owen	Newcastle	26	9
Wayne Rooney	Man Utd	20	7

■ Probable ■ Possible **QG** Qualification Games

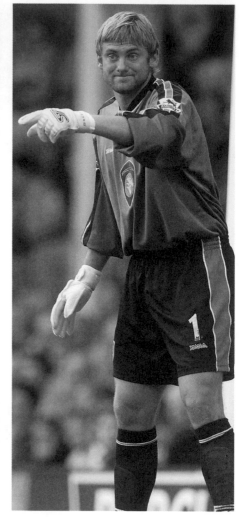

PAUL ROBINSON
TOTTENHAM

Paul Robinson is the third of England's keepers to have suffered relegation from the Premiership.

A highly rated youngster, he surprised the Premiership by taking over the Leeds' No. 1 jersey from England regular Nigel Martyn soon after his professional debut in 1998. He was still there when their financial problems came home to roost and relegation followed.

Back in the Premiership with Spurs, he put together a run of clean sheets in 2004/5 and Robinson's era as England's No. 1 began.

Playing record	12 mths lge	wcq
Appearances:	39	9
Minutes played:	3484	810
Percentage played:	92.2%	90.0%
Goals conceded:	38	3
Clean sheets:	12	6
Cards:	Y1, R0	Y0, R0
Defensive rating:	92mins	270mins
Defensive ranking:	15th	5th

AGE 26 **WORLD RANKING 350**

DAVID JAMES
MAN CITY

David James has had more than his fair share of goalkeeping disasters, which detracts from his spells of solid security.

At Liverpool, he was nicknamed 'Calamity James' after his mistakes and he had to rebuild his career at Aston Villa and West Ham. Kevin Keegan selected James to replace the injured David Seaman at Manchester City and the keeper immediately made a difference. The 2004/5 season saw James only conceding 39 goals in 38 games, including two shut-outs against Chelsea.

Playing record	12 mths lge	wcq
Appearances:	41	1
Minutes played:	3690	90
Percentage played:	100.0%	10.0%
Goals conceded:	44	2
Clean sheets:	10	0
Cards:	Y1, R0	Y0, R0
Defensive rating:	84mins	-
Defensive ranking:	16th	-

AGE 35 **WORLD RANKING 290**

ROBERT GREEN
NORWICH

Robert Green was a star in Norwich's promoted team in 2003/4 and was called into the England squad in March 2004.

Norwich had a torrid time in the top league, finishing 19th with Green the worst performing keeper on show. He played every match and conceded 75 goals – almost two a game.

Green stayed with Norwich despite their relegation and won his first England cap last summer against Columbia.

The last keeper relegated with a worse record was Paul Robinson - 76 goals with Leeds!

Playing record	LGE	wcq
Appearances:	38	-
Minutes played:	3392	-
Percentage played:	99%	-
Goals conceded:	75	-
Clean sheets:	6	-
Cards:	Y0, R0	Y-, R-
Defensive rating:	45	-

Green's stats are for the 2004/5 season.

AGE 26 **WORLD RANKING –**

KEY GOALKEEPER

PAUL ROBINSON TOTTENHAM

"If England have a good World Cup Paul Robinson may be regarded as the best keeper of the tournament."
Not surprisingly, Martin Jol rates his own player highly but could he really be the best keeper at the World Cup?
Spurs currently have the fourth best defensive record in the Premiership. Last season Robinson started well, letting in only three goals in the first six games, and finished with 40 goals conceded from 36. He saved 4.5 shots on target for every goal conceded which is below the Premiership average of 5.5. Stats don't tell the whole story though, and Robinson's performances have been solid and professional for two seasons. He's not a flamboyant keeper but a calming influence and mistakes are rare.

"Best keeper of the tournament?"

THE MANAGER

Sven-Goran Eriksson was the first foreign coach to be given the England manager's job when he took over from Kevin Keegan in 2001.

The Football Association announced last January that by mutual agreement Eriksson is to step down from his post at the end of the 2006 World Cup finals.

The FA plan to appoint a successor before this summer's tournament, but the new man will not have a hands-on role during the finals. Eriksson, 58, has insisted that he will be in sole charge of the squad in Germany.

England have experienced a number of highs and lows during Eriksson's reign. The famous 5-1 victory over Germany in Munich back in September 2001, which helped the side qualify for the 2002 World Cup finals, remains his finest moment.

The 3-1 home defeat by Australia in February 2003 and a 4-1 thumping by Denmark in Copenhagen in August 2005 were definite lows and provoked a lot criticism about Eriksson's approach to friendly internationals.

However, England's record under the Swede in competitive matches is impressive. In 33 matches, they have won 23, drawn seven and lost just three times.

He has only ever lost one qualifier but that game against Northern Ireland highlighted his cool detachment and made it seem like helplessness in the face of a team losing its way (and its heads) on the pitch. His substitutions have been criticised and have rarely been effective. Against this, the players remain vocal in their support for their media-besieged manager.

His CV as a club coach is impressive. He won an Italian league and cup double, the Uefa Super Cup and European Cup Winners Cup with Lazio, the Uefa Cup and Swedish title with IFK Gothenburg and three Portuguese league titles with Benfica.

KEY DEFENDER

JOHN TERRY CHELSEA – TOP 12 DEFENDER

England are blessed with many imperious centre halves - but the undisputed king among them isn't Ledley but John Terry.

Before Euro 2004, Rio Ferdinand and Sol Campbell were seen as the best pairing and Terry was among a pack of promising reserves who gave England cover.

Then two things happened; Ferdinand was banned for missing a drugs test and Chelsea won the Premiership. Terry played in all bar one of England's Euro 2004 games. He followed that by leading Chelsea to the league title and the best defensive record in Europe. He played in 36 league games, during which Chelsea only conceded 13 goals. Now, the question is; who should play with Terry?

AGE 25 **WORLD RANKING 4**

RIO FERDINAND
MAN UTD

At a cool £30m, Manchester United made Rio Ferdinand the world's most expensive defender after the 2002 World Cup.

The England centre back pairing was rated the best at the tournament and the unruffled Ferdinand was supposed to secure the Old Trafford defence for years to come. It didn't quite work out like that after a missed drugs test, an eight month ban and some laziness accusations from Sven. However, Ferdinand still commanded a Defensive rating of 140 last season, putting him in Europe's top 20.

Playing record	12 mths lge	wcq
Appearances:	38	8
Minutes played:	3387	657
Percentage played:	91.8%	73.0%
Goals conceded:	36	2
Clean sheets:	17	6
Cards:	Y2, R1	Y0, R0
Defensive rating:	94mins	328mins
Defensive ranking:	45th	18th

AGE 27 | **WORLD RANKING 139**

GARY NEVILLE
MAN UTD

Most pictures of Gary Neville show his commitment. His face usually embodies gritty determination as he busts a gut to get down the flank or strives that extra inch to win a tackle.

Often, he's open-mouthed, eyes glaring, caught mid-bellow, lambasting or entreating a team-mate to do better. His drive has turned a talented but possibly limited full back into one of the world's best. Whenever, Neville has made a mistake (and there's been a few) he's come back stronger.

Playing record	12 mths lge	wcq
Appearances:	22	6
Minutes played:	1858	481
Percentage played:	50.4%	53.4%
Goals conceded:	21	2
Clean sheets:	12	5
Cards:	Y2, R1	Y0, R0
Defensive rating:	88mins	240mins
Defensive ranking:	56th	22nd

AGE 31 | **WORLD RANKING 681**

ASHLEY COLE
ARSENAL

Ashley Cole's performance against Cristiano Ronaldo in the quarter-finals at Euro 2004 was billed as one of the great football head-to-heads.

It lived up to expectations with an in-form Ronaldo taking on Cole every chance he got and the Arsenal defender just about repelling him every time. Injury looks increasingly likely to limit Cole's match fitness with a recent setback in a reserve game in late February.

Unless he recovers swiftly, it could deprive England of their dashing left back in June.

Playing record	12 mths lge	wcq
Appearances:	21	8
Minutes played:	1857	720
Percentage played:	50.3%	80.0%
Goals conceded:	14	4
Clean sheets:	12	5
Cards:	Y3, R0	Y0, R0
Defensive rating:	133mins	180mins
Defensive ranking:	9th	35th

AGE 25 | **WORLD RANKING 303**

JAMIE CARRAGHER
LIVERPOOL

While the cameras caught Stevie Gerrard kissing the Champions League trophy, most Liverpool fans were praising another Merseysider – Jamie Carragher.

Shipping three goals to AC Milan in the final was the exception. The rule stated that Liverpool won the trophy with their defensive displays. Prior to the final, they had let in just one goal in four games against champions-elect Juventus and Chelsea.

Carragher has discovered defensive class to go with his energy and determination.

Playing record	12 mths lge	wcq
Appearances:	39	5
Minutes played:	3510	419
Percentage played:	92.9%	46.6%
Goals conceded:	32	3
Clean sheets:	19	2
Cards:	Y6, R0	Y0, R0
Defensive rating:	110mins	140mins
Defensive ranking:	33rd	48th

AGE 28 | **WORLD RANKING 194**

DAVID BECKHAM
REAL MADRID

England's inspirational captain in the 5-1 defeat of Germany and qualifying run-in to 2002, David Beckham is appearing at his third World Cup.

Despite handing over the roles of England star (to Rooney), midfield inspiration (to Gerrard) and penalty taker (to Lampard), Beckham is still a significant performer. Only two Barcelona players had better midfield stats in Spain's Primera Liga last season and, most importantly, his long passing and delivery from out wide is as effective as ever.

Playing record	12 mths lge	wcq
Appearances:	35	8
Minutes played:	2932	668
Percentage played:	77.6%	74.2%
Goals scored:	1	2
Goals conceded:	35	4
Cards:	Y12, R2	Y1, R1
Power rating:	46mins	48mins
Power ranking:	29th	62nd

AGE 31 | **WORLD RANKING 78**

FRANK LAMPARD
CHELSEA – TOP 12 MIDFIELDER

For the last four seasons, Frank Lampard has been Chelsea's most consistent performer.

The difference now is that Chelsea are one of the best two club sides in Europe and Lampard is finally getting the recognition he deserves. Last season the only midfield players close to his goal total of 19 were PSV's (now Barcelona's) Mark van Bommel and Lyon's Juninho. This season he's at it again with only Gerrard and Michael Ballack keeping pace. He's still improving and is deadly around the box.

Playing record	12 mths lge	wcq
Appearances:	40	10
Minutes played:	3600	889
Percentage played:	95.2%	98.8%
Goals scored:	20	5
Goals conceded:	23	5
Cards:	Y5, R0	Y0, R0
Power rating:	47mins	52mins
Power ranking:	32nd	80th

AGE 27 | **WORLD RANKING 1**

JOE COLE
CHELSEA

Joe Cole is finally fulfilling the potential that football coaches prophesised when he was in the West Ham youth team.

Then, his close control and jinking runs were earmarking him as a future England 'great'.

Instead, West Ham were relegated in 2002/3 with Cole a battling but besieged captain. His £6.6m move to Chelsea left him as a bit-part player. Sven was playing him; but usually out of position on the left flank, mainly in friendlies and often talking up some defensive flaw. Now he's in on merit and top man in the Uruguay friendly.

Playing record	12 mths lge	wcq
Appearances:	37	7
Minutes played:	2544	443
Percentage played:	67.3%	49.2%
Goals scored:	9	2
Goals conceded:	18	2
Cards:	Y9, R0	Y1, R0
Power rating:	48mins	44mins
Power ranking:	41st	49th

AGE 24 | **WORLD RANKING 37**

MICHAEL CARRICK
TOTTENHAM

Regularly highlighted as the country's best deep-lying holding player on Match of the Day this season, Michael Carrick is another ex-Hammer battering on England's door.

He came through the youth ranks at West Ham with Lampard, Ferdinand and Cole but stayed with the side after relegation in 2002/3. He was brought back to the Premiership by Tottenham after a year but ignored by the manager Jacques Santini early in the 2004/5 season.

When Santini departed and Martin Jol took over, Carrick became a regular. This season he's been joined by Edgar Davids and Jermaine Jenas in a more powerful midfield unit with a Champions League place as the goal.

Carrick protects the back four, sprays passes around and prompts the Spurs attack from deep. He hardly ever puts in a poor performance and impressed against Uruguay.

AGE 24 | **WORLD RANKING –**

KEY MIDFIELDER

STEVEN GERRARD LIVERPOOL – TOP 12 MIDFIELDER

Steve Gerrard is capable of undoing top club defences and imposing his high-energy game on world-class midfields.

There have been games for Liverpool in the last two seasons when he has looked head-and shoulders above the other 21 players sharing the pitch. Equally, there have been England games when has struggled to fit into the system and looked anonymous.

Gerrard has a ferocious shot and 18 goals in 36 appearances are the mark of a midfielder in form and full of self-belief.

In recent games, he and Frank Lampard have proved they can play effectively together without the need for a holding player. There isn't room for one in England's best line-up and both players are capable ball-winners for their clubs.

AGE 26 **WORLD RANKING 13**

KEY STRIKER

MICHAEL OWEN NEWCASTLE

Michael Owen is a penalty box predator. He can be out of a game for 85 minutes and still score the two goals that win it.

The 18-year-old, who netted the solo goal of the 1998 World Cup, now saves his speed for shorter runs.

Injury hindered his form at Liverpool and lack of opportunity at Real Madrid but for England, he has never stopped scoring.

Playing record	12 mths lge	wcq
Appearances:	26	9
Minutes played:	1854	791
Percentage played:	49.0%	87.9%
Goals scored:	13	3
Percentage share:	34.21	17.65
Cards:	Y1, R0	Y1, R0
Strike rate:	143mins	264mins
Strike rate ranking:	15th	49th

AGE 26 **STRIKER** **WORLD RANKING 362**

WAYNE ROONEY
MAN UTD - TOP 12 STRIKER

Where best to play Wayne Rooney? For England, he has played as part of a twin strike-force and, more usually, 'in-the-hole' linking attack to midfield.

At United he's been played wide on the flank as part of a 4-3-3 formation and in, what Martin Jol believes is his best position, the attacking point of the midfield diamond with two forwards in front of him. Given England's wealth of midfield talent, this is the least likely option.

And, Rooney says, "I'll play anywhere; I'd play centre half if I was asked to."

Playing record	12 mths lge	wcq
Appearances:	40	7
Minutes played:	3203	613
Percentage played:	86.8%	68.1%
Goals scored:	16	0
Percentage share:	21.92	0.00
Cards:	Y11, R0	Y2, R0
Strike rate:	200mins	-
Strike rate ranking:	46th	-

AGE 20 | **WORLD RANKING 31**

PETER CROUCH
LIVERPOOL

Peter Crouch has been written off more times than Roman Abramovich's cheque signature.

He rarely got a kick in three seasons at Aston Villa, he was relegated with Southampton and he couldn't score for four months with Liverpool. Yet he's survived it all to become an important off the bench option for England. His height is what defenders focus on but Crouch has a good touch, a sharp turn and leads the line intelligently. Even when he's not scoring he can be effective – but now he's scoring.

Playing record	12 mths lge	wcq
Appearances:	36	2
Minutes played:	2686	115
Percentage played:	71.1%	12.8%
Goals scored:	12	0
Percentage share:	24.49	0.00
Cards:	Y4, R1	Y0, R0
Strike rate:	224mins	-
Strike rate ranking:	57th	-

AGE 25 | **WORLD RANKING 731**

JERMAIN DEFOE
TOTTENHAM

Jermain Defoe looked a good prospect in the Championship with 11 goals in the first half of the 2003/4 season.

He moved to Spurs for the second half and looked even better, scoring on his debut and hitting seven in a struggling side. He hit 22 goals in all competitions next season and scored a vital qualifying goal against Poland on his England debut. He looked a definite for Germany but has been in and out of the Spurs side as their strikers are rotated and is now battling for the fourth forward place.

Playing record	12 mths lge	wcq
Appearances:	40	6
Minutes played:	2380	281
Percentage played:	63.0%	31.2%
Goals scored:	11	1
Percentage share:	20.00	5.88
Cards:	Y4, R0	Y0, R0
Strike rate:	216mins	281mins
Strike rate ranking:	55th	51st

AGE 23 | **WORLD RANKING 531**

DEFENDERS

LEDLEY KING
TOTTENHAM

Tottenham captain Ledley King is regularly winning rave reviews from Alan Hansen for his displays this season.

In a new partnership with another impressive young England centre half, Michael Dawson, King is building his reputation. He has also turned in some accomplished displays as holding midfielder for his club and for England.

Playing record	12 mths lge	wcq
Appearances:	34	4
Minutes played:	3036	300
Percentage played:	80.3%	33.3%
Goals conceded:	35	4
Clean sheets:	8	1
Cards:	Y2, R0	Y0, R0
Defensive rating:	87mins	75mins
Defensive ranking:	60th	78th

AGE 25 | **WORLD RANKING 604**

WAYNE BRIDGE
FULHAM

A horrifying injury for Wayne Bridge ended his 2004/5 season early.

A collision with Paul Robinson in England's recent friendly against Uruguay has interrupted his comeback with a six week lay-off.

Playing record	12 mths lge	wcq
Appearances:	8	2
Minutes played:	720	180
Percentage played:	19.0%	20.0%
Goals conceded:	9	3
Clean sheets:	4	0
Cards:	Y0, R0	Y0, R0
Defensive rating:	-	-
Defensive ranking:	-	-

AGE 25 | **WORLD RANKING –**

LUKE YOUNG
CHARLTON

Luke Young has developed into one of the most consistent Premiership defenders.

At 1.83m tall, Young can play centre half but will go to Germany as proven cover for Gary Neville at right-back.

Playing record	12 mths lge	wcq
Appearances:	39	4
Minutes played:	3510	360
Percentage played:	92.9%	40.0%
Goals conceded:	60	2
Clean sheets:	12	2
Cards:	Y5, R0	Y0, R0
Defensive rating:	58mins	180mins
Defensive ranking:	107th	33rd

AGE 26 | **WORLD RANKING 1049**

WES BROWN
MAN UNITED

Wes Brown didn't play in any of the qualification games as it seemed his early promise had come to nothing.

However, he's overcome a long run of nagging injury problems to put together a run of games and reminded everyone just how strong he is and how well he times a tackle. He's won back his United place against stiff competition and a place in Sven's squad for the friendly against Uruguay.

AGE 26 | **WORLD RANKING 219**

SOL CAMPBELL
ARSENAL

Sol Campbell had the unenviable task of replacing Tony Adams.

He did do brilliantly for Arsenal and England but injuries have sapped his confidence and he's missing vital games ahead of Germany.

Playing record	12 mths lge	wcq
Appearances:	19	3
Minutes played:	1653	243
Percentage played:	44.8%	27.0%
Goals conceded:	17	0
Clean sheets:	9	3
Cards:	Y2, R0	Y0, R0
Defensive rating:	97mins	-
Defensive ranking:	42nd	-

AGE 31 | **WORLD RANKING 759**

MIDFIELDERS

OWEN HARGREAVES
BAYERN MUNICH

Owen Hargreaves has been out injured for Bayern Munich but shouldn't be counted out of the England squad yet.

He was been ill-used by Sven as a late sub in most of his recent appearances for the national team. It hasn't helped endear him to the England fans and it hasn't given him a chance to display the form he shows for Bayern Munich in the Bundesliga.

Playing record	12 mths lge	wcq
Appearances:	18	4
Minutes played:	1112	46
Percentage played:	32.5%	5.1%
Goals scored:	2	0
Goals conceded:	6	0
Cards:	Y2, R0	Y0, R0
Power rating:	37mins	-
Power ranking:	4th	-

AGE 25 | **WORLD RANKING 209**

JERMAINE JENAS
TOTTENHAM

Jermaine Jenas' form dipped alarmingly at Newcastle last season

Since moving to Spurs, however, his form has improved and he has also rediscovering the eye for goal that marked his early career.

Playing record	12 mths lge	wcq
Appearances:	35	2
Minutes played:	2707	79
Percentage played:	71.6%	8.8%
Goals scored:	4	0
Goals conceded:	31	0
Cards:	Y5, R1	Y0, R0
Power rating:	87mins	-
Power ranking:	140th	-

AGE 23 | **WORLD RANKING 318**

KIERAN RICHARDSON
MAN UNITED

Kieran Richardson took to the white shirt of England with remarkable confidence.

He left behind relegation struggles at West Brom and stepped out against the US, scoring two goals - the first a stunning free kick.

Playing record	12 mths lge	woq
Appearances:	28	2
Minutes played:	1761	18
Percentage played:	47.7%	2.0%
Goals scored:	3	0
Goals conceded:	25	0
Cards:	Y4, R0	Y0, R0
Power rating:	55mins	-
Power ranking:	66th	-

AGE 21	WORLD RANKING 721

STRIKER

DARREN BENT
CHARLTON

Darren Bent has come up on the outside as a possible England striker for Germany.

As befits a man of such pace, he has overtaken a lot of other candidates on the run-in to the tournament. Scoring 20 goals for Ipswich in a failed bid to reach the Premiership last season, probably wouldn't have caught Sven's attention but being on target for a similar total for Charlton certainly did. He had hit 13 league goals in 26 matches for his new club before his England debut against Uruguay.

Whether he did enough then to convince Sven to replace Defoe or take a fifth striker is more doubtful, but if he keeps on scoring for Charlton...

AGE 22	WORLD RANKING 472

ONE TO WATCH

SHAUN WRIGHT-PHILLIPS CHELSEA

The flying winger at Manchester City who scored on his England debut ran into something of a brick wall after his £21m move to Chelsea.

Shaun Wright-Phillips could not get a start for the champions and even lost his place on the bench. A February cup-tie against Everton suggested that he was back to his jinking best and terrorising the Uruguayans confirmed it.

Playing record	12 mths lge	wcq
Appearances:	30	3
Minutes played:	1686	184
Percentage played:	44.6%	20.4%
Goals scored:	1	0
Goals conceded:	14	1
Cards:	Y0, R0	Y0, R0
Power rating:	54mins	-
Power ranking:	60th	-

AGE 24	MIDFIELDER	WORLD RANKING 328

ROUTE TO THE FINALS

Paraguay finished fourth in the South America qualifying group and secured their place at the World Cup finals with a game in hand after beating Venezuela 1-0 in Maracaibo last October.

Werder Bremen striker Nelson Valdez secured victory with the only goal of the game on 65 minutes but Paraguay were made to work hard for the points as Venezuela dominated play for long periods.

Although Paraguay made it safely through to Germany, their qualifying campaign was dogged by inconsistent displays.

FINAL QUALIFYING TABLE
S AMERICA GROUP

	P	W	D	L	GF	GA	Pts
Brazil	18	9	7	2	35	17	34
Argentina	18	10	4	4	29	17	34
Ecuador	18	8	4	6	23	19	28
Paraguay	18	8	4	6	23	23	28
Uruguay	18	6	7	5	23	28	25
Colombia	18	6	6	6	24	16	24
Chile	18	5	7	6	18	22	22
Venezuela	18	5	3	10	20	28	18
Peru	18	4	6	8	20	28	18
Bolivia	18	4	2	12	20	37	14

#	Date	Venue	Opponent	FIFA ranking	Result		Scorers
1	06 Sep 03	Away	Peru	68	L	4 1	Gamarra 24
2	10 Sep 03	Home	Uruguay	18	W	4 1	Cardozo 26, 58, 72, Paredes 53
3	15 Nov 03	Home	Ecuador	35	W	2 1	Santacruz 29, Cardozo 75
4	18 Nov 03	Away	Chile	72	W	0 1	Paredes 30
5	31 Mar 04	Home	Brazil	1	D	0 0	
6	01 Jun 04	Away	Bolivia	96	L	2 1	Cardozo 33
7	06 Jun 04	Away	Argentina	3	D	0 0	
8	05 Sep 04	Home	Venezuela	66	W	1 0	Gamarra 52
9	09 Oct 04	Away	Colombia	25	D	1 1	Gavilan 77
10	13 Oct 04	Home	Peru	68	D	1 1	Paredes 13
11	17 Nov 04	Away	Uruguay	18	L	1 0	
12	27 Mar 05	Away	Ecuador	35	L	5 2	Cardozo 10pen, Cabanas 14
13	30 Mar 05	Home	Chile	72	W	2 1	Morinigo 37, Cardozo 59
14	05 Jun 05	Away	Brazil	1	L	4 1	Santacruz 72
15	08 Jun 05	Home	Bolivia	96	W	4 1	Gamarra 17, Santacruz 45, JC.Caceres 54, J.Nunez 68
16	03 Sep 05	Home	Argentina	3	W	1 0	Santacruz 14
17	08 Oct 05	Away	Venezuela	66	W	0 1	Haedo Valdez 64
18	12 Oct 05	Home	Colombia	25	L	0 1	

| Average FIFA ranking of opposition | 43 |

MAIN PLAYER PERFORMANCES IN QUALIFICATION

Match	1 2 3 4 5 6 7 8 9 10 11 12 13 14 15 16 17 18	Appearances	Started	Subbed on	Subbed off	Mins played	% played	Goals	Yellow	Red
Venue	A H H A H A A H A H A A H A H H A H									
Result	L W W W D L D W D D L L W L W W W L									
Goalkeepers										
Ricardo Tavarelli		2	2	0	0	180	11.1	0	0	0
Justo Villar		15	15	0	0	1350	83.3	0	1	0
Defenders										
Francisco Arce		5	5	0	0	450	27.8	0	0	0
Julio Cesar Caceres		15	15	0	1	1332	82.2	1	1	0
Denis Caniza		12	12	0	0	1080	66.7	0	4	0
Paulo Da Silva		14	11	3	0	1013	62.5	0	1	0
Carlos Alberto Gamarra		15	15	0	0	1341	82.8	3	2	0
Julio Manzur		5	4	1	0	369	22.8	0	2	0
Jorge Nunez		5	5	0	1	420	25.9	1	0	0
Midfielders										
Roberto Miguel Acuna		3	3	0	0	270	16.7	0	0	0
Edgar Barreto		7	3	4	2	371	22.9	0	0	0
Carlos Bonet		8	8	0	5	575	35.5	0	0	0
Julio Dos Santos		4	3	1	3	258	15.9	0	0	0
Julio Cesar Enciso		9	9	0	1	809	49.9	0	1	0
Diego Gavilan		12	5	7	5	505	31.2	1	2	0
Angel Ortiz		12	10	2	1	887	54.8	0	1	1
Carlos Paredes		13	13	0	2	1159	71.5	3	3	0
Forwards										
Salvador Cabanas		7	5	2	3	434	26.8	1	1	0
Jose Cardozo		15	14	1	7	1162	71.7	7	1	0
Nelson Cuevas		12	3	9	1	447	27.6	0	1	0
Cristian Fatecha		2	2	0	0	180	11.1	0	0	0
Nelson Haedo Valdez		4	3	1	1	285	17.6	1	0	0
Roque Santa Cruz		12	12	0	2	1007	62.2	4	0	0

FINAL PROSPECTS

The eccentric – but often very effective – Jose Luis Chilavert no longer holds centre stage in the Paraguay team.

The former captain and goalkeeper, renowned for taking free kicks and scoring his fair share of goals with his left-footed thunderbolts, has now retired from the international game.

The current Paraguay side, however, has more depth with good players in most positions. Coach Anibal Ruiz's team has built up a reputation for playing attractive football with Jose Cardozo, Nelson Valdez and the (currently doubtful) Bayern striker Roque Santa Cruz all capable of scoring goals.

They may have been encouraged by Sweden's rare wobble in their March friendly against the Republic of Ireland.

England and Sweden will be favourites to qualify but Paraguay can be expected to keep it tight at the back and battle for possession in midfield.

THE MANAGER

Uruguayan-born coach Anibal 'Mano' Ruiz took temporary charge of the team from Italian Cesare Maldini after the 2002 World Cup finals and was given the job on a permanent basis in April 2003.

Ruiz, 64, was coach of the Paraguay youth team and has given a number of his former charges their opportunity at full international level.

Prior to taking over the national team Ruiz coached several Paraguayan clubs, including Asuncion giants Olimpia. A young midfielder from Olimpia, Jose Montiel, was blooded by Ruiz during qualifying and may now join Udinese.

Anibal Ruiz

GROUP FIXTURES

KEY PLAYER

CARLOS PAREDES REGGINA

Paraguay are hoping Roque Santa Cruz recovers from injury but even if fit, Santa Cruz is rarely in the Bayern Munich side. Carlos Paredes is at least playing regularly in Reggina's midfield in Serie A. He began with Olimpia in Asuncion in 1995, winning five Paraguayan titles before moving to Porto in 2000 and onto Reggina in 2002. He scored six goals in 28 games last season.

Playing record	12 mths lge	wcq
Appearances:	32	13
Minutes played:	2608	1159
Percentage played:	64.4%	71.5%
Goals scored:	8	3
Goals conceded:	44	15
Cards:	Y3, R1	Y3, R0
Power rating:	84mins	61mins
Power ranking:	131st	93rd

AGE 29 **MIDFIELDER** **WORLD RANKING 709**

Asunció

Zone	South America
Population	6,444,679
Capital	Asuncion
Language	Spanish
Top league	Liga Paraguaya
Major clubs	**Capacities**
Cerro Porteno	25,000
Olimpia	22,000
Libertad	10,000

Where likely squad players play:

In Paraguay	12
In Premiership	0
In other major five European Leagues	5
Outside the major European Leagues	6

Number of Paraguayan players playing:

In Premiership	0
In other major five European Leagues	11

World Cup record

1930 -	Group 2nd	1974 -	Did not qualify
1934 -	Did not enter	1978 -	Did not qualify
1938 -	Did not enter	1982 -	Did not qualify
1950 -	Group 3rd	1986 -	Round 2
1954 -	Did not qualify	1990 -	Did not qualify
1958 -	Group 3rd	1994 -	Did not qualify
1962 -	Did not qualify	1998 -	Last 16
1966 -	Did not qualify	2002 -	Last 16
1970 -	Did not qualify		

THE SQUAD

Goalkeepers	Club side	Age	QG
Derlis Gomez	Sportivo Luqueno	33	1
Ricardo Tavarelli	Porto Alegre	35	2
Justo Villar	Newell's Old Boys	28	15
Defenders			
Francisco Arce	Asuncion	35	5
Julio Cesar Caceres	River Plate	26	15
Denis Caniza	Cruz Azul	31	12
Paulo Da Silva	Toluca	26	14
Carlos Alberto Gamarra	Palmeiras Sao Paulo	35	15
Julio Manzur	Santos	25	5
Jorge Nunez	Estudiantes	28	5
Pedro Sarabia	CP Asuncion	30	3
Delio Cesar Toledo	Real Zaragoza	29	3
Midfielders			
Roberto Miguel Acuna	Deportivo	34	3
Guido Alvarenga	Libertad Asuncion	35	3
Edgar Barreto	NEC Nijmegen	21	7
Carlos Bonet	Liberted Asuncion	28	8
Jorge Campos	Liberted Asuncion	35	3
Julio Dos Santos	Cadiz	23	4
Julio Cesar Encisco	Olimpia Asuncion	31	9
Diego Gavilan	Newells Old Boys	26	12
Mauro Monges	Rosario Central	23	4
Jose Montiel	Olimpia Asuncion	18	2
Angel Ortiz	Atletico Lanus	28	12
Carlos Paredes	Reggina	29	13
Forwards			
Salvador Cabanas	Jaquares Chiapas	25	7
Jose Cardozo	San Lorenzo	35	15
Nelson Cuevas	Pachuca	26	12
Cristian Fatecha	General Caballero	24	2
Nelson Haedo Valdez	Werder Bremen	22	4
Cesar Ramirez	Flamengo	29	4
Roque Santa Cruz	Bayern Munich	24	12

■ Probable ■ Possible **QG** Qualification Games

TRINIDAD & TOBAGO

ROUTE TO THE FINALS

Trinidad & Tobago booked their trip to Germany when they beat Bahrain in the CONCACAF-Asia play-off after finishing fourth in the American qualifying group.

Wrexham's Dennis Lawrence scored the only goal of the second leg away against Bahrain after the first leg played in Port of Spain had finished 1-1.

The defender headed the crucial goal after 64 minutes when he met Dwight Yorke's well-flighted corner.

The Soca Warriors needed to beat the mighty Mexico in their last group match on 12 October 2005 to make it through to the play-off against Bahrain and they started badly by going a goal down and missing a penalty.

Coventry striker Stern John weighed in with two goals to secure a last-gasp 2-1 win for the Warriors, a victory that saw them pip Guatemala to a play-off place.

Coach Leo Beenhakker was appointed midway through the qualifiers in May 2005 and he guided the side to their first World Cup finals at the 11th attempt.

For final qualification table see USA.

	Date	Venue	Opponent	FIFA ranking	Result			Scorers
1	18 Aug 04	Away	StVincent/Grenadines	131	W	0	2	McFarlane 80, 85
2	04 Sep 04	Away	St Kitts/Nevis	122	W	1	2	McFarlane 45, S.John 89
3	08 Sep 04	Home	Mexico	6	L	1	3	S.John 39
4	10 Oct 04	Home	St Kitts/Nevis	122	W	5	1	A.Riley 8og, S.John 24, 80, Glenn 71, Nixon 88
5	13 Oct 04	Away	Mexico	6	L	3	0	
6	17 Nov 04	Home	StVincent/Grenadines	131	W	2	1	Sam 84, Eve 90
7	09 Feb 05	Home	United States	8	L	1	2	Eve 87
8	26 Mar 05	Away	Guatemala	60	L	5	1	Edwards 32
9	30 Mar 05	Home	Costa Rica	22	D	0	0	
10	04 Jun 05	Home	Panama	88	W	2	0	S.John 34, Lawrence 71
11	08 Jun 05	Away	Mexico	6	L	2	0	
12	17 Aug 05	Away	United States	8	L	1	0	
13	03 Sep 05	Home	Guatemala	60	W	3	2	Latapy 48, S.John 85, 86
14	07 Sep 05	Away	Costa Rica	22	L	2	0	
15	08 Oct 05	Away	Panama	88	W	0	1	S.John 61
16	12 Oct 05	Home	Mexico	6	W	2	1	S.John 43, 69
17	16 Nov 05	Away	Bahrain	51	W	0	1	Lawrence 49
	Average FIFA ranking of opposition			55				

MAIN PLAYER PERFORMANCES IN QUALIFICATION

Match	1 2 3 4 5 6 7 8 9 10 11 12 13 14 15 16 17	Appearances	Started	Subbed on	Subbed off	Mins played	% played	Goals	Yellow	Red
Venue	A A H H A H H A H H A A H A A H A									
Result	W W L W L W L L D W L L W L W W W									
Goalkeepers										
Shaka Hislop		5	4	1	0	405	26.5	0	0	0
Clayton Ince		2	2	0	0	180	11.8	0	0	0
Kelvin Jack		10	10	0	1	855	55.9	0	0	0
Defenders										
Marvin Andrews		15	15	0	0	1350	88.2	0	1	0
David Atiba Charles		4	4	0	1	313	20.5	0	0	0
Ian Cox		6	4	2	0	458	29.9	0	0	0
Cyd Gray		2	2	0	0	180	11.8	0	2	0
Avery John		8	8	0	0	719	47.0	0	4	1
Dennis Lawrence		14	14	0	1	1198	78.3	2	1	1
AmtonPierre		3	3	0	0	270	17.6	0	1	0
Marlon Rojas		6	6	0	1	485	31.7	0	1	0
Brent Sancho		10	9	1	0	857	56.0	0	1	0
Midfielders										
Christopher Birchall		7	7	0	1	623	40.7	0	1	0
Carlos Edwards		10	10	0	3	854	55.8	1	1	0
Angus Eve		8	6	2	0	607	39.7	2	2	0
Kenwyne Jones		12	9	3	4	799	52.2	0	3	0
Russell Latapy		5	4	1	1	369	24.1	1	1	0
Brent Rahim		7	4	3	4	439	28.7	0	2	0
Silvio Spann		9	5	4	3	503	32.9	0	2	0
Densil Theobald		8	4	4	3	347	22.7	0	1	0
Aurtis Whitley		8	7	1	4	509	33.3	0	1	0
Forwards										
Stern John		16	16	0	2	1384	90.5	10	0	0
Errol McFarlane		5	4	1	4	330	21.6	3	0	0
Anthony Rougier		4	4	0	1	315	20.6	0	2	0
Dwight Yorke		11	11	0	0	990	64.7	0	2	0

FINAL PROSPECTS

The Trinidad & Tobago squad in Germany is likely to feature a record number of players from the English Football League but few, if any from the Premiership.

Coventry's Stern John leads the attack and hit 12 goals in qualifying. The Soca Warriors will be well prepared by Leo Beenhakker, but will not be expected to beat either England or Sweden in their Group B matches.

Their most famous player Dwight Yorke, the former Manchester United striker, has recently been playing his club football for FC Sydney in Australia and will be 35 by the time the World Cup finals are in full swing.

Yorke came out of international retirement in 2005 and played every minute of the last 11 qualifiers. He plays in a deeper role than United fans would expect but will have a leading part to play in Germany.

THE MANAGER

Leo Beenhakker, took control of the Trinidad & Tobago squad in May 2005 after his predecessor Bertile St Clair was sacked in the wake of the disappointing goalless draw against Costa Rica.

He is one of the most experienced coaches in world football.

The 64-year-old Beenhakker has been in charge of the Holland and Saudi Arabia national sides, as well as head coach at some of Europe's most prestigious clubs, including Ajax, Feyenoord, Real Madrid and Real Zaragoza.

He has worked wonders with the limited resources of the tiny island nation. He also worked his experienced players hard to galvinise the squad.

Leo Beenhakker

GROUP FIXTURES

SWEDEN	Sat 10 June	1700 BST
ENGLAND	Thur 15 June	1700 BST
PARAGUAY	Tue 20 June	2000 BST

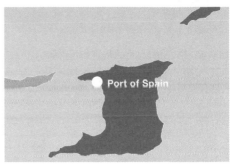

Port of Spain

Zone	North, Central America & Caribbean
Population	1,077,046
Capital	Port-of-Spain
Language	English
Top league	Pro League
Major clubs	**Capacities**
Defence Force	27,000
San Juan Jabloteh	27,000
W Connection FC	10,000

Where likely squad players play:

In Premiership	1
In other major five European Leagues	0
Outside major European Leagues	22

Number of Trinidad & Tobago players playing:

In Premiership	1
In other major five European Leagues	0

World Cup record

1930 -	Did not enter	1974 -	Did not qualify
1934 -	Did not enter	1978 -	Did not qualify
1938 -	Did not enter	1982 -	Did not qualify
1950 -	Did not enter	1986 -	Did not qualify
1954 -	Did not enter	1990	Did not qualify
1958 -	Did not enter	1994 -	Did not qualify
1962 -	Did not enter	1998 -	Did not qualify
1966 -	Did not qualify	2002 -	Did not qualify
1970 -	Did not qualify		

THE SQUAD

Goalkeepers	Club side	Age	QG
Shaka Hislop	West Ham	37	5
Clayton Ince	Coventry	33	2
Kelvin Jack	Dundee	30	10
Defenders			
Marvin Andrews	Rangers	30	15
David Atiba Charles	Couva	28	4
Ian Cox	Gillingham	35	6
Avery John	New England Rev	30	8
Dennis Lawrence	Wrexham	32	14
Amton Pierre	Mucarapo	28	3
Marlon Rojas	Salt Lake City	26	6
Brent Sancho	Gillingham	29	10
Midfielders			
Christopher Birchall	Port Vale	22	7
Andre Boucaud	Aldershot	21	3
Carlos Edwards	Luton	27	10
Angus Eve	San Juan Jabloteh	33	8
Kenwyne Jones	Southampton	22	12
Russell Latapy	Falkirk	37	5
Brent Rahim	-	27	7
Silvio Spann	Yokohama	24	9
Densil Theobald	Falkirk	23	8
Aurtis Whitley	San Juan Jabloteh	29	8
Forwards			
Arnold Dwarika	Guangzhou Riz	32	3
Gary Glasgow	Guangzhou Riz	30	1
Cornell Glenn	Columbus Crewe	24	6
Stern John	Coventry	29	16
Stockley Mason	Caledonia	30	1
Errol McFarlane	Al-Nijmeh Beirut	28	5
Nigel Pierre	San Juan Jabloteh	27	1
Anthony Rougier	Rochester USA	34	4
Hector Sam	Port Vale	28	4
Jason Scotland	St Johnstone	27	3
Scott Sealy	Kansas City Wizards	25	5
Dwight Yorke	Sydney FC	34	11

■ Probable ■ Possible **QG** Qualification Games

KEY PLAYER

DWIGHT YORKE SYDNEY FC

Graham Taylor unearthed Dwight Yorke on an Aston Villa tour of the Caribbean in 1989. Yorke was injury-prone at Villa but impressed enough when fit for Manchester United to pay £12.6m for him.
Teaming up with Andy Cole at United, Yorke made an immediate impact and his beaming smile accompanied 47 goals in 95 league appearances. He was the club's main striker when they completed their unique treble in 1999 but the arrival of Ruud van Nistelrooy in 2001 limited Yorke's appearances.
His form dipped at Blackburn but he is hugely influential for the Soca Warriors and recently persuaded former Rangers star Russell Latapy to come out of international retirement and make himself available for the side.

AGE 35 | **STRIKER** | **WORLD RANKING –**

ROUTE TO THE FINALS

Sweden qualified for their 11th World Cup finals after finishing second behind Croatia in European Group 8.

The Swedes won eight of their ten qualifiers, but 1-0 defeats at home and away against Croatia saw the Croats claim top spot despite both sides finishing with 24 points.

Apart from those narrow losses against Croatia, Sweden's qualifying campaign was stunning. They made a clean sweep of all their other matches and recorded home and away victories over Hungary and Bulgaria.

Sweden scored 30 goals and conceded just four. Their well-organised defence also managed to keep six clean sheets.

Juventus striker Zlatan Ibramimovic was the star of Sweden's qualifying campaign, scoring eight goals. Arsenal's Freddie Ljungberg was impressive, finding the net seven times with his penetrative running from midfield, while former Celtic star Henrik Larsson weighed in with five goals.

The Swedish defence usually performs far better than their club form would lead you to expect but they were surprisingly found out by the Republic of Ireland in a March friendly when they conceded three goals to Steve Staunton's team.

FINAL QUALIFYING TABLE
EUROPE GROUP 8

	P	W	D	L	GF	GA	Pts
Croatia	10	7	3	0	21	5	24
Sweden	10	8	0	2	30	4	24
Bulgaria	10	4	3	3	17	17	15
Hungary	10	4	2	4	13	14	14
Iceland	10	1	1	8	14	27	4
Malta	10	0	3	7	4	32	3

	Date		Opponent	FIFA ranking		Score	Scorers
1	04 Sep 04	Away	Malta	132	W	0 7	Ibrahimovic 4, 11, 14, 71, Ljungberg 46, 74, Larsson 76
2	08 Sep 04	Home	Croatia	21	L	0 1	
3	09 Oct 04	Home	Hungary	67	W	3 0	Ljungberg 26, Larsson 50, A.Svensson 67
4	13 Oct 04	Away	Iceland	93	W	1 4	Larsson 23, 38, Allback 27, Wilhelmsson 44
5	26 Mar 05	Away	Bulgaria	42	W	0 3	Ljungberg 17, 90pen, Edman 73
6	04 Jun 05	Home	Malta	132	W	6 0	Jonson 6, A.Svensson 18, Wilhelmsson 30, Ibrahimovic 40, Ljungberg 57, Elmander 81
7	03 Sep 05	Home	Bulgaria	42	W	3 0	Ljungberg 60, Mellberg 75, Ibrahimovic 90
8	07 Sep 05	Away	Hungary	67	W	0 1	Ibrahimovic 90
9	08 Oct 05	Away	Croatia	21	L	1 0	
10	12 Oct 05	Home	Iceland	93	W	3 1	Ibrahimovic 30, Larsson 42, Kallstrom 90
	Average FIFA ranking of opposition			71			

MAIN PLAYER PERFORMANCES IN QUALIFICATION

Match Venue Result	1 2 3 4 5 6 7 8 9 10 A H H A A H H A A H W L W W W W W W L W	Appearances	Started	Subbed on	Subbed off	Mins played	% played	Goals	Yellow	Red
Goalkeepers										
Magnus Hedman		1	0	1	0	61	6.8	0	0	0
Andreas Isaksson		10	10	0	1	839	93.2	0	0	0
Defenders										
Christoffer Andersson		1	1	0	0	90	10.0	0	1	0
Erik Edman		7	7	0	1	588	65.3	1	1	0
Petter Hansson		1	1	0	0	90	10.0	0	1	0
Teddy Lucic		10	10	0	1	889	98.8	0	0	0
Olof Mellberg		10	10	0	1	871	96.8	1	0	0
Johan Mjallby		1	1	0	1	45	5.0	0	0	0
Alexander Ostlund		9	8	1	0	762	84.7	0	3	0
Midfielders										
Niclas Alexandersson		8	4	4	1	425	47.2	0	0	0
Mattias Jonson		6	3	3	3	246	27.3	1	1	0
Kim Kallstrom		5	1	4	1	147	16.3	1	0	0
Tobias Linderoth		10	10	0	1	875	97.2	0	0	0
Fredrik Ljungberg		10	10	0	1	865	96.1	7	1	0
Mikael Nilsson		3	1	2	0	164	18.2	0	0	0
Anders Svensson		8	8	0	5	625	69.4	2	0	0
Christian Wilhelmsson		10	8	2	4	707	78.6	2	0	0
Forwards										
Marcus Allback		7	2	5	0	249	27.7	1	0	0
Johan Elmander		2	0	2	0	39	4.3	1	0	0
Zlatan Ibrahimovic		8	7	1	2	650	72.2	8	2	0
Henrik Larsson		8	8	0	2	673	74.8	5	0	0

FINAL PROSPECTS

Sweden have a good World Cup record, having been runners-up when they hosted the tournament in 1958, and semi-finalists twice in 1950 and 1994.

They will go to Germany expecting to reach the last 16 after December's draw in Leipzig, put them in the same group as England, Trinidad & Tobago and Paraguay.

Sweden coach Lars Lagerback is well respected by his players and has managed to produce an attractive team that combines a miserly defence with a free-scoring attack.

Aston Villa's Olof Mellberg will captain the side and is a key player in the centre of defence. He may not be as quick as he once was over the ground, but his excellent football brain and leadership skills on the park will be crucial to Sweden's chances.

Lagerback will look to Juventus striker Zlatan Ibramimovic to lead the front line with skill and power, as he did so effectively in the qualifiers. Barcelona's Henrik Larsson, who is due to return to his home-club Helsingborg after the finals in Germany, will also hope to be in the goals. This will almost certainly be his last major tournament.

> **"Sweden play the English formation of 4-4-2 and always do well against England at international competition level."**
> Martin Jol

If there are no upsets in earlier matches against Trinidad & Tobago and Paraguay, Sweden's third and final Group B match against England in Cologne will decide who finishes top of the group table.

Sweden always do well against England at international level. The two countries have played each other ten times and although all the results have been close, Sweden have won four times and the rest have all been draws. England are still waiting for their first victory over the Swedes.

An in-form Sweden will fancy their chances against either Poland or Germany in the last 16 and are a good bet to reach the quarter-finals even if they finish runners-up to England in the group stage.

GROUP FIXTURES

TRINIDAD & T.	Sat 10 June 1700 BST
PARAGUAY	Thu 15 June 2000 BST
ENGLAND	Tue 20 June 2000 BST

Zone	Europe
Population	9,002,000
Capital	Stockholm
Language	Swedish
Top league	Allsvenskan

Major clubs	Capacities
Malmo	26,500
IFK Goteborg	16,500
AIK	36.600

Where likely squad players play:

In Premiership	2	In Spain	2
In Holland	2	In France	3
In Italy	1	In Germany	0

Number of Swiss players playing:

In Premiership	4	In Spain	1
In Holland	10	In France	5
In Italy	1	In Germany	1

World Cup record

1930 -	Did not enter	1974 -	Round 2
1934 -	Quarter-finals	1978 -	Group 4th
1938 -	Fourth place	1982 -	Did not qualify
1950 -	Third place	1986 -	Did not qualify
1954 -	Did not qualify	1990 -	Group 4th
1958 -	Runners-up	1994 -	Third place
1962 -	Did not qualify	1998 -	Did not qualify
1966 -	Did not qualify	2002 -	Last 16
1970 -	Group 3rd		

THE SQUAD

Goalkeepers	Club side	Age	QG
Magnus Hedman	Floating	33	1
Andreas Isaksson	Rennes	24	10
Eddie Gustafsson	Ham-Kam		
Defenders			
Christoffer Andersson	Lillestrom	27	1
Mikael Dorsin	Rosenborg	24	0
Erik Edman	Rennes	27	7
Petter Hansson	Heerenveen	29	1
Teddy Lucic	Floating	33	10
Olof Mellberg	Aston Villa	28	10
Johan Mjallby	Levante	35	1
Alexander Ostlund	Southampton	27	9
Midfielders			
Daniel Andersson	Malmo	28	-
Niclas Alexandersson	Lillestrom	34	8
Mattias Jonson	Djurgardens	32	6
Kim Kallstrom	Rennes	23	5
Tobias Linderoth	FC Copenhagen	27	10
Fredrik Ljungberg	Arsenal	29	10
Mikael Nilsson	Panathinaikos	27	3
Anders Svensson	Elfsborg	29	8
Christian Wilhelmsson	Anderlecht	26	10
Forwards			
Marcus Allback	FC Copenhagen	32	7
Johan Elmander	Brondby	25	2
Zlatan Ibrahimovic	Juventus	24	8
Henrik Larsson	Barcelona	34	8
Markus Rosenberg	Ajax	24	0

KEY PLAYER

ZLATAN IBRAHIMOVIC JUVENTUS

Zlatan Ibrahimovic is a goal-scoring sensation at Juventus. He has made an almost seamless transition from Swedish league football via Ajax in Holland, to Italy's Serie A.

Arsenal tried to sign Ibrahimovic from his hometown club Malmo but the 1.93m tall striker opted instead for a move to Ajax in 2001. He collected Dutch league and cup

winners' medals before Juventus paid £12.5m for him in the summer of 2004. He immediately had an impact, scoring 16 goals in the club's Serie A title win next season.

His combination of skill, aerial strength and predatory finishing has lifted him to superstar status.

Ibrahimovic is one of our Top 12 Strikers.

AGE 20   **STRIKER**   **WORLD RANKING** 43

■ Probable ■ Possible **QG** Qualification Games

KEY GOALKEEPER

ANDREAS ISAKSSON
RENNES

Andreas Isaksson took over from the dependable Magnus Hedman as Sweden's first choice keeper at Euro 2004.

The much-admired Hedman's injuries and struggle to hold down a first-team place at Celtic propelled the 23-year old into the Swedish team and he now holds the place on ability. As a youngster, he was signed by Juventus but elected to return to the Allsvenskan League in Sweden for first team experience with Djurgarden. He replaced Petr Cech at Rennes last season and made 38 appearances. He has recovered from a four-month lay-off with a thigh injury this season.

Playing record	12 mths lge	wcq
Appearances:	28	10
Minutes played:	2463	839
Percentage played:	65.2%	93.2%
Goals conceded:	42	3
Clean sheets:	10	7
Cards:	Y1, R1	Y0, R0
Defensive rating:	59mins	280mins
Defensive ranking:	24th	4th

AGE 24	WORLD RANKING 685

KEY DEFENDERS

OLOF MELLBERG
ASTON VILLA

The Aston Villa defender Olof Mellberg is Sweden's captain and the key player in a settled back four.

His centre back partner Teddy Lucic (formerly of Leeds and Bayer Leverkusen) is out of top class football but the pair are solid for Sweden, only conceding four goals in ten qualifying games.

Powerful in the air and a natural leader, Mellberg adds steel across the back line. He doesn't have a good scoring record but is still a target at free kicks and corners.

He topped Villa's defensive charts last season recording nine clean sheets in 30 league appearances.

Playing record	12 mths lge	wcq
Appearances:	30	10
Minutes played:	2642	871
Percentage played:	71.6%	96.8%
Goals conceded:	40	4
Clean sheets:	8	6
Cards:	Y5, R0	Y0, R0
Defensive rating:	66mins	218mins
Defensive ranking:	99th	24th

AGE 28	WORLD RANKING 1219

ERIK EDMAN
RENNES

Eric Edman impressed at Tottenham last season, not least when he unleashed a stunning 35-yarder to score past Jerzy Dudek at Anfield.

He has played for Helsingborg in Sweden and Heerenveen in Holland. When Young-Pyo Lee came in at left back for Spurs, Edman moved to Rennes, joining a growing Swedish contingent, including Isaksson and Kallstrom. He was part of the Swedish squad in 2002 but didn't play and gained his tournament experience in Euro 2004.

During qualifying, Edman scored a free kick against Bulgaria in a 3-0 away win.

Playing record	12 mths lge	wcq
Appearances:	38	7
Minutes played:	3341	588
Percentage played:	88.4%	65.3%
Goals conceded:	36	3
Clean sheets:	13	4
Cards:	Y7, R0	Y1, R0
Defensive rating:	93mins	196mins
Defensive ranking:	49th	29th

AGE 27	WORLD RANKING 1134

KEY MIDFIELDERS

KIM KALLSTROM
RENNES

A team-mate of Andreas Isaksson at Rennes is attacking midfielder Kim Kallstrom.

He also moved from Djurgarden to the French club and looks their most in-form player this season. Nicknamed Kongo Kim, he was first capped in 2001 and scored five goals in 28 league appearances last season.

Playing record	12 mths lge	wcq
Appearances:	37	5
Minutes played:	3093	147
Percentage played:	81.8%	16.3%
Goals scored:	8	1
Goals conceded:	47	0
Cards:	Y6, R1	Y0, R0
Power rating:	72mins	-
Power ranking:	113rd	-

AGE 23	WORLD RANKING 490

THE MANAGER

Lars Lagerback is now in sole charge of the Sweden national team

His former co-manager, Tommy Soderberg, stepped down after Euro 2004, where the Swedes were eliminated after the second round.

The 62-year-old Lagerback first joined the Sweden set-up as Soderberg's assistant and made co-manager in 2000.

While the two men shared responsibility for the Sweden squad, Lagerback was seen as the shrewd tactician, with Soderberg taking care of man-management and motivation.

However, in his fours years as manager Lagerback has demonstrated the full range of qualities required of a national team boss, not least his polite but honest dealings with the media.

Lagerback, who never reached the top flight as a player, is now one of the most respected national coaches in Europe.

Lars Lagerback

KEY STRIKER

HENRIK LARSSON
BARCELONA

Henrik's Larsson's decision to retire from international football before Euro 2004 , led to an outcry in Sweden and he was eventually persuaded to play on.

He did so to great effect scoring three times in four matches.

When he is on the pitch, a goal is always likely. He has scored some of the most memorable headed goals of the last five years, climbing at the far post, or diving full length to power past the keeper. He links play brilliantly and moves to a devastating effect in the penalty area. Still a potent threat although he is playing less at Barcelona.

Playing record	12 mths lge	wcq
Appearances:	19	8
Minutes played:	678	673
Percentage played:	17.9%	74.8%
Goals scored:	6	5
Percentage share:	6.67	16.67
Cards:	Y0, R0	Y0, R0
Strike rate:	-	135mins
Strike rate ranking:	-	21st

AGE 34   **WORLD RANKING —**

ONE TO WATCH

FREDDIE LJUNGBERG ARSENAL

Freddie Ljungberg always seems to be straining every sinew to reach a cross or collect or pass everyone else has given up on. Ljungberg can play wide, on either flank or behind a main striker. He impressed for Sweden in the 1998 World Cup and Arsenal signed him for £3m. His influence quickly grew and he has scored twice in FA Cup finals.

Playing record	12 mths lge	wcq
Appearances:	26	10
Minutes played:	1939	865
Percentage played:	51.3%	96.1%
Goals scored:	3	7
Goals conceded:	19	3
Cards:	Y1, R0	Y1, R0
Power rating:	59mins	29mins
Power ranking:	79th	7th

AGE 29   **MIDFIELD**   **WORLD RANKING 79**

12th ANDRIY SHEVCHENKO
AC MILAN

Andriy Shevchenko is one of the most devastating strikers of his generation.

He combines pace and skill with a predator's instinct in front of goal. The youngster, who was evacuated from Chernobyl aged nine and originally turned away by Dinamo Kiev for failing a dribbling test, won five league titles with the Ukrainian team before moving to Italian giants AC Milan. He top-scored for Milan last season with 17 league goals plus five in the Champions League. He was European Footballer of the Year in 2004.

Playing record	12 mths lge	wcq
Appearances:	30	9
Minutes played:	2393	775
Percentage played:	59.1%	71.8%
Goals scored:	18	6
Percentage share:	20.45	33.33
Cards:	Y0, R0	Y0, R0
Strike rate:	133mins	129mins
Strike rate ranking:	13th	18th

AGE 29 **WORLD RANKING 47**

11th DIDIER DROGBA
CHELSEA

Didier Drogba is a physically strong and imposing striker, who is a handful for any marker.

He is a capable rather than a deadly finisher with a penchant for the unexpected. He also creates valuable space for team-mates. Drogba was one of the stars of the Ivory Coast's World Cup qualifying campaign, scoring nine goals. He first came to the fore at unfashionable Guingamp in the French league, before a year at Marseille and a move to Chelsea for £24m in summer 2004.

Playing record	12 mths lge	wcq
Appearances:	28	9
Minutes played:	1802	725
Percentage played:	47.7%	80.6%
Goals scored:	9	9
Percentage share:	11.54	45.00
Cards:	Y5, R0	Y1, R0
Strike rate:	200mins	81mins
Strike rate ranking:	44th	4th

AGE 28 **WORLD RANKING 45**

10th ZLATAN IBRAHIMOVIC
JUVENTUS

Swedish striker Zlatan Ibrahimovic has been knocking the goals in on a regular basis for Juventus since the Turin club paid Ajax £12.5m for him.

He's an imposing player but also an intelligent one, although at times his qualities are eclipsed by the descent of the red mist. He hit eight goals in ten qualifiers to help Sweden reach the World Cup finals and he forms a deadly partnership with Henrik Larsson. Ibrahimovic top-scored for Juve with 16 last season but is third in their ranks this time.

Playing record	12 mths lge	wcq
Appearances:	39	8
Minutes played:	2689	650
Percentage played:	66.4%	72.2%
Goals scored:	13	8
Percentage share:	15.29	26.67
Cards:	Y6, R0	Y2, R0
Strike rate:	207mins	81mins
Strike rate ranking:	48th	6th

AGE 24 **WORLD RANKING 43**

9th RUUD VAN NISTELROOY
MAN UTD

Holland striker Ruud van Nistelrooy overcame a career-threatening knee injury when he was at PSV Eindhoven to become a goal-scoring legend at Manchester United.

He is a powerful, natural finisher, who is good in the air and on the ground but deadliest in the six-yard box.

Van Nistelrooy has formed a good understanding in the Holland team with fellow striker Dick Kuijt of Feyenoord that should be a threat to any defence at the World Cup finals.

Playing record	12 mths lge	wcq
Appearances:	33	10
Minutes played:	2670	800
Percentage played:	72.4%	74.1%
Goals scored:	21	7
Percentage share:	28.77	25.93
Cards:	Y6, R0	Y1, R0
Strike rate:	127mins	114mins
Strike rate ranking:	11th	15th

AGE 29 **WORLD RANKING 42**

8th MIROSLAV KLOSE
W BREMEN

A tall, predatory striker with good all-round skills, Miroslav Klose is extremely dangerous in the air and his gung-ho attitude has made him a favourite amongst the German fans.

He rose to fame on the back of five goals for Germany in the finals of the 2002 World Cup. The Polish-born Klose has found a new lease of life after joining Werder Bremen from Bundesliga rivals Kaiserslautern at the beginning of 2004/5 and struck 15 league goals for them.

Playing record	12 mths lge	int
Appearances:	28	7
Minutes played:	2171	554
Percentage played:	63.5%	33.6%
Goals scored:	21	2
Percentage share:	25.61	5.56
Cards:	Y3, R0	Y0, R0
Strike rate:	103mins	277mins
Strike rate ranking:	3rd	50th

AGE 28 **WORLD RANKING 41**

7th LUCA TONI
FIORENTINA

The late developing Luca Toni has similarities with Liverpool's Peter Crouch – only he scores more goals!

A tall centre forward, who can be hit-and-miss in the air, he spent many years mis-starting his career at a series of small or unfashionable clubs.

That all changed last season when his 20 goals in 35 appearances for Palermo, lifted them to sixth place, earned a national team call-up and a £6m move to Fiorentina. Just look at his goals scored total.

Playing record	12 mths lge	wcq
Appearances:	43	8
Minutes played:	3817	264
Percentage played:	94.2%	29.3%
Goals scored:	35	5
Percentage share:	51.47	26.32
Cards:	Y6, R0	Y0, R0
Strike rate:	109mins	53mins
Strike rate ranking:	6th	1st

AGE 29 **WORLD RANKING 34**

6th WAYNE ROONEY
MAN UTD

Wayne Rooney was only 18 when he took Euro 2004 by storm and scared the living daylights out of seasoned international defenders.

But England's hopes of glory faded after he injured a foot in the quarter-finals against Portugal. The wonder-kid, who has since joined Manchester United from Everton, remains the inspiration for club and country. Rooney is still only 20 and has the raw talent to become the greatest player ever to represent his country.

Playing record	12 mths lge	wcq
Appearances:	40	7
Minutes played:	3203	613
Percentage played:	86.8%	68.1%
Goals scored:	16	0
Percentage share:	21.92	0.00
Cards:	Y11, R0	Y2, R0
Strike rate:	200mins	-
Strike rate ranking:	43rd	-

AGE 20 **WORLD RANKING 31**

5th THIERRY HENRY
ARSENAL

Thierry Henry's devastating pace and accuracy in front of goal have made him one of the deadliest strikers in football and a living legend at Arsenal.

He was only 20 when he won a place in France's 1998 World Cup-winning squad. He was also in the French team that later triumphed at Euro 2000. After a brief, unhappy spell on the wing at Juventus, Henry moved to Highbury, where he has taken goal scoring to a new level. He passed 200 goals for them in February.

Playing record	12 mths lge	wcq
Appearances:	29	6
Minutes played:	2565	472
Percentage played:	69.5%	52.4%
Goals scored:	24	3
Percentage share:	32.88	18.75
Cards:	Y2, R0	Y0, R0
Strike rate:	107mins	157mins
Strike rate ranking:	5th	25th

AGE 28 **WORLD RANKING 19**

4th

DAVID TREZEGUET
JUVENTUS

Striker David Trezeguet is already in the history books as the man who scored the 'golden goal' winner that saw France beat Italy 2-1 in the final of the Euro 2000 tournament in Rotterdam.

The Juventus striker has been in great scoring form this season after suffering a series of injuries. He fell out of favour in France after a red card against Israel, but remains one of the best finishers in Europe and will form a formidable striking double act with Thierry Henry in Germany.

Playing record	12 mths lge	wcq
Appearances:	34	2
Minutes played:	2298	180
Percentage played:	56.7%	20.0%
Goals scored:	22	1
Percentage share:	25.88	6.25
Cards:	Y0, R0	Y1, R0
Strike rate:	104mins	-
Strike rate ranking:	4th	-

3rd

RONALDO
REAL MADRID

Ronaldo is one of the most formidable strikers the world has ever seen.

He survived a mid-career crisis – caused by injuries and illness – to recapture the astonishing form he showed as a younger player. The forward scored both goals when Brazil beat Germany 2-0 in the 2002 World Cup final and hit ten goals during Brazil's qualifying campaign. He was heckled over his fitness levels at the Bernabeu and fell out with the crowd but still struck 21 league goals for Real Madrid last year.

Playing record	12 mths lge	wcq
Appearances:	33	15
Minutes played:	2754	1285
Percentage played:	72.9%	79.3%
Goals scored:	20	10
Percentage share:	24.39	28.57
Cards:	Y0, R0	Y1, R0
Strike rate:	138mins	128mins
Strike rate ranking:	14th	17th

2nd

DIRK KUIJT
FEYENOORD

Feyenoord striker Dirk Kuijt is one of the most coveted players in Europe - a big-money transfer waiting to happen.

The Holland international started his career at FC Utrecht but it was only after he moved to Feyenoord that the goals really start to flow. He is a skilful, accurate finisher who has already netted more than 100 goals in the Dutch league.

His form is so good that the Bundesliga's best striker, Bayern Munich's Roy Makaay, is confined to the bench for Holland.

Playing record	12 mths lge	wcq
Appearances:	41	11
Minutes played:	3659	978
Percentage played:	94.5%	90.6%
Goals scored:	33	3
Percentage share:	28.95	11.11
Cards:	Y0, R0	Y1, R0
Strike rate:	111mins	326mins
Strike rate ranking:	7th	55th

| AGE 28 | WORLD RANKING 17 |

| AGE 29 | WORLD RANKING 9 |

| AGE 25 | WORLD RANKING 8 |

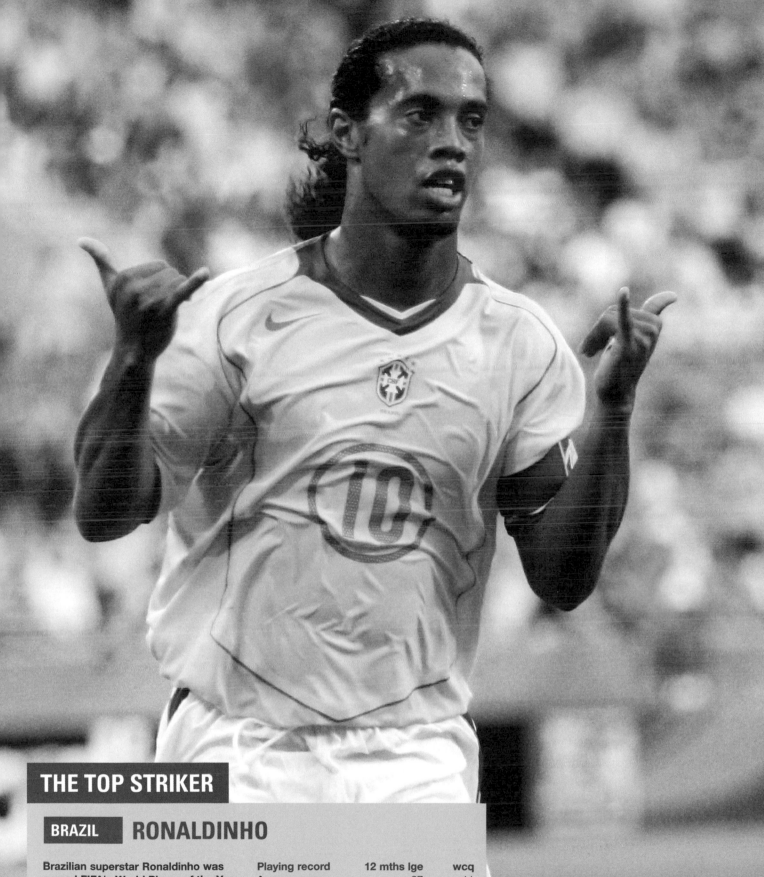

THE TOP STRIKER

BRAZIL **RONALDINHO**

Brazilian superstar Ronaldinho was
named FIFA's World Player of the Year
in December – for the second
consecutive year.

The multi-talented Ronaldinho used to be
a little goal shy but he's hitting the net with
ease this season. He will go to Germany
confident that he can inspire another
triumph for the reigning world champions.

Playing record	12 mths lge	wcq
Appearances:	37	11
Minutes played:	3266	909
Percentage played:	86.4%	56.1%
Goals scored:	17	4
Percentage share:	18.89	11.43
Cards:	Y9, R0	Y3, R0
Strike rate:	192mins	227mins
Strike rate ranking:	41st	41st

1st

AGE 26 **BARCELONA** **WORLD RANKING 5**

Position	1st	2nd	3rd	4th	5th	6th	7th	8th
Group	E	F	C	A	D	H	B	G
Total FIFA ranking	89	93	95	96	101	109	117	138

ARGENTINA V IVORY COAST
ARGW DRAW — Hamburg, Saturday 10th June 2000 BST

Ivory Coast will be doubly up for this game. They will be desperate to get over the tears of the African Cup of Nations final defeat by Egypt in a penalty shoot-out and equally keen to impress in their first World Cup.
There's a bit of club rivalry too in pitting Chelsea's two main strikers, Hernan Crespo and Didier Drogba, against each other.

Argentina may be slow-starters here without a settled defence if Ayala and Heinze are missing. The powerful Olympiakos midfielder Gnegneri Yaya Toure (Kolo's little brother) made a big impression in the Champions League group stages and along with Didier Zokora will be charged with stifling the Argentinian midfield and protecting the defence.

SERB & MONT V HOLLAND
HOLW HOLW — Leipzig, Sunday 11th June 1400 BST

A look at Serbia and Montenegro's team-sheet and it's easy to see them pointless in this group but take a look at their results. Ignore a recent reverse against South Korea as they sent a weakened squad on that tour. They have played Spain twice, Belgium twice, Italy and Bulgaria recently and no one has beaten them.

They will struggle to penetrate though, especially as Mateja Kezman has been misfiring for Atletico Madrid.
Ruud van Nistelrooy will be vital to this young Dutch side – they didn't play in Euro 2004 and they will need to be settled by the striker and Edwin van der Sar.

ARGENTINA V SERB & M
ARGW ARGW — Gelsenkirchen, Fri 16th June 1400 BST

If the earlier results have gone with our predictions, both sides will be playing for a win here.
A more open game will suit Argentina and Riquelme will find the freedom to orchestrate play in midfield and could give Julio Cruz a chance up front. Cruz is scoring goals and forcing his way into the team at Inter, and could be the perfect complement to Hernan Crespo.

HOLLAND V IVORY COAST
HOLW DRAW — Stuttgart, Friday 16th June 1700 BST

Put the Ivory Coast defence under the microscope and it shows they perform pretty well. Only three goals conceded in the African Cup of Nations; just seven goals in ten games in a strong qualifying group.
Holland have the fire-power to break through but may need more than one goal.

The Ivory Coast's Yaya Toure

HOLLAND V ARGENTINA
ARGW DRAW — Frankfurt, Wednesday 21st June 2000 BST

The most lip-smacking tie in the group stages sees the new young Dutch generation against the traditional South American superpower. The chances are, a draw won't be good enough for both countries. The Dutch defence is solid but Argentina have fire power on the pitch and the bench. Crespo or Riquelme could nick a goal. Roberto Ayala – if he's fit – must be the key to

keeping the Dutch from scoring. Castelen, Robben and Landzaat can get around the back and Ayala's calm in the centre will be crucial.

" I think that both teams will already have qualified for the second stage, in which case Argentina will be the more lethal."
Martin Jol

IVORY COAST V SERB & MONT
IVCW IVCW — Munich, Wednesday 21st June 2000 BST

Depending on what happens before in this group it could well be a case of both playing for pride. However, it could be a case of the Ivory Coast needing a win to proceed in the

tournament. If so then their mix of experience and youth could carry them through with the partnership of Aruna Dindane and Drogba proving crucial.

MARTIN JOL'S VIEW

Every team has two or three star players but Argentina have masses. They play the best football on the planet. They are skilful, merciless and artistic – but efficient too.

The team is built around playmaker Riquelme. He showed how good he is in the game against England in Basle. My player, Ledley King could not stop talking about his fabulous skill. It's strange that he didn't fit in at Barcelona, but he is still Argentina's best player and will be one of the players the tournament, while Coloccini and Sorin (best left back in the world) will be two of the top defenders

The only thing they lack is world-class strikers. Leo Messi has great promise and if he delivers in Germany, Argentina will join Brazil as favourites for the tournament. If he's not ready, they will rely on Crespo, who is dangerous for any defence.

Holland are a big question mark. I am not sure what to expect, especially as the defence has lost many experienced players. The positions of Reiziger, Frank de Boer and Stam have now been taken by Kromkamp, Boulahrouz and Joris Mathijsen.

Holland will have the youngest team by far and that is a deliberate choice by Marco van Basten.

The coach has eliminated some problem players who are are not his favourites such as Seedorf. Davids, van Bommel and Makaay, and he will use domestic players like Landzaat, Maduro and Opdam.

"Holland are a big question mark. I am not sure what to expect, especially as the defence has lost many experienced players."

He trusts the players he knows from his days as reserve-team coach at Ajax. The only defender with any major experience is Andre Ooijer. The same is true for Cocu, 35, in the midfield. They could provide a balance for the lack of experience of the others. If they are not in the team, Holland will struggle. Therefore, I hope – not for me but for Oranje – that Edgar Davids will make the squad. A fit Davids could be very useful for this young team.

The strike force is formidable with Ruud van Nistelrooy, Dirk Kuijt and, most of all, Arjen Robben – players who could frighten any defence.

Van Nistelrooy is a 'box player' and needs his team-mates to make chances. If they provide him with the ball, he will be lethal.

Robben, one of the best flank players in the world, could be a sensation. Like Rooney, Messi, or Ballack, Robben could be the player of the tournament.

I hope that van Basten is right and that unknown players like Boulahrouz, Sneijder, and van der Vaart make a name for themselves. If not, Holland will discover why Group D is called the 'Group of Death'.

Ivory Coast are easily the strongest of the African nations. They have a good mix of experience (Drogba, Kolo Toure, Kalou, Zokora and goalkeeper Tizie) and younger talents – even among the 'older' players, nobody is over 27. Their younger players are all excellent. Very impressive are Eboue from Arsenal, Fae, Doumbia, Dindane and Arouna Kone.

> ### "Robben, one of the best flank players in the world, could be a sensation."

The beautiful thing about the Ivory Coast is that they play a European style of Football (Henri Michel's well-organised 4-4-2) with a lot of confidence. It's combined with African flair but they can be as uncompromising as Argentina. The Elephants could well be one of the surprise teams of the tournament.

Serbia and Montenegro are a great footballing nation but after the political problems in the area, they lack young talent. Red Star and Partizan used to produce many good young players but less so now.

Mateja Kezman didn't get a chance at Chelsea, but was Europe's top-scorer when at PSV. Other talented players, include Zigic (a tower of a player at 2.02m), Vidic and Mladen Krstajic. In big tournaments, they have disappointed but there is a good harmony in this team.

"Coloccini and Sorin will be two of the top defenders at the World Cup"

MARTIN JOL'S PREDICTIONS FOR THE TOP TWO TEAMS FROM THIS GROUP

Schedule of play is on page 80

GROUP STAGE

FIRST GROUP C

> ARGENTINA

LAST SIXTEEN

v SECOND GROUP D

> ARGENTINA v MEXICO

QUARTER-FINALS

v FIRST GROUP A or SECOND GROUP B

> GERMANY v ARGENTINA

SECOND GROUP C

> HOLLAND

v FIRST GROUP D

> PORTUGAL v HOLLAND

v FIRST GROUP B or SECOND GROUP A

> ENGLAND v PORTUGAL

GROUP C
ARGENTINA, HOLLAND, IVORY COAST, SERBIA & MONTENEGRO

GROUP D
MEXICO, PORTUGAL, IRAN, ANGOLA

GROUP A
GERMANY, POLAND, COSTA RICA, ECUADOR
GROUP B
ENGLAND, SWEDEN, PRAGUAY, TRINIDAD & TOBAGO

England v Argentina could be a mouth-watering quarter-final tie if one wins their group and the other finishes runner-up.

ROUTE TO THE FINALS

It's a rare day that Argentina struggle to qualify for the World Cup. They measure their readiness for the tournament in the two games against arch rivals Brazil.

The first qualifying tussle for 2006 took place in Brazil's fourth largest city Belo Horizonte in June 2004. It was the sixth game of Argentina's campaign and they had already drawn against Chile and Colombia. Ronaldo scored three penalties although Argentina had the better possession and a late flurry when Juan Pablo Sorin pulled one back.

June 2005 saw Brazil in Buenos Aires, new coach Jose Pekerman was still experimenting with his line-up but Juan Riquelme was a fixture and scored – a fierce left foot strike after leaving two defenders with his turn. Hernan Crespo's clinical finishing added goals either side of this and Argentina could afford to lose to Paraguay and still finish joint top of the group.

A change of coach in qualifying has led to a rearrangement of the midfield, Pekerman ended with a quartet quite different from those who started the campaign.

For final qualification table see Paraguay.

	Date	Venue	Opponent	FIFA ranking	Result		Scorers
1	06 Sep 03	Home	Chile	72	D	**2 2**	Kily Gonzalez 31, Aimar 35
2	09 Sep 03	Away	Venezuela	66	W	**0 3**	Aimar 7, Crespo 25, Cesar Delgado 32
3	15 Nov 03	Home	Bolivia	96	W	**3 0**	D'Alessandro 55, Crespo 61, Aimar 63
4	19 Nov 03	Away	Colombia	25	D	**1 1**	Crespo 27
5	30 Mar 04	Home	Ecuador	35	W	**1 0**	Crespo 60
6	02 Jun 04	Away	Brazil	1	L	**3 1**	Sorin 79
7	06 Jun 04	Home	Paraguay	30	D	**0 0**	
8	04 Sep 04	Away	Peru	68	W	**1 3**	Rosales 14, Coloccini 66, Sorin 90
9	09 Oct 04	Home	Uruguay	18	W	**4 2**	L.Gonzalez 6, Figueroa 31, 54, Zanetti 44
10	13 Oct 04	Away	Chile	72	D	**0 0**	
11	17 Nov 04	Home	Venezuela	66	W	**3 2**	Rey 3og, Riquelme 46, Saviola 65
12	26 Mar 05	Away	Bolivia	96	W	**1 2**	Figueroa 57, Galletti 63
13	30 Mar 05	Home	Colombia	25	W	**1 0**	Crespo 65
14	04 Jun 05	Away	Ecuador	35	L	**2 0**	
15	08 Jun 05	Home	Brazil	1	W	**3 1**	Crespo 3, 40, Riquelme 18
16	03 Sep 05	Away	Paraguay	30	L	**1 0**	
17	09 Oct 05	Home	Peru	68	W	**2 0**	Riquelme 81pen, Guadalupe 90og
18	12 Oct 05	Away	Uruguay	18	L	**1 0**	
	Average FIFA ranking of opposition			46			

MAIN PLAYER PERFORMANCES IN QUALIFICATION

Match	1 2 3 4 5 6 7 8 9 10 11 12 13 14 15 16 17 18	Appearances	Started	Subbed on	Subbed off	Mins played	% played	Goals	Yellow	Red
Venue	H A H A H A H A H A H A H A H A H A									
Result	D W W D W L D W W D W W W L W L W L									
Goalkeepers										
Roberto Abbondancieri		11	11	0	0	990	61.1	0	0	0
Pablo Cavallero		6	6	0	0	540	33.3	0	1	0
Leonardo Franco		1	1	0	0	90	5.6	0	1	0
Defenders										
Roberto Ayala		11	11	0	0	990	61.1	0	4	0
Fabricio Coloccini		7	7	0	0	630	38.9	1	2	0
Gabriel Ivan Heinze		10	9	1	0	803	49.6	0	4	1
Gabriel Milito		5	5	0	1	427	26.4	0	0	0
Facundo Quiroga		3	3	0	0	270	16.7	0	1	0
Walter Samuel		9	9	0	0	806	49.8	0	2	1
Javier Zanetti		12	11	1	0	1010	62.3	1	2	0
Midfielders										
Pablo Aimar		8	6	2	4	513	31.7	3	2	0
Esteban Cambiasso		8	7	1	1	617	38.1	0	1	1
Andres D'Alessandro		9	5	4	3	482	29.8	1	4	0
Cristian Gonzalez		8	8	0	2	615	38.0	0	1	1
Luis Gonzalez		12	10	2	6	753	46.5	1	4	0
Javier Mascherano		7	6	1	1	548	33.8	0	2	0
Juan Riquelme		9	8	1	2	723	44.6	3	0	0
Juan Pablo Sorin		13	11	2	0	1018	62.8	2	1	0
Forwards										
Hernan Crespo		11	11	0	4	929	57.3	7	0	0
Cesar Delgado		10	9	1	7	634	39.1	1	0	0
Lucho Figueroa		5	4	1	3	329	20.3	3	0	0
Javier Saviola		10	5	5	3	527	32.5	1	2	0
Carlos Tevez		8	3	5	1	438	27.0	0	2	0

FINAL PROSPECTS

Just before plotting Argentina's successful qualifying win over Brazil, coach Jose Pekerman declared his side a team in transition.

Sure enough, just 21 days later, the two teams met again in the final of Confederations Cup and Pekerman had six changes in the starting line-up. The result was also different, an emphatic Adriano inspired win for Brazil.

Argentina's defence looked experimental without Roberto Ayala or Walter Samuel and with Gabriel Heinze forced to play in the centre.

Seven more changes for the England game in November before Pekerman was experimenting again against Qatar. His rather strange problem is that there is no shortage of talent spread between top and lower league teams in Europe and those still playing in Argentina. Another problem is injuries to some of his certainties; Heinze and Ayala have long-term injuries and are struggling to be fit for the World Cup.

Likely starters for the opening fixture against Ivory Coast will be Crespo possibly with Corinthians' Carlos Tevez playing just behind him. However, there is the exciting prospect of seeing Barcelona youngster Lionel Messi, in the line-up. Julio Cruz is playing and scoring more for much improved Inter Milan, also netting for Argentina in their November game against Qatar to improve his chances.

Riquelme who often dictates a game as well as scores – 15 for Villarreal last season, will run midfield.

> **"My player Ledley King could not stop talking about the fabulous skill of Juan Riquelme after the England Argentina game."**
> Martin Jol

Sorin will play on the flank as skipper with Esteban Cambiasso as the likely ball-winner. Aimar seems destined for the bench. Maxi Rodriguez has hit scoring form and played as an advanced midfielder against England.

It's in defence where injuries may disrupt their plans. If everyone's fit Argentina are capable of winning Group C, grinding out a win against Brazil in the semis and going all the way.

GROUP FIXTURES

IVORY COAST	Sat 10 June 2000 BST
SERBIA & MONT	Fri 16 June 1400 BST
HOLLAND	Wed 21 June 2000 BST

Buenos Aires

Zone	South America
Population	39,763,809
Capital	Buenos Aires
Language	Spanish
Top league	Primera Division
Major clubs	**Capacities**
River Plate	65,600
Boca Juniors	57,400
Independiente	52,800

Where likely squad players play:

In Premiership	2	In Spain	11
In Holland	0	In France	0
In Italy	4	In Germany	0

Number of Argentinian players playing:

In Premiership	6	In Spain	48
In Holland	2	In France	9
In Italy	25	In Germany	8

World Cup record

1930 -	Runners-up	1974 -	Round 2
1934 -	Round 1	1978 -	Champions
1938 -	Withdrew	1982 -	Round 2
1950 -	Withdrew	1986 -	Champions
1954 -	Did not enter	1990 -	Runners-up
1958 -	Group 4th	1994 -	Last 16
1962 -	Group 3rd	1998 -	Quarter-finals
1966 -	Quarter-finals	2002 -	Group 3rd
1970 -	Did not qualify		

THE SQUAD

Goalkeepers	Club side	Age	QG
Roberto Abbondancieri	Boca Juniors	33	11
Pablo Cavallero	Levante	32	6
Leonardo Franco	Atl Madrid	29	1
Defenders			
Roberto Ayala	Valencia	33	11
Nicolas Burdisso	Inter Milan	25	2
Fabricio Coloccini	Deportivo	24	7
Gabriel Ivan Heinze	Man Utd	28	10
Gabriel Milito	Real Zaragoza	25	5
Diego Placente	Celta Vigo	29	4
Facundo Quiroga	Wolfsburg	28	3
Clemente Rodriguez	Spartak Moscow	24	2
Gonzalo Rodriguez	Villarreal	22	1
Walter Samuel	Inter Milan	28	9
Javier Zanetti	Inter Milan	32	12
Midfielders			
Pablo Aimar	Valencia	26	8
Matias Almeyda	Parma	32	4
Sebastian Battaglia	Villarreal	25	2
Esteban Cambiasso	Inter Milan	25	8
Andres D'Alessandro	Portsmouth	25	9
Luis Gonzalez	Porto	25	12
Kily Gonzalez	Inter Milan	31	11
Javier Mascherano	Corinthians	22	7
Juan Riquelme	Villarreal	27	9
Juan Pablo Sorin	Villarreal	30	13
Pablo Zabaleta	Espanyol	21	1
Forwards			
Hernan Crespo	Chelsea	30	11
Cesar Delgado	Cruz Azul Ciudad	24	10
Luciano Figueroa	Villarreal	25	5
Luciano Galletti	Atl Madrid	25	3
Lionel Messi	Barcelona	18	3
Maxi Rodriguez	Atl Madrid	25	3
Javier Saviola	Seville	24	10
Carlos Tevez	Corinthians	22	8

■ Probable ■ Possible **QG** Qualification Games

KEY PLAYER

JUAN RIQUELME VILLARREAL

Juan Riquelme has reinvented himself to become the best playmaker in football. Three seasons ago, he was an expensive misfit in an under-performing Barcelona side. It cost the Catalan club over £10m to bring Riquelme to Europe from Argentinian club Boca Juniors in 2002. He spent half the season on the bench and was loaned out to Primera Liga rivals Villarreal at the end of it, having never settled at the Nou Camp. At Villarreal, he rediscovered his form and hit eight goals in the league and another four in the club's run to the semi-finals of the Uefa Cup. In 2004/5, Riquelme inspired Villarreal to third in La Liga –scoring 15 league goals from midfield.

Riquelme is a Top 12 Midfielder and so is Argentina's Esteban Cambiasso.

AGE 27   **MIDFIELDER**   **WORLD RANKING** 12

KEY GOALKEEPER

ROBERTO ABBONDANCIERI
BOCA JUNIORS

Roberto Abbondancieri took over the gloves from Pablo Cavallero seven games into qualifying.

The Boca Juniors player spelt his name with a 'c' but switched to a 'z' as a reminder of his Italian heritage. He was South American goalkeeper of the year in 2003 and is currently holding off the challenge of Atletico Madrid's Leo Franco as Argentina's No. 1.

Franco had a stunning year in Spanish League football in 2004/5 conceding only a goal every 104 minutes on average in a team which finished 11th.

LEONARDO FRANCO
ATLETICO MADRID

Playing record	12 mths lge	wcq
Appearances:	36	1
Minutes played:	3113	90
Percentage played:	84.4%	5.6%
Goals conceded:	28	2
Clean sheets:	19	0
Cards:	Y3, R0	Y1, R0
Defensive rating:	111mins	-
Defensive ranking:	7th	-

AGE 29	WORLD RANKING 235

KEY DEFENDERS

WALTER SAMUEL
INTER MILAN

Inter Milan are at their most competitive in Serie A for a while and the rugged defending of Walter Samuel is a key factor.

He's played more games than the rest of the Inter back line so far this season and is making up for a poor spell at Real Madrid, where he had the worst record of their four main defenders in 2004/5. His revival at Inter was recently interrupted when he received a three-match ban for allegedly spitting against Pavel Nedved.

Samuel is a danger in the air at set pieces as England's defence found out in the friendly in November.

Playing record	12 mths lge	wcq
Appearances:	38	9
Minutes played:	3339	806
Percentage played:	82.4%	49.8%
Goals conceded:	31	11
Clean sheets:	19	3
Cards:	Y10, R2	Y2, R1
Defensive rating:	108mins	73mins
Defensive ranking:	35th	79th

AGE 28	WORLD RANKING 163

FABRICIO COLOCCINI
DEPORTIVO LA CORUNA

Coloccini is a memorable figure on the football pitch with his mop of ginger hair in afro style.

He's highly rated – not least by Martin Jol and fellow Premiership manager Rafael Benitez, who would like to take him to Liverpool.

Coloccini became a regular in Argentina's qualifying progress after missing the first seven games of the campaign.

At Deportivo La Coruna in Spain the centre-back frequently finds his name in the referee's book, so it is possible if selected the Argentinians will be without him at some stage during the competition due to a match suspension.

Playing record	12 mths lge	wcq
Appearances:	29	7
Minutes played:	2362	630
Percentage played:	64.0%	38.9%
Goals conceded:	31	7
Clean sheets:	9	2
Cards:	Y7, R2	Y2, R0
Defensive rating:	76mins	90mins
Defensive ranking:	73rd	71st

AGE 24	WORLD RANKING 668

JAVIER ZANETTI
INTER MILAN

Javier Zanetti must have trodden on every blade of grass of Inter Milan's San Siro.

The versatile club captain can play midfield or in defence but has appeared in pretty well every position since joining Inter from Argentinian side Banfield in 1995.

His decade at the club has only been rewarded by an Italian Cup trophy as Juventus and AC Milan have enjoyed dominance over their old rivals, but his reputation as the ultimate professional hasn't been tarnished. He won Serie A's fair play award in 2004/5.

He usually plays either right back or in midfield protecting the defence. He has over a century of caps for Argentina and is likely to overtake the Argentinean appearance record during the World Cup finals. The current holder is David Beckham's former adversary Diego Simeone who had 106 appearances when he retired.

This will be Zanetti's final World Cup tournament and he deserves to go out on a high.

Playing record	12 mths lge	wcq
Appearances:	32	12
Minutes played:	2815	1010
Percentage played:	71.1%	62.3%
Goals scored:	0	1
Goals conceded:	20	14
Cards:	Y3, R0	Y2, R0
Power rating:	53mins	48mins
Power ranking:	55th	66th

AGE 32	WORLD RANKING 88

KEY DEFENDER

ROBERTO AYALA VALENCIA

Roberto Ayala is a cool calm central defender with pace and a firm tackle. He has been in and (more often) out with an injured knee over the last 18 months. His absence shows; Valencia's form dipped while he was out in 2004/5 and Michael Owen struck twice after Ayala went off in the friendly against England in Basle in November.

Playing record	12 mths lge	wcq
Appearances:	28	11
Minutes played:	2368	990
Percentage played:	64.2%	61.1%
Goals conceded:	30	6
Clean sheets:	8	6
Cards:	Y3, R0	Y4, R0
Defensive rating:	79mins	165mins
Defensive ranking:	68th	41st

AGE 33   **DEFENDER**   **WORLD RANKING 559**

THE MANAGER

Jose Pekerman, 57, the successful former youth team coach, took over.

Bielsa had begun the qualifying campaign with Juan Sebastian Veron and Pablo Aimar pulling the central midfield strings. Pekerman played Villarreal's Juan Riquelme there.

In Pekerman's first game against Uruguay – a 4-2 win – Riquelme's club-mate, Sorin, was made captain, while yet another 'Yellow Submarine', Luciano Figueroa, scored two goals.

Most of Pekerman's team-sheets will beat most of the opposition they come up against, but finding the best blend for the rigours of the World Cup finals is trickier. They used 50 players in 18 games in qualifying and his search for the right combination is hampered by injuries to three key players.

Coach Marcelo 'El Loco' Bielsa was in his sixth year in charge of Argentina when he surprisingly resigned in September 2004, just two weeks after guiding them to their first Olympic title.

KEY STRIKERS

KEY MIDFIELDERS

PABLO AIMAR
VALENCIA

Diego Maradona said of Pablo Aimar, "Pablo is the only current footballer I would pay to watch".

Aimar is a fabulous playmaker for Valencia but for Argentina is often on and off the bench.

Playing record	12 mths lge	wcq
Appearances:	35	8
Minutes played:	2700	513
Percentage played:	73.2%	31.7%
Goals scored:	7	3
Goals conceded:	27	6
Cards:	Y3, R0	Y2, R0
Power rating:	59mins	51mins
Power ranking:	76th	78th

AGE 26 | **WORLD RANKING 169**

JUAN PABLO SORIN
VILLARREAL

Juan Pablo Sorin is Argentina's captain and a left-sided wing-back who can play either defence or midfield.

For Argentina, it's usually midfield.

After less than successful earlier spells in Europe at Juventus and Barcelona, his career made headway in France for Paris St Germain, helping them to the runners-up spot in 2003/4.

He joined Spanish side Villarreal the following season and it is here, alongside compatriot Juan Riquelme, that Sorin has settled and flourished.

Playing record	12 mths lge	wcq
Appearances:	30	13
Minutes played:	2258	1018
Percentage played:	58.3%	62.8%
Goals conceded:	33	10
Clean sheets:	7	7
Cards:	Y6, R0	Y1, R0
Defensive rating:	68mins	102mins
Defensive ranking:	94th	65t

AGE 30 | **WORLD RANKING 892**

ESTEBAN CAMBIASSO
INTER MILAN

Cambiasso's career took off when he swapped Real Madrid reserves for Inter Milan in 2004. He instantly became the key player in the centre of their midfield. He's a Top 12 Player.

AGE 25 | **WORLD RANKING 35**

LIONEL MESSI
BARCELONA

Barcelona's teen sensation Lionel Messi may have rubbed Chelsea's Jose Mourinho up the wrong way but he usually does this to defenders as Asier Del Horno found out.

He left Argentina for Spain as a frail 13-year-old and this has been his breakthrough season. A lot is expected and he has yet to disappoint.

Playing record	12 mths lge	wcq
Appearances:	18	3
Minutes played:	773	127
Percentage played:	20.9%	7.8%
Goals scored:	7	0
Goals conceded:	4	0
Cards:	Y2, R0	Y0, R0
Power rating:	-	-
Power ranking:	-	-

AGE 18 | **WORLD RANKING –**

MAXI RODRIGUEZ
ATL MADRID

Playing record	12 mths lge	wcq
Appearances:	41	3
Minutes played:	3314	175
Percentage played:	89.8%	10.8%
Goals scored:	13	0
Goals conceded:	40	4
Cards:	Y4, R0	Y1, R0
Power rating:	63mins	-
Power ranking:	92nd	-

AGE 25 | **WORLD RANKING 473**

KEY STRIKER

HERNAN CRESPO CHELSEA

Hernan Crespo's goal scoring has made him one of the most expensive players in the history of the game. So far, he has cost his clubs nearly £70m in transfer fees.
A natural, predatory finisher, Crespo offers superb off the ball running combined with an ability to score from anywhere – close in, with his head or from distance as he did against Wigan on this season's first game.

Playing record	12 mths lge	wcq
Appearances:	21	11
Minutes played:	1124	929
Percentage played:	30.5%	57.3%
Goals scored:	9	7
Percentage share:	11.84	24.14
Cards:	Y1, R0	Y0, R0
Strike rate:	125mins	133mins
Power ranking:	11th	20th

AGE 30 **STRIKER** **WORLD RANKING 129**

IVORY COAST

ROUTE TO THE FINALS

Ivory Coast's historic first qualification for the World Cup finals all rested on a penalty. With two games to go, African Group 3 favourites Cameroon had 17 points to the 19 secured by the Ivory Coast.

Cameroon had inflicted the only defeat on the 'Elephants' – a 2-0 win in Yaounde achieved with the help of a late Samuel Eto'o goal. So, when Cameroon visited Abidjan for the return it was expected to decide the group. Didier Drogba hit two goals for the Elephants but was outscored by Cameroon's Osasuna striker Achille Webo, who recorded a stunning hat-trick, sinking Elephants hopes. However, both teams still had one last game to play.

In the final games, Kanga Akale struck early for the Elephants against Sudan and two second half goals by Lens striker Aruna Dindane earned a win.

Cameroon were up against third - place Egypt. At the end of 90 minutes the two sides were level but Cameroon were awarded an injury time penalty kick. Pierre Wome took it and hit the woodwork. The Ivory Coast qualified after winning the group by a solitary point.

FINAL QUALIFYING TABLE
AFRICA GROUP 3

	P	W	D	L	GF	GA	Pts
Ivory Coast	10	7	1	2	20	7	22
Cameroon	10	6	3	1	18	10	21
Egypt	10	5	2	3	26	15	17
Libya	10	3	3	4	8	10	12
Sudan	10	1	3	6	6	22	6
Benin	10	1	2	7	9	23	5

					FIFA ranking			
1	06 Jun 04	Home	Libya	72	W	2 0	Dindane 35, Drogba 63pen
2	20 Jun 04	Away	Egypt	29	W	1 2	Dindane 22, Drogba 75
3	04 Jul 04	Away	Cameroon	24	L	2 0	
4	05 Sep 04	Home	Sudan	99	W	5 0	Drogba 12pen, Dindane 15, 64, Yapi Yapo 25, B.Kone 56
5	10 Oct 04	Away	Benin	121	W	0 1	Dindane 48
6	27 Mar 05	Home	Benin	121	W	3 0	Kalou 7, Drogba 19, 59
7	03 Jun 05	Away	Libya	72	D	0 0	
8	19 Jun 05	Home	Egypt	29	W	2 0	Drogba 41, 49
9	04 Sep 05	Home	Cameroon	24	L	2 3	Drogba 38, 47
10	08 Oct 05	Away	Sudan	99	W	1 3	Akale 22, Dindane 51, 73
	Average FIFA ranking of opposition			69			

MAIN PLAYER PERFORMANCES IN QUALIFICATION

Match	1 2 3 4 5 6 7 8 9 10	Appearances	Started	Subbed on	Subbed off	Mins played	% played	Goals	Yellow	Red
Venue	H A A H A H A H H A									
Result	W W L W W W D W L W									
Goalkeepers										
Boubacar Barry		1	1	0	0	90	10.0	0	1	0
Gerard Gnanhouan		1	1	0	0	90	10.0	0	0	0
Jean Jacques Tizie		8	8	0	0	720	80.0	0	0	0
Defenders										
Arthur Boka		7	7	0	0	630	70.0	0	2	0
Cyril Domoraud		9	8	1	0	765	85.0	0	1	0
Emmanuel Eboue		2	1	1	1	82	9.1	0	0	0
Emerse Fae		3	0	3	0	73	8.1	0	1	0
Blaise Kouassi		5	4	1	1	364	40.4	0	1	0
Abdoulaye Meite		7	5	2	1	484	53.8	0	1	0
Olivier Tebily		1	1	0	1	71	7.9	0	0	0
Siaka Tiene		4	4	0	2	322	35.8	0	0	0
Kolo Toure		10	10	0	1	855	95.0	0	0	0
Midfielders										
Guy Demel		3	1	2	0	113	12.6	0	0	0
Serge Die		2	2	0	2	127	14.1	0	0	0
Aboulaye Djire		1	1	0	0	90	10.0	0	1	0
Tchiressoa Guel		9	9	0	5	707	78.6	0	0	0
Yaya Toure		1	1	0	0	90	10.0	0	0	0
Didier Zokora		9	9	0	0	809	89.9	0	0	1
Marco Zoro		4	4	0	2	295	32.8	0	2	0
Forwards										
Kanga Akale		4	1	3	1	191	21.2	0	0	0
Aruna Dindane		10	10	0	1	888	98.7	7	1	0
Didier Drogba		9	9	0	5	725	80.6	9	1	0
Bonaventure Kalou		9	9	0	3	746	82.9	1	0	0
Arouna Kone		4	0	4	0	26	2.9	0	0	0
Bakary Kone		5	0	5	0	110	12.2	1	0	0
Gilles Yapi Yapo		6	3	3	1	292	32.4	1	0	0

FINAL PROSPECTS

The Ivory Coast is investing more than it can afford in football so there is more than just pride at stake in the national team's place in the World Cup finals.

The success of Kolo Toure at Arsenal and Didier Drogba (former French footballer of the Year at Marseille in 2003/4) means the war-torn West African state suddenly views football as its primary export. Over 300 soccer academies have sprung up around Abidjan and the next generation of West African footballers will be cheering on their heroes.

The team has a strong spine and a stunning strike force. It will almost certainly take points even in the 'Group of Death'.

Coach Michel Henri has them well organised and playing to their strengths, which include natural athleticism and frightening pace.

"The beautiful thing about the Ivory Coast is that they play a European style of football."
Martin Jol

Toure marshals central defence, which can call on the vastly experienced Cyril Domoraud, who numbers Monaco, Espanyol and Inter Milan among his previous clubs. Abdoulaye Meite is a key figure in Marseille's defence, with Marc Zoro, Arsenal's Emmanuel Eboue and Arthur Boka making up a solid defensive unit. In goal they have the experience of Jean Jaques Tizie,

In midfield, Didier Zokora is arguably the top ball-winner in French football and has recently been joined by Toure's brother, Yaya, from Olympiakos. Kanga Akale has as many tricks as Cristiano Ronaldo but more pace. However, it's up front that the Elephants are blessed with talent. So much so, that skipper Bonaventure Kalou, top-scorer for Auxerre last season, plays in midfield and Aruna Kone is on he bench. Drogba and Aruna Dindane up front thumped 16 goals in qualifying between them.

Dindane missed most of the African Cup of Nations after a family tragedy and without him to support Drogba the goals dried up. If he's back, and they survive the group, it will be a tournament the Elephants won't forget.

GROUP FIXTURES

ARGENTINA	Sat 10 June 2000 BST
HOLLAND	Fri 16 June 1700 BST
SERBIA & MONT	Wed 21 June 2000 BST

KEY PLAYER

DIDIER DROGBA CHELSEA

Didier Drogba shares the striking duties at Chelsea with Argentina's Hernan Crespo. When one's on the pitch, the other is usually on the bench, yet both are automatic first choices for their countries.

The Ivory Coast look to Drogba ahead of any other player. He hit nine goals in qualifying as the second highest scorer in the five African groups.

The forward takes flack from Mark Lawrenson for his occasional clumsiness in front of goal but makes up for it with his strength and work-rate. For the Elephants, he is still the striker with the golden touch that drove Marseille to the Uefa Cup final in 2004 with his goals and was voted the French league's top player.

Top 12 players: Toure and Drogba

| AGE 28 | STRIKER | WORLD RANKING 45 |

Abidjan

Zone	Africa
Population	17,528,516
Capital	Yamoussoukro (official), Abidjan (de facto).
Language	French
Top league	Premiere Division
Major clubs	**Capacities**
Asec Mimosas	50,000
Africa SN	50,000
Stade Abidjan	20,000

Where likely squad players play:

In Premiership	3	In Spain	0
In Holland	1	In France	12
In Italy	1	In Germany	1
Outside Europe			5

Number of Ivorian players playing:

In Premiership	4	In Spain	1
In Holland	3	In France	20
In Italy	5	In Germany	2

World Cup record

1930 -	Did not enter	1974 -	Did not qualify
1934 -	Did not enter	1978 -	Did not qualify
1938 -	Did not enter	1982 -	Did not enter
1950 -	Did not enter	1986 -	Did not qualify
1954 -	Did not enter	1990 -	Did not qualify
1958 -	Did not enter	1994 -	Did not qualify
1962 -	Did not enter	1998 -	Did not qualify
1966 -	Did not enter	2002 -	Did not qualify
1970 -	Did not enter		

THE SQUAD

Goalkeepers	Club side	Age	QG
Boubacar Barry	Beveren	26	1
Gerard Gnanhouan	Sochaux	27	1
Jean Jacques Tizie	Esperance	33	8
Defenders			
Arthur Boka	Strasbourg	23	7
Cyril Domoraud	Creteil	34	9
Emmanuel Eboue	Arsenal	23	2
Blaise Kouassi	Troyes	31	5
Abdoulaye Meite	Marseille	25	7
Olivier Tebily	Birmingham	30	1
Siaka Tiene	St Etienne	24	4
Habib Kolo Toure	Arsenal	25	10
Midfielders			
Kanga Akale	Auxerre	25	4
Guy Demel	Hamburg	24	3
Serge Die	Nice	28	2
Aboulaye Djire	Beveren	25	1
Almamy Doumbia	AS Melfi	22	1
Emerse Fae	Nantes	22	3
Tchiressoa Guel	Ankaraguku	30	9
Bonaventure Kalou	Paris SG	28	9
Tiene Siaka	St Etienne	-	1
Yaya Toure	Olympiakos	23	1
Gilles Yapi Yapo	Nantes	24	6
Didier Zokora	St Etienne	25	9
Marco Zoro	Messina	22	4
Forwards			
Aruna Dindane	Lens	25	10
Didier Drogba	Chelsea	28	9
Arouna Kone	PSV Eindhoven	22	4
Bakary Kone	Nice	24	5

■ Probable ■ Possible **QG** Qualification Games

KEY GOALKEEPER

JEAN JACQUES TIZIE
ESPERANCE

Jean-Jacques Tizie almost cost the Elephants their place in the World Cup finals when he had an off day in the vital qualifying defeat away against the Cameroon.

However, the team scraped through in the final game and the veteran keeper came back from that performance to prove a key part of the best defence on show at the African Cup of Nations.

His nickname in the Ivorian team is 'The Shepherd' because of the feeling of security he gives the side. He has terrific reflexes and is an excellent line keeper, currently playing in Tunisia for Esperance.

Boubacar Barry of Beveren and Gerrard Gnanhouan were both given one game each at the end of the qualifying games to show what they could do. Both conceded goals which could have been costly.

Coach Henri Michel is grooming younger keepers to take over from Tizie but he will select him for the World Cup finals because of his bond with the other defenders.

AGE 33 | **WORLD RANKING** –

KEY DEFENDERS

HABIB KOLO TOURE
ARSENAL

Kolo Toure is the key figure at the heart of the Elephants' defence.

He earned rave reviews in the African Cup of Nations where he helped take the Elephants to the final.

He is one of our Top 12 Defenders.

ABDOULAYE MEITE
MARSEILLE

Abdoulaye Meite is another defender playing for a top European side.

The Parisian-born player qualified through his parents but took some convincing to play for the side.

Playing record	12 mths lge	wcq
Appearances:	23	7
Minutes played:	1963	484
Percentage played:	53.2%	53.8%
Goals conceded:	27	3
Clean sheets:	5	5
Cards:	Y3, R0	Y1, R0
Defensive rating:	73mins	161mins
Defensive ranking:	86th	44th

AGE 25 | **WORLD RANKING 130**

EMMANUEL EBOUE
ARSENAL

Emmanuel Eboue has recently erupted out of the reserves for both club and country.

Signed by Arsene Wenger in January 2005 from Belgian side Beveren, Eboue was primarily used in the reserves and given first team experience in cup games. Arsenal's injury problems changed all that and he was promoted to play right back. He had a good game against Robinho in Madrid.

Eboue barely featured in qualifying but became a fixture for the Ivory Coast in their African Cup of Nations run to the final.

Playing record	12 mths lge	wcq
Appearances:	7	2
Minutes played:	231	82
Percentage played:	6.4%	9.1%
Goals conceded:	4	0
Clean sheets:	4	2
Cards:	Y0, R0	Y0, R0
Defensive rating:	-	-
Defensive ranking:	-	-

AGE 23 | **WORLD RANKING** –

KEY MIDFIELDERS

GNERI YAYA TOURE
OLYMPIAKOS

Gneri Yaya Toure has impressed for Olympiakos in the Champions League this season and is another holding midfield player who used the African Cup of Nations to force his way into the squad.

AGE 23 | **WORLD RANKING** –

BONAVENTURE KALOU
PARIS SG

The skipper of the Elephants is Bonaventure Kalou, an experienced campaigner in top European teams.

He first played for Feyenoord in Holland for four years, before moving to Auxerre in the French league in 2003.

He has always contributed good goals from midfield. Eight in 29 appearances last season led to a move to PSG.

Playing record	12 mths lge	wcq
Appearances:	27	9
Minutes played:	2095	746
Percentage played:	56.8%	82.9%
Goals scored:	5	1
Percentage share:	11.11	5.00
Cards:	Y9, R0	Y0, R0
Strike rate:	419mins	746mins
Power ranking:	79th	64th

AGE 28 | **WORLD RANKING 53**

KEY STRIKER

ARUNA DINDANE
LENS

Aruna Dindane missed the African Cup of Nations when he returned home to deal with a personal tragedy - and the Elephants badly missed his goals.

Playing record	12 mths lge	wcq
Appearances:	18	10
Minutes played:	1178	888
Percentage played:	31.2%	98.7%
Goals scored:	5	7
Goals conceded:	10	7
Cards:	Y3, R1	Y1, R0
Power rating:	74mins	44mins
Power ranking:	113rd	51st

AGE 25 | **WORLD RANKING 704**

THE MANAGER

Coach Henri Michel has experience of both World Cups and African teams. In the past, he has coached six national teams, starting with his native France.

The 58-year-old took over the reins of France when they were 1984 European champions and led the Michel Platini inspired team into a World Cup semi final where they lost to West Germany.

He has coached Cameroon, Morocco, Tunisia and Saudi Arabia. He experienced the lows of the qualification campaign after the Elephants lost to Cameroon, when the nation blamed Michel for what they believed was a failure to get to Germany.

"The defeat to Cameroon in the penultimate match of the qualifiers was treated like a national disaster," said Michel. "It is unbelievable the importance of football to Africa."

When the side finally qualified, Michel didn't attend the celebrations and half expects to be sacked before Germany.

Henri Michel

ONE TO WATCH

DIDIER ZOKORA ST ETIENNE

Didier Zokora is the latest in a long line of French League players to be dubbed 'the new Vieira'. An effective midfield ball-winner the Elephants star plays his club football at St Etienne, although other clubs are interested. He seldom scores but last season Zokora's 35 games for St Etienne saw only 28 goals conceded, the sixth best midfield record in the league

Playing record	12 mths lge	wcq
Appearances:	33	9
Minutes played:	2873	809
Percentage played:	72.6%	89.9%
Goals scored:	0	0
Goals conceded:	25	7
Cards:	Y6, R1	Y0, R1
Power rating:	87mins	54mins
Power ranking:	134th	83rd

AGE 25 | **MIDFIELDER** | **WORLD RANKING 306**

ROUTE TO THE FINALS

The little known team from Serbia and Montenegro surprised everyone during qualifying.

They condemned Spain to the play-offs, eclipsed Belgium and bettered local rivals Bosnia-Herzegovina in Europe Group 7.

They did it with the best defensive record in the entire qualifying tournament, conceding only one goal from ten matches in a tough group.

Well, the first game wasn't so tough, San Marino away, but Bosnia-Herzegovina are no walkovers and Spain have some highly-prized strikers. Yet, Spain were drawing with teams that the Balkan nation were beating.

Serbia met Spain in their fifth game and drew 0-0 in Belgrade. The return in September saw Spanish captain, Raul, score the only goal that keeper Dragoslav Jevric was to concede in the campaign. However, Mateja Kezman stabbed home an equaliser and that gave them control of the group.

They still had work to do and Kezman needed to find his scoring form twice more to gain wins away in Lithuania and after only five minutes of a tight and tense home win over neighbours Bosnia.

FINAL QUALIFYING TABLE
EUROPE GROUP 7

	P	W	D	L	GF	GA	Pts
Serbia and Mont	10	6	4	0	16	1	22
Spain	10	5	5	0	19	3	20
Bosnia-Herz	10	4	4	2	12	9	16
Belgium	10	3	3	4	16	11	12
Lithuania	10	2	4	4	8	9	10
San Marino	10	0	0	10	2	40	0

	Date	Venue		FIFA ranking			Result	Scorers
1	04 Sep 04	Away	San Marino	160	W		0 3	Vukic 4, Jestrovic 15, 83
2	09 Oct 04	Away	Bosnia	74	D		0 0	
3	13 Oct 04	Home	San Marino	160	W		5 0	Milosevic 35, D.Stankovic 45, 50,3 Koroman 52, Vukic 69
4	17 Nov 04	Away	Belgium	47	W		0 2	Vukic 10, Kezman 59
5	30 Mar 05	Home	Spain	6	D		0 0	
6	04 Jun 05	Home	Belgium	47	D		0 0	
7	03 Sep 05	Home	Lithuania	97	W		2 0	Kezman 18, Ilic 75
8	07 Sep 05	Away	Spain	6	D		1 1	Kezman 68
9	08 Oct 05	Away	Lithuania	97	W		0 2	Kezman 42, Vukic 88
10	12 Oct 05	Home	Bosnia	74	W		1 0	Kezman 5
	Average FIFA ranking of opposition			77				

MAIN PLAYER PERFORMANCES IN QUALIFICATION

Match	1 2 3 4 5 6 7 8 9 10	Appearances	Started	Subbed on	Subbed off	Mins played	% played	Goals	Yellow	Red
Venue	A A H A H H H A A H									
Result	W D W W D D W D W W									
Goalkeepers										
Dragoslav Jevric		10	10	0	0	900	100.0	0	0	0
Defenders										
Nenad Djordjevic		2	1	1	1	70	7.8	0	1	0
Ivica Dragutinovic		8	8	0	1	690	76.7	0	0	0
Goran Gavrancic		10	10	0	0	900	100.0	0	0	0
Mladen Krstajic		9	9	0	0	810	90.0	0	1	0
Marjan Markovic		3	2	1	0	214	23.8	0	0	0
Albert Nadj		2	2	0	1	163	18.1	0	1	0
Nemanja Vidic		5	5	0	0	444	49.3	0	2	1
Milivoje Vitakic		1	0	1	0	30	3.3	0	0	0
Midfielders										
Nenad Brnovic		3	0	3	0	52	5.8	0	1	0
Predrag Djordjevic		6	6	0	0	540	60.0	0	3	0
Igor Duljaj		9	7	2	1	629	69.9	0	0	1
Sasa Ilic		4	2	2	2	166	18.4	1	0	0
Ognjen Koroman		6	5	1	2	474	52.7	1	3	0
Aleksandar Lukovic		2	1	1	0	93	10.3	0	0	0
Milos Maric		1	0	1	0	7	0.8	0	0	0
Dragan Mladenovic		5	2	3	2	271	30.1	0	1	0
Dejan Stankovic		9	9	0	2	720	80.0	2	0	0
Zvonimir Vukic		8	7	1	2	602	66.9	4	3	0
Forwards										
Nenad Jestrovic		1	1	0	0	90	10.0	2	0	0
Mateja Kezman		7	5	2	3	507	56.3	5	1	0
Darko Kovacevic		1	0	1	0	91	10.1	0	0	0
Danijel Ljuboja		4	3	1	1	286	31.8	0	1	0
Savo Milosevic		6	6	0	5	392	43.6	1	0	0
Nikola Zigic		4	2	2	2	204	22.7	0	1	0

FINAL PROSPECTS

If ever there was a team that seemed more than the sum of its parts it is the current Serbia & Montenegro side.

The only star name in the squad is Inter Milan's midfielder Dejan Stankovic. Former Chelsea forward Kezman is one of the few other members of their line-up most people would have heard of during their qualifying campaign. Even the names that you think you recognise you don't! Sasa Ilic isn't the former Charlton and Portsmouth goalkeeper but the goal-scoring central midfielder who captained Partizan Belgrade to the last 16 of the Uefa Cup in 2004/5 before moving to Galatasaray.

Since they conceded only one goal in qualifying, the back four are attracting attention. Sir Alex Ferguson paid £7m in the January transfer window to bring central defender Nemanja Vidic from Spartak Moscow to Old Trafford but he has yet to look settled.

Dynamo Kiev right-back Goran Gavrancic, Seville left-back Ivica Dragutinovic and the experienced Mladen Krstajic of Schalke make up a secure back four.

Strangely, ever-present goalkeeper Jevric wasn't even the best keeper at Vitesse Arnhem last year. He conceded 23 goals in the first 17 games and was replaced leaving at the end of the season for Ankaraspor – relegation strugglers in Turkey.

"Mateja Kezman never got a chance at Chelsea, but was European league top-scorer at PSV Eindhoven"
Martin Jol

Goals are a struggle for the team – eight of the 16 they scored in qualifying came against San Marino. Kezman hit five and lines up with the 2.02m Red Star Belgrade striker Nikola Zigic up front with all-time top cap earner and top goalscorer, Savo Milosevic, largely confined to cameos.

When you put it all into the blue of Serbia, the same national pride that drives near-neighbours Croatia is unleashed and they step up a class. They have plenty of spirit and belief but will probably be found out in Group C and are likely to finish bottom of the group.

GROUP FIXTURES

HOLLAND	Sun 11 June 1400 BST
ARGENTINA	Fri 16 June 1400 BST
IVORY COAST	Wed 21 June 2000 BST

KEY PLAYER

MATEJA KEZMAN ATL MADRID

Mateja Kezman was a goal-machine in Holland. He top-scored for PSV in 2003/4 with 31 goals in just 29 league games. He didn't settle at Chelsea with just 11 starts and seven goals but ironically he did begin scoring more regularly for Serbia and Montenegro. He moved to Atletico Madrid to rediscover his scoring form but five goals in 15 starts is more Chelsea than PSV.

Playing record	12 mths lge	wcq
Appearances:	18	7
Minutes played:	1382	507
Percentage played:	37.5%	56.3%
Goals scored:	5	5
Percentage share:	10.42	31.25
Cards:	Y6, R0	Y1, R0
Strike rate:	276mins	101mins
Power ranking:	61st	13th

AGE 27   **STRIKER**   **WORLD RANKING** 1291

Belgrade

Zone	Europe
Population	10,842,744
Capital	Belgrade
Language	Serbian
Top league	Meridian Superliga
Major clubs	**Capacities**
Red Star Belgrade	51,000
Partizan Belgrade	32,700
OFK Beograd	18,000

Where likely squad players play:

In Premiership	2
In other major five European Leagues	7
Outside major European Leagues	14

Number of Serbia & Motenegro players playing:

In Premiership	5	In Spain	9
In Holland	7	In France	6
In Italy	6	In Germany	7

World Cup record (1994 - 2002 as Yugoslavia)

1930 -	Did not enter	1974 -	Did not enter
1934 -	Did not enter	1978 -	Did not enter
1038	Did not enter	1982 -	Did not enter
1950 -	Did not enter	1900 -	Did not enter
1954 -	Did not enter	1990 -	Did not enter
1958 -	Did not enter	1994 -	Banned
1962 -	Did not enter	1998 -	Last 16
1966 -	Did not enter	2002 -	Did not qualify
1970 -	Did not enter		

THE SQUAD

Goalkeepers	Club side	Age	QG
Dragoslav Jevric	Ankaraspor	31	10
Oliver Kovacevic	CSKA	31	0
Defenders			
Nenad Djordjevic	Partizan	26	2
Ivica Dragutinovic	Seville	30	8
Goran Gavrancic	Dinamo Kiev	27	10
Mladen Krstajic	Schalke	32	9
Marjan Markovic	Dinamo Kiev	24	3
Albert Nadj	Partizan	31	2
Nemanja Vidic	Man Utd	24	5
Milivoje Vitakic	Lille	29	1
Midfielders			
Nenad Brnovic	Partizan	26	3
Predrag Djordjevic	Piraeus	33	6
Igor Duljaj	Shakhtar Donetsk	26	9
Sasa Ilic	Galatasary	28	4
Ognijen Koroman	Portsmouth	27	6
Aleksandar Lukovic	Red Star Belgrade	23	2
Milos Maric	Olympiakos	24	1
Dragan Mladenovic	Red Star Belgrade	30	5
Dejan Stankovic	Inter Milan	27	9
Simon Vukcevic	S Ramenskoye	20	1
Zvonimir Vukic	Partizan	26	8
Forwards			
Nenad Jestrovic	Al-Ain	30	1
Mateja Kezman	Atl Madrid	27	7
Darko Kovacevic	Real Sociedad	32	1
Danijel Ljuboja	Stuttgart	28	4
Savo Milosevic	Osasuna	32	6
Marko Pantelic	Hertha Berlin	27	2
Mirkio Vucinic	Lecce	22	1
Nikola Zigic	Red Star Belgrade	25	4

■ Probable ■ Possible **QG** Qualification Games

KEY GOALKEEPER

DRAGOSLAV JEVRIC
ANKARASPOR

Dragoslav Jevric is an unlikely goalkeeper to have the best defensive record in World Cup qualifying.

When the Serbia & Montenegro player started out on qualifying, he was playing for Vitesse Arnhem in Holland. While he was keeping clean sheets for Serbia, he was conceding 23 goals in 17 games at Vitesse. Halfway through the 2004/5 season, the Dutch side brought in former Utrecht and Portsmouth keeper Harald Wapenaar to take over from the Serbian.

Jevric was on the bench and switched clubs in the close season to Ankaraspor in Turkey only to find himself pitched into a relegation battle.

Still he kept everything out for Serbia until Raul of Spain beat him in Madrid – the only goal he conceded.

While his club form was going through a rocky patch, he was formidable behind a fairly settled defence for Serbia & Montenegro. He played every minute of qualifying and had still not picked the ball out of his net after the first seven games.

AGE 32   **WORLD RANKING –**

KEY DEFENDERS

NEMANJA VIDIC
MAN UTD

Nemanja Vidic joined Manchester United for £7 million from Spartak Moscow.

A tough tackling central defender with pace and presence, Vidic came to their attention for his defensive displays against Spain and Belgium in qualifying and United thought they were buying another Jaap Stam. However, he has yet to duplicate Stam-standard performances in a United defence that has looked shaky since January.

It could knock his confidence for Serbia where stunning defence made up for a misfiring attack in qualifying.

Playing record	12 mths lge	wcq
Appearances:	3	5
Minutes played:	202	444
Percentage played:	5.5%	49.3%
Goals conceded:	5	1
Clean sheets:	1	4
Cards:	Y1, R0	Y2, R1
Defensive rating:	-	444mins
Defensive ranking:	-	12th

AGE 24   **WORLD RANKING –**

MLADEN KRSTAJIC
SCHALKE

Playing record	12 mths lge	wcq
Appearances:	33	9
Minutes played:	2925	810
Percentage played:	85.5%	90.0%
Goals conceded:	34	1
Clean sheets:	13	8
Cards:	Y9, R0	Y1, R0
Defensive rating:	86mins	810mins
Defensive ranking:	63rd	6th

AGE 32   **WORLD RANKING 354**

IVICA DRAGUTINOVIC
SEVILLE

Playing record	12 mths lge	wcq
Appearances:	16	8
Minutes played:	1378	690
Percentage played:	37.3%	76.7%
Goals conceded:	19	1
Clean sheets:	5	7
Cards:	Y3, R0	Y0, R0
Defensive rating:	73mins	690mins
Defensive ranking:	87th	7th

AGE 30   **WORLD RANKING 1865**

KEY MIDFIELDERS

ZVONIMIR VUKIC
PARTIZAN

Attacking midfielder Zvonimir Vukic was Portsmouth's last minute loan signing from Shakhtar Donetsk in August 2005.

He made his name during a four-year stint with Partizan Belgrade where he scored 53 times, including 22 in one year.

He struggled at Portsmouth, so returning manager Harry Redknapp cancelled the player's loan in January and he moved back to Belgrade, where he has undergone a foot operation.

Vukic is a deep-lying playmaker for the national side, who often takes charge at set pieces

AGE 27   **WORLD RANKING –**

THE MANAGER

Ilija Petkovic has had two spells in charge of the international teams. He was briefly put in charge of Yugoslavia's in June 2000 but left after a year. Three years later, he was invited back again - his job hadn't changed but the country had.

In the final stage of the break-up of the former Yugoslavia, the country was renamed Serbia and Montenegro.

Petkovic sees defence as the key to success, saying: "Now we are hard workers like the other European teams. In the past we were the European Brazilians but we have changed."

The 60-year-old Petkovic, was assistant to Slobodan Santrac for two years in Yugoslavia's 1998 World Cup campaign. As a player, he won 43 caps and scored six goals for the national team between 1968 and 1974. He played the bulk of his club football with first division OFK Belgrade, for whom he racked up more than 500 matches in over 15 years, and with whom he began his coaching career.

Ilija Petkovic

KEY STRIKER

NIKOLA ZIGIC
RED STAR BELGRADE

The last two games of qualifying saw Nikola Zigic start for Serbia and Montenegro.

The Red Star Belgrade striker is taller even than Peter Crouch, standing 2.02m and presents a unique challenge for opposing defences. He has scored three goals in ten caps for Serbia but didn't add to his total during qualifying.

AGE 25	WORLD RANKING –

SAVO MILOSEVIC
OSASUNA

Savo Milosevic has compiled a record 96 caps playing for Yugoslavia and then Serbia.

He's also the all-time top scorer with 35 goals. He began the qualifying campaign but gave way to Mateja Kezman towards the end.

The well-travelled former Aston Villa striker will go to Germany as he is a talismanic member of the side but be used sparingly.

AGE 32	WORLD RANKING 796

ONE TO WATCH

DEJAN STANKOVIC INTER MILAN

A teenage prodigy at Red Star Belgrade, Dejan Stankovic became a hot property when he scored twice on his on his debut for Serbia and Montenegro in 1998. The play-making midfielder is now captain of the national side and has shown his class in eight seasons in Serie A, winning a Scudetto title in 2000 with Lazio and moving to Inter Milan in 2004.

Playing record	12 mths lge	wcq
Appearances:	28	9
Minutes played:	2095	720
Percentage played:	52.9%	80.0%
Goals scored:	2	2
Goals conceded:	16	1
Cards:	Y5, R0	Y0, R0
Power rating:	52mins	55mins
Power ranking:	51st	85th

AGE 27	MIDFIELDER	WORLD RANKING 179

HOLLAND

ROUTE TO THE FINALS

On the back of a thrilling 3-2 game in Euro 2004, Holland and the Czech Republic were drawn together again in qualifying for the World Cup.

Many things favoured the highly rated Czechs: Ruud van Nistelrooy was injured and Holland were rebuilding under a new coach, Marco van Basten.

His first game in charge was against the Czechs. He kept faith with Edwin van der Sar and Edgar Davids and pulled in Pierre van Hooijdonk up front.

However, there was no de Boer, Reiziger, Overmars, Stam or Seedorf. Instead, Andre Ooijer, John Heitinga, Nigel de Jong made for an inexperienced defence, while Wesley Sneijder, Romeo Castelen and Rafael van der Vaart had an average age of 20 in midfield. The Dutch won though, thanks to two goals by van Hooijdonk and the new generation was launched. It came down to the penultimate game against the Czechs in Prague where a 2-0 win gave Holland the group.

FINAL QUALIFYING TABLE
EUROPE GROUP 1

	P	W	D	L	GF	GA	Pts
Holland	12	10	2	0	27	3	32
Czech Rep	12	9	0	3	35	12	27
Romania	12	8	1	3	20	10	25
Finland	12	5	1	6	21	19	16
Macedonia	12	2	3	7	11	24	9
Armenia	12	2	1	9	9	25	7
Andorra	12	1	2	9	4	34	5

				FIFA ranking			
1	08 Sep 04	Home	Czech Republic	3	W	**2 0**	van Hooijdonk 33, 84
2	09 Oct 04	Away	Macedonia	93	D	**2 2**	Bouma 43, Kuijt 66
3	13 Oct 04	Home	Finland	41	W	**3 1**	Sneijder 39, van Nistelrooy 41, 63
4	17 Nov 04	Away	Andorra	113	W	**0 3**	Cocu 21, Robben 31, Sneijder 78
5	26 Mar 05	Away	Romania	29	W	**0 2**	Cocu 1, Babel 84
6	30 Mar 05	Home	Armenia	116	W	**2 0**	Castelen 3, van Nistelrooy 34
7	04 Jun 05	Home	Romania	29	W	**2 0**	Robben 26, Kuijt 46
8	08 Jun 05	Away	Finland	41	W	**0 4**	van Nistelrooy 36, Kuijt 77, Cocu 84, van Persie 87
9	03 Sep 05	Away	Armenia	116	W	**0 1**	van Nistelrooy 63
10	07 Sep 05	Home	Andorra	113	W	**4 0**	van der Vaart 23, A.Lima Sola 27og, van Nistelrooy 43, 89
11	08 Oct 05	Away	Czech Republic	3	W	**0 2**	van der Vaart 32, Opdam 39
12	12 Oct 05	Home	Macedonia	93	D	**0 0**	
	Average FIFA ranking of opposition			66			

MAIN PLAYER PERFORMANCES IN QUALIFICATION

Match	1 2 3 4 5 6 7 8 9 10 11 12	Appearances	Started	Subbed on	Subbed off	Mins played	% played	Goals	Yellow	Red
Venue	H A H A A H H A A H A H									
Result	W D W W W W W W W W W D									
Goalkeepers										
Edwin Van der Sar		12	12	0	0	1080	100.0	0	0	0
Defenders										
Khalid Boulahrouz		6	6	0	1	506	46.9	0	1	0
Wilfred Bouma		2	2	0	0	180	16.7	1	0	0
Nigel de Jong		7	5	2	0	473	43.8	0	0	0
John Heitinga		4	4	0	0	360	33.3	0	0	0
Lucius		3	3	0	2	181	16.8	0	0	0
Joris Mathijsen		3	2	1	0	188	17.4	0	0	0
Mario Melchiot		2	1	1	0	155	14.4	0	1	0
Andre Ooijer		2	2	0	0	180	16.7	0	0	0
Barry Opdam		6	6	0	0	540	50.0	1	0	0
Giovanni Van Bronckhorst		10	8	2	1	703	65.1	0	3	0
Midfielders										
Phillip Cocu		8	8	0	2	629	58.2	3	0	1
Edgar Davids		4	3	1	0	297	27.5	0	0	0
Denny Landzaat		10	9	1	2	734	68.0	0	1	0
Hedwiges Maduro		7	3	4	1	310	28.7	0	0	0
Wesley Sneijder		7	5	2	2	513	47.5	2	1	0
Mark van Bommel		6	5	1	3	389	36.0	0	1	0
Rafael van der Vaart		9	6	3	2	571	52.9	2	2	0
Robin van Persie		6	3	3	2	307	28.4	1	1	0
Forwards										
Romeo Castelen		5	4	1	3	289	26.8	1	0	0
Dirk Kuijt		11	11	0	2	978	90.6	3	1	0
Roy Makaay		4	0	4	0	117	10.8	0	0	0
Arjen Robben		6	6	0	2	457	42.3	2	0	0
Pierre van Hooijdonk		3	2	1	2	167	15.5	2	1	0
Ruud van Nistelrooy		10	10	0	3	800	74.1	7	1	0

FINAL PROSPECTS

The Dutch easily headed the toughest qualifying group and have moved into a top four FIFA Ranking.

It helps that Holland have the best strike force outside Brazil. Ruud van Nistelrooy hit seven in qualifying and Dirk Kuijt was Europe's top scorer last season with 29 league goals for Feyenoord. There's just no room for the best striker in the Bundesliga, Roy Maakay.

Kuijt's club-mate Romeo Castelen is an exciting young right-winger who supplements the forward line.

Midfield is harder to call as van Basten constantly mixes and matches. He uses either the ever-reliable Phillip Cocu or the ultra-competitive Edgar Davids, alongside a battalion of young stars. Hedwiges Maduro is typical, picked for the Oranje only three matches and 27 days after his league debut for Ajax.

> **"Holland will have the youngest team by far and that is a deliberate choice by Marco van Basten"**
> **Martin Jol**

Young defender John Heitinga has been tried in midfield, Denny Landzaat of AZ Alkmaar competes with Arjen Robben on the left of midfield and Rafael van der Vaart's return to form at Hamburg means he usually starts.

The rise of Alkmaar as a European team, has seen central defenders Joris Mathijsen and Barry Opdam playing for the national side but Hamburg's Khalid Boulahrouz is likely to start ahead of Mathijsen while PSV's versatile Andre Ooijer is a late bloomer whose powerful club form has been rewarded.

Full backs will probably be Barcelona's Giovanni van Bronkhorst on the left and Jan Kromkamp (now at Liverpool) on the right. However, van Bronkhorst is in midfield for Barca and van Basten recently criticised Kromkamp for his choice of club.

It says a lot for the strength in depth of Dutch football that van Basten probably doesn't know his best XI, but whoever he pulls in seems to perform and gets him a result.

Most importantly, unlike previous Dutch teams, van Basten's selections leave their egos at home, so it's their form rather than their sulks that make the headlines.

GROUP FIXTURES

SERBIA & MONT	Sun 11 June 1400 BST
IVORY COAST	Fri 16 June 1700 BST
ARGENTINA	Wed 21 June 2000 BST

Amsterdam

Zone		Europe
Population		16,427,825
Capital		Amsterdam
Language		Dutch
Top league		Eredivisie
Major clubs		**Capacities**
PSV Eindhoven		36,500
Feyenoord		51,200
Ajax		51,900

Where likely squad players play:

In Holland			11
In Premiership			6
In Italy	0	In France	0
In Spain	2	In Germany	3

Number of Dutch players playing:

In Holland			288
In Premiership			21
In Italy	3	In France	0
In Spain	2	In Germany	15

World Cup record

1930 -	Did not enter	1974 -	Runners-up
1934 -	Round 1	1978 -	Runners-up
1938 -	Round 1	1982 -	Did not qualify
1950 -	Did not enter	1986 -	Did not qualify
1954 -	Did not enter	1990 -	Last 16
1958 -	Did not qualify	1994 -	Quarter-finals
1962 -	Did not qualify	1998 -	Fourth place
1966 -	Did not qualify	2002 -	Did not qualify
1970 -	Did not qualify		

THE SQUAD

Goalkeepers	Club side	Age	QG
Edwin Van der Sar	Man Utd	35	12
Defenders			
Khalid Boulahrouz	Hamburg	24	7
Wilfred Bouma	Aston Villa	27	2
Tim de Cler	AZ Alkmaar	27	1
Nigel de Jong	Hamburg	21	7
John Heitinga	Ajax	22	4
Jan Kromkamp	Liverpool	25	4
Lucius	PSV Eindhoven	29	3
Joris Mathijsen	AZ Alkmaar	26	3
Mario Melchiot	Birmingham	29	2
Andre Ooijer	PSV Eindhoven	31	2
Barry Opdam	AZ Alkmaar	30	6
Gio Van Bronckhorst	Barcelona	31	10
Midfielders			
Romeo Castelen	Feyenoord	23	5
Phillip Cocu	PSV Eindhoven	35	8
Edgar Davids	Tottenham	33	4
Denny Landzaat	AZ Alkmaar	30	10
Hedwiges Maduro	Ajax	21	7
Arjen Robben	Chelsea	22	6
Wesley Sneijder	Ajax	22	7
Mark van Bommel	Barcelona	29	6
Rafael van der Vaart	Hamburg	23	9
Robin van Persie	Arsenal	22	6
Ron Vlaar	Feyenoord	21	1
Forwards			
Ryan Babel	Ajax	20	3
Dirk Kuijt	Feyenoord	25	11
Roy Makaay	Bayern Munich	31	4
Pierre van Hooijdonk	Fenerbahce	36	3
Ruud van Nistelrooy	Man Utd	29	10
Jan Vennegoor	PSV Eindhoven	27	0
Klaas Jan Huntelaar	Ajax	22	0

■ Probable ■ Possible **QG** Qualification Games

KEY PLAYER

ARJEN ROBBEN CHELSEA

Arjen Robben had a record last season. He was the Premiership player most likely to see his team score when he was on the pitch. Chelsea would hit the net every 32 minutes on average when Robben was playing – that's nearly three goals a game! The Dutch winger can go in and out of form but he's delivering right now with a deadly turn of pace, balance and a strong finish.

Playing record	12 mths lge	wcq
Appearances:	23	6
Minutes played:	1313	457
Percentage played:	35.6%	42.3%
Goals scored:	6	2
Goals conceded:	9	0
Cards:	Y3, R1	Y0, R0
Power rating:	45mins	29mins
Power ranking:	27th	9th

AGE 22   **MIDFIELDER**   **WORLD RANKING 36**

KEY GOALKEEPER

EDWIN VAN DER SAR
MAN UTD

Edwin van der Sar has plenty of experience of penalties. He started his Dutch international career in 1995 and was in goal for Holland in Euro 96, the World Cup in 1998 and Euro 2000 – all of which saw his team go out on penalties.

It was his save from Olof Mellberg in a quarter-final penalty shootout against Sweden that helped Holland reach the last four at Euro 2004.

A secure, and frequently inspired keeper, van der Sar kept goal for Ajax, Juventus and Fulham before moving to Manchester United for £2m in 2005. He made over 150 appearances for Fulham in his four seasons at the club.

Playing record	12 mths lge	wcq
Appearances:	40	12
Minutes played:	3510	1080
Percentage played:	95.1%	100.0%
Goals conceded:	44	3
Clean sheets:	15	10
Cards:	Y2, R0	Y0, R0
Defensive rating:	80mins	360mins
Defensive ranking:	18th	3rd

AGE 35 **WORLD RANKING 124**

KEY DEFENDERS

ANDRE OOIJER
PSV EINDHOVEN

Playing record	12 mths lge	wcq
Appearances:	33	2
Minutes played:	2864	180
Percentage played:	75.8%	16.7%
Goals conceded:	15	0
Clean sheets:	23	2
Cards:	Y7, R0	Y0, R0
Defensive rating:	191mins	-
Defensive ranking:	2nd	-

AGE 31 **WORLD RANKING 29**

KHALID BOULAHROUZ
HAMBURG

With the wonderful nickname of Khalid the Cannibal, Boulahrouz is supposed to 'eat up' opposing forwards.

He had just moved from RKC Waalwijk in Holland to Hamburg when Marco van Basten pulled him into the Dutch qualifiers. By the time the Dutch had qualified with a clean sheet against the Czech Republic, Boulahrouz was part of a settled central defensive partnership.

At Hamburg, he and Dutch colleague Rafael van der Vaart have helped changed the Bundesliga team from just mid-table battlers.

Playing record	12 mths lge	wcq
Appearances:	28	7
Minutes played:	2520	534
Percentage played:	75.7%	49.4%
Goals conceded:	29	2
Clean sheets:	9	6
Cards:	Y8, R0	Y1, R0
Defensive rating:	87mins	267mins
Defensive ranking:	55th	21st

AGE 24 **WORLD RANKING 439**

JAN KROMKAMP
LIVERPOOL

Playing record	12 mths lge	wcq
Appearances:	4	4
Minutes played:	41	325
Percentage played:	1.1%	30.1%
Goals conceded:	1	0
Clean sheets:	3	4
Cards:	Y0, R0	Y2, R0
Defensive rating:	-	-
Defensive ranking:	-	-

AGE 25 **WORLD RANKING 1854**

BARRY OPDAM
AZ ALKMAAR

Barry Opdam is the perfect example of a late developer. He made his professional debut for AZ Alkmaar in September 1996 and almost nine years later won his first senior cap for Holland against Romania in June 2005 at the grand old age of 29.

One of the reasons why Opdam's career blossomed late is that he is now playing with a fine group of young players at AZ.

AZ have broken into the group of three clubs that usually dominate Dutch football. They had a wonderful season in 2004/5, finishing third in the league with a fine Uefa Cup run.

Club coach Louis van Gaal believes Opdam is the key player in AZ's newfound success. He is desperate to tie the defender down beyond his current contract deal that ends summer 2007 but Opdam is looking to move.

Playing record	12 mths lge	wcq
Appearances:	30	7
Minutes played:	2368	603
Percentage played:	62.6%	55.8%
Goals conceded:	40	3
Clean sheets:	9	6
Cards:	Y6, R1	Y0, R0
Defensive rating:	59mins	201mins
Defensive ranking:	101st	29th

AGE 30 **WORLD RANKING 1237**

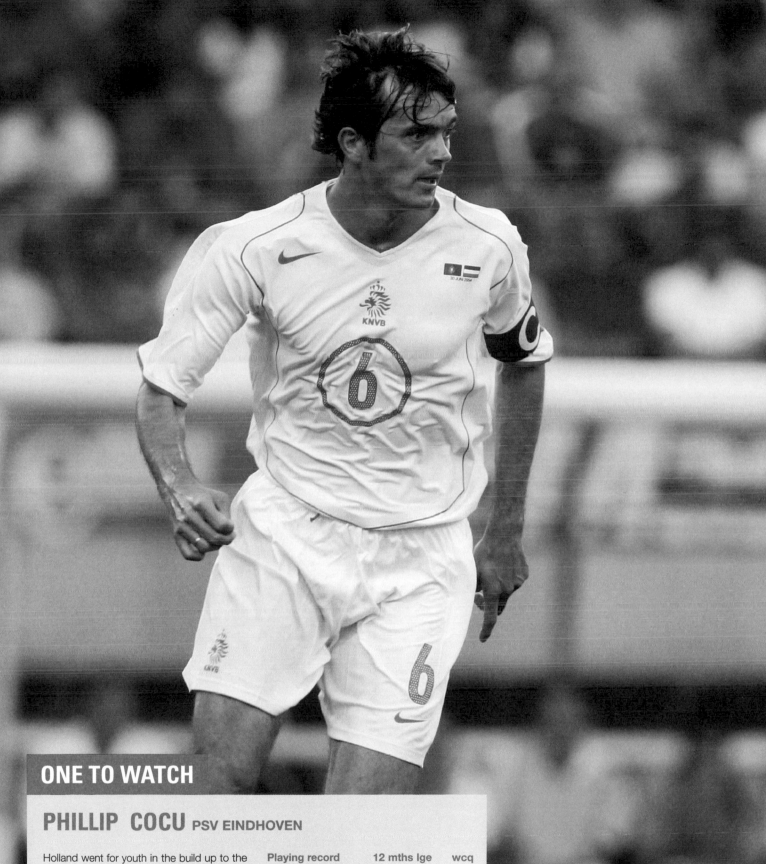

ONE TO WATCH

PHILLIP COCU PSV EINDHOVEN

Holland went for youth in the build up to the 2006 World Cup but welded it together with the canny experience and grit of Phillip Cocu. After six years at Barcelona, Cocu is back in Holland, continuing to play at the highest level. He was hugely influential for PSV last season, particularly in the Champions League.

He is a Top 12 Midfielder.

Playing record	12 mths lge	wcq
Appearances:	37	8
Minutes played:	3262	629
Percentage played:	88.4%	58.2%
Goals scored:	10	3
Goals conceded:	18	2
Cards:	Y4, R1	Y0, R1
Power rating:	43mins	35mins
Power ranking:	16th	18th

| AGE 35 | MIDFIELDER | WORLD RANKING 16 |

THE MANAGER

Marco van Basten scored a miracle goal to win the 1988 European Championship for Holland. If he can win the World Cup in his first two years as a manager, it will be a bigger miracle.

He's broken Alan Hansen's golden rule that you don't win anything with kids by bringing a seemingly endless stream of youngsters into the Dutch side.

Van Basten, 42, took over from Dick Advocaat (now in charge of South Korea) following Euro 2004. He swiftly moved on from the previous generation of stars and then left out the current Barcelona midfielder Mark van Bommel – although he has since thrown him a lifeline.

Having surprised the Dutch public with one crop of youngsters, van Basten then bloodied another, constantly switching new players in and out. However, he's consistently won games and qualified ahead of bogey side, the Czechs. The Dutch press still aren't quite won over though.

KEY MIDFIELDERS

The Dutch midfield is hard to call as van Basten constantly mixes and matches.

Hedwiges Maduro is typical; picked for the Oranje only three matches and 27 days after he made his debut for Ajax. The winger **Denny Landzaat**, of AZ Alkmaar, has been the most consistently played midfielder in qualifying. **Rafael van der Vaart** moved to Hamburg in the summer and has struck nine goals in 17 to return for the Dutch side.

The ultra-competitive **Edgar Davids** came back into the squad in the Autumn of last year and winger **Romeo Castelen** is a van Basten favourite who lost his place through injury but subsequently came back into form.

HEDWIGES MADURO

AJAX

Hedwiges Maduro had already impressed Marco van Basten when he was coach of the reserve team at Ajax.

Van Basten was prepared to back his judgement and pulled the player – who can also play in defence – into his international team in an astonishingly short time after his professional debut. Having bloodied the youngster against Armenia, he then included him in the vital game against the Czechs.

Playing record	12 mths lge	wcq
Appearances:	32	7
Minutes played:	2789	310
Percentage played:	75.6%	28.7%
Goals conceded:	37	0
Clean sheets:	12	7
Cards:	Y2, R0	Y0, R0
Defensive rating:	75mins	-
Defensive ranking:	75th	-

AGE 21	WORLD RANKING 699

DENNY LANDZAAT

AZ ALKMAAR

Denny Landzaat is another player to have used AZ Alkmaar's success in Europe as a springboard to the Dutch side.

He made ten appearances in the qualifying tournament and is likely to start in Germany despite competition from Arjen Robben, Romeo Castelen and Robin van Persie.

Pllaying record	12 mths lge	wcq
Appearances:	37	10
Minutes played:	3276	734
Percentage played:	86.7%	68.0%
Goals scored:	11	0
Goals conceded:	46	1
Cards:	Y3, R0	Y1, R0
Power rating:	39mins	39mins
Power ranking:	6th	27th

AGE 30	WORLD RANKING 111

ROMEO CASTELEN

FEYENOORD

Playing record	12 mths lge	wcq
Appearances:	27	5
Minutes played:	2284	289
Percentage played:	60.4%	26.8%
Goals scored:	14	1
Goals conceded:	34	3
Cards:	Y1, R0	Y0, R0
Power rating:	29mins	36mins
Power ranking:	1st	21st

AGE 23	WORLD RANKING 128

KEY STRIKERS

KLAAS JAN HUNTELAAR

AJAX

Here's van Basten's surprise pick for the finals - the untried Klaas Jan Huntelaar

The Heereneveen youngster hit 17 goals last season and as many again before he was signed by Ajax in January this season.

AGE 22	WORLD RANKING 56

DIRK KUIJT

FEYENOORD

Every big club seems interested in Feyenoord's Dirk Kuijt – and no wonder, his 29 league goals made him the top striker in Europe last season.

His partnership with Ivory Coast teen sensation Salomon Kalou (20 goals) and Romeo Castelen (10) made Feyenoord the best attacking side on the continent.

Kuijt (we've adopted the Dutch spelling) is a Top 12 Striker.

AGE 25	WORLD RANKING 8

KEY STRIKER

RUUD VAN NISTELROOY MAN UTD

Ruud van Nistelrooy is a classic penalty box predator. He won't make many goals for others or score many from outside the box. He is a natural goal-scorer, with pace, strength, courage and a sixth sense in timing his runs into the box.
Following his £19m move to Manchester United he reached the milestone of 100 goals in less than three seasons.

Van Nistelrooy has struck a good partnership with Dirk Kuijt in attack.
He and United team-mate Edwin van der Sar are vital players for Holland. These two may be the only two with international tournament experience if van Basten continues with his youth selection policy.
Top 12 players: van Nistelrooy, Kuijt, Cocu and Ooijer.

AGE 29 | **STRIKER** | **WORLD RANKING 42**

Position	1st	2nd	3rd	4th	5th	6th	7th	8th
Group	E	F	C	A	D	H	B	G
Total FIFA ranking	89	93	95	96	101	109	117	138

MEXICO V IRAN
MEXW MEXW — Nuremberg, Sunday 11th June 1700 BST

Iran are well-organised and only five games in the last 28 have seen them concede more than one goal. They notched up 11 clean sheets in that time. However, they do not have a track record of scoring against top-class defences in the few games that they have come up against them. They enjoyed good possession against Germany in late 2004 without finding the back of the net.

Mexico have a strong defence, confidence in their system and any number of players who can hit the net.

Francisco Fonseca will be the player they look to to spark the attack if Borgetti is rusty.

ANGOLA V PORTUGAL
PORW PORW — Cologne, Sunday 11th June 2000 BST

This is Angola's cup final. Portugal is the old colonial power and several Angolans have links to the Portuguese league.

While this has similar ingredients for the upset that befell France against Senegal, Angola have less experience of top league football than the Senegalese had. They are also coming off a poor African Cup of Nations while the Portuguese are flying but may be hampered by their high expectations.

Pedro Mantorras is the top striking act in the Angolan team, playing Champions League football for Benfica and could make an impact for the Africans.

MEXICO V ANGOLA
MEXW MEXW — Hanover, Friday 16th June 2000 BST

The Angolans will either be riding the crest of belief if they have gained a point against Portugal or a slump of spirit following any kind of defeat. Either way this game will be less intense for them and Mexico will be looking to build their goal difference to top the group. If Blanco is truly back in the fold for Mexico, he could be played behind the two main strikers as he was recently to good effect in a recent win against Norway.

PORTUGAL V IRAN
PORW PORW — Frankfurt, Saturday 17th June 1400 BST

The slow-starting Portuguese should be cranking through the gears after a win against Angola. The Iran strikers will struggle against the no-nonsense defending of Carvalho and Andrade while the Portuguese midfield is combative enough to snuff out Karimi.

If Deco starts to exert the same kind of control and possession he does for Barcelona, there's enough talent on the pitch and the bench to win by two goals.

IRAN V ANGOLA
IRAW DRAW — Leipzig, Wednesday 21 June 1500 BST

The battle for the wooden spoon should be a close affair. Both teams can point to recent narrow wins over Togo in their form guide and both have the ability to score against anything but world-class defences.

Ali Daei, at 37, will be on his last hurrah for Iran and his leadership qualities will insist every Iranian player takes some pride back home with them after the group stage.

Iran's Ali Daei

PORTUGAL V MEXICO
PORW DRAW — Gelsenkirchen, Wednesday 21 June 1500 BST

The heavyweight game of Group D could easily peter out into a tame draw. Whether you come first or second in this group, you face a fearsome prospect in the last 16 so there may not be much to play for. Both sides have strong defences and are secure in possession so goals will be hard to come by. An early goal could mean we have a classic on our hands. In midfield, Brazilian Antonia Naelsen 'Zinha' will be up against his former countryman Deco in midfield. Both are small but influential playmakers and Zinha is Mexico's best chance of unlocking Portugal's defence.

MARTIN JOL'S VIEW

I was very impressed with Mexico during the 2005 Confederations Cup. They played good and attacking football and used their wingers well. Jared Borgetti, who now plays for Bolton and is the first Mexican player in the Premiership, was one of their best players.

Mexico played attacking football down the flanks with plenty of crosses aimed at Borgetti, who is very good with his head. He scored 14 goals during the World Cup qualification.

Playing millions of games makes Mexico one of the highest rated countries in world football. They are currently sixth in the FIFA World Ranking list and they have a bright future. Last October they were hugely impressive in winning the Under-17 World Cup tournament.

Portugal have - with 10 million people - only 10% of Mexico's population. You can compare them a bit with Holland, playing attractive football but falling at the last hurdle.

"What I like very much is the fact Portugal play with real wingers."

It isn't easy to pick out special players from their squad. Almost everybody plays at a good international level. I mention Jorge Andrade and Ricardo Carvalho – both central defenders – and Miguel a very good right back.

They have good midfield players in Costinha, Deco, Maniche and Tiago, who all won the Champions League with Porto under Jose Mourinho. They have something of everything – now that includes a lot of experience with several top European clubs.

In Simao and Cristiano Ronaldo, they have good wingers too. I expect Ronaldo to be one of the best and most exciting players of the World Cup.

Striker Pauleta broke Eusebio's all-time Portuguese record of 41 goals. He was the European qualifying groups' top scorer too with 11 goals.

But their main attraction still is Figo.

What I like very much is the fact they play with real wingers. During the last European Championship in their own country they reached the final but I still expect everybody will underestimate them, despite the fact that they won their qualifying group with seven points to spare, and that after a 2-2 draw against Liechtenstein in an away game!

Iran is one of the mystery teams, but it is a great footballing country with some stars like Ali Karimi, who is playing well at Bayern Munich, and is known as Asia's Maradona. Not only Bayern, but also Real Madrid were interested in signing him.

"In short Iran have the potential to be a surprise team during the tournament."

Mehdi Mahdavikia, is playing as a winger for Hamburg while the old fox Ali Daei also proved his worth in the Bundesliga. Vahid Hashemian is at Hannover 96 and very good in the air.

In short Iran has the potential to be a surprise team during the tournament.

Angola are real dark horses but the fact that they won their group above Nigeria shows that they are capable of something. Mantorras is their star player and has been since a very young age. He made Benfica Champions of Portugal, in 2004/5 – their first title for 11 years – and during the season, Mantorras was more influential than the coach Giovanni Trapattoni. Fabrice Akwa is another of their players to watch. In the decisive qualifier in Rwanda he scored the winning goal ten minutes from time. However, I don't expect much from Angola.

PAULETA BROKE EUSEBIO'S ALL-TIME PORTUGUESE RECORD OF 41 GOALS

MARTIN JOL'S PREDICTIONS FOR THE TOP TWO TEAMS FROM THIS GROUP

Schedule of play is on page 80

GROUP STAGE	LAST SIXTEEN	QUARTER-FINALS
FIRST GROUP D	v SECOND GROUP C	v FIRST GROUP B or SECOND GROUP A
PORTUGAL →	**PORTUGAL v HOLLAND** →	**ENGLAND v PORTUGAL**
SECOND GROUP D	v FIRST GROUP C	v FIRST GROUP A or SECOND GROUP B
MEXICO →	**MEXICO v ARGENTINA** →	**ARGENTINA v GERMANY**
GROUP D MEXICO, IRAN, ANGOLA, PORTUGAL	**GROUP C** ARGENTINA, IVORY COAST, SERBIA & MONTENEGRO, HOLLAND	**GROUP A** GERMANY, COSTA RICA, POLAND, ECUADOR **GROUP B** ENGLAND, PARAGUAY, TRINIDAD & TOBAGO, SWEDEN

Catch the likely group D decider, Mexico verses Portugal, as the winners could meet the winners of England's group in the quarters.

ROUTE TO THE FINALS

Mexico and the United States are the superpowers of the CONCACAF and the qualifiers are about local bragging rights.

They finished all square – on 22 points with each side winning one of the head-to-heads. However, Mexico were streets ahead in goalscoring including the preliminaries, hitting nearly double the USA's 35 goal total.

Jared Borgetti has had little chance to show his finishing skills at Bolton but the 'Desert Fox' struck 14 times in 18 games as Mexico hit 67 in total. Mexico gained early ascendancy over the US with Borgetti scoring first in front of a 120,000 Azteca Stadium crowd. Antonio

Naelsen beat Kasey Keller to take Mexico 2-0 up before Eddie Lewis hit a US consolation. An experiment of moving Barcelona defender Rafael Marquez into midfield in a 3-5-2 formation backfired in the return game.

FINAL QUALIFYING TABLE
N/C AMERICA & CAR STAGE 3

	P	W	D	L	GF	GA	Pts
USA	10	7	1	2	16	6	22
Mexico	10	7	1	2	22	9	22
Costa Rica	10	5	1	4	15	14	16
Trinidad & Tobago	10	4	1	5	10	15	13
Guatemala	10	3	2	5	16	18	11
Panama	10	0	2	8	4	21	2

#	Date	Venue	Opponent	FIFA ranking	Result	Score	Scorers
1	08 Sep 04	Away	Trinidad & Tobago	57	W	1 3	Arellano 1, 80, Borgetti 19
2	06 Oct 04	Home	StVincent/Grenadines	131	W	7 0	Borgetti 31, 68, 77, 89, Lozano 54, 63, Santana 81
3	10 Oct 04	Away	StVincent/Grenadines	131	W	0 1	Borgetti 25
4	13 Oct 04	Home	Trinidad & Tobago	57	W	3 0	Zinha 19, Lozano 55, 84
5	13 Nov 04	Away	St Kitts/Nevis	122	W	0 5	Altamirano 31, Fonseca 40, 57, Santana 49, 90
6	17 Nov 04	Home	St Kitts/Nevis	122	W	8 0	Altamirano 10pen, L.Perez 21, 49, 78, Fonseca 44, 56, Osomo 52, Santana 67
7	09 Feb 05	Away	Costa Rica	22	W	1 2	Lozano 8, 10
8	27 Mar 05	Home	United States	8	W	2 1	Borgetti 30, Zinha 32
9	30 Mar 05	Away	Panama	88	D	1 1	Morales 26
10	04 Jun 05	Away	Guatemala	60	W	0 2	Zinha 41, G.Cabrera 45og
11	08 Jun 05	Home	Trinidad & Tobago	57	W	2 0	Borgetti 63, L.Perez 88
12	17 Aug 05	Home	Costa Rica	22	W	2 0	Borgetti 63, Fonseca 86
13	03 Sep 05	Away	United States	8	L	2 0	
14	07 Sep 05	Home	Panama	88	W	5 0	L.Perez 31, Marquez 54, Borgetti 59, Fonseca 75, Pardo 76
15	08 Oct 05	Home	Guatemala	60	W	5 2	Franco 19, Fonseca 48, 51, 62, 66
16	12 Oct 05	Away	Trinidad & Tobago	57	L	2 1	Lozano 38
	Average FIFA ranking of opposition			68			

Not including pre-qualifying games

MAIN PLAYER PERFORMANCES IN QUALIFICATION

Match	Appearances	Started	Subbed on	Subbed off	Mins played	% played	Goals	Yellow	Red
1 2 3 4 5 6 7 8 9 10 11 12 13 14 15 16									
Venue: A H A H A H A H A A H H H A H H A									
Result: W W W W W W W W D W W W L W W L									
Goalkeepers									
Jose Corona	2	2	0	0	180	12.5	0	0	0
Moises Munoz	2	2	0	0	180	12.5	0	0	0
Oswaldo Sanchez	11	11	0	0	990	68.8	0	0	0
Defenders									
Salvador Carmona	5	5	0	0	450	31.3	0	2	0
Rafael Marquez	9	9	0	2	760	52.8	1	2	0
Marlo Mendez	7	5	2	2	426	29.6	0	0	0
Ricardo Osorio	6	6	0	0	540	37.5	0	1	0
Pavel Pardo	6	6	0	0	540	37.5	1	2	0
Gonzalo Pineda	10	4	6	1	452	31.4	0	1	0
Francisco Rodriguez	11	11	0	0	958	66.5	0	0	0
Carlos Salcido	12	12	0	1	1063	73.8	0	0	0
Hugo Sanchez	6	5	1	0	523	36.3	0	0	0
Midfielders									
Israel Lopez	4	4	0	1	287	19.9	0	0	0
Jaime Lozano	9	9	0	4	732	50.8	7	0	0
Ramon Morales	8	4	4	2	403	28.0	1	1	0
Luis Perez	11	8	3	2	713	49.5	5	3	0
Juan Pablo Rodriguez	5	4	1	0	377	26.2	0	0	0
Antonin Naelsen 'Zinha'	9	9	0	5	708	49.2	3	0	0
Forwards									
Jesus Arellano	4	4	0	2	331	23.0	2	0	0
Jared Echavarria Borgetti	12	12	0	3	1004	69.7	10	0	0
Fonseca	11	10	1	3	858	59.6	10	0	0
Sergio Santana	4	1	3	0	149	10.3	4	0	0

FINAL PROSPECTS

Mexico have qualified from the group stages of the last three World Cup finals and within this group will do so again.

They are comfortable on the ball and their neat possession game confounded top-class opponents in last summer's Confederations Cup where they beat Brazil 1-0 and only lost to Argentina after a penalty shoot-out in the semi-finals. The FIFA World Ranking works in their favour but they have been a top ten side for several years.

By the time they play Portugal, both countries should have qualified for the later stages, so a draw looks likely between two entertaining sides. The last 16 tie may end Mexico's interest.

Apart from Borgetti, 'El Tri' expect goals from Pumas midfielder Jaime Lozano, who hit 11 in qualifying, and Francisco 'Jose' Fonseca.

Rafael Marquez is one of our top 12 form defenders at the World Cup.

THE MANAGER

Argentine-born Ricardo La Volpe has the Mexicans playing a more attacking brand of football, bringing the best out of the deadly Borgetti.

As befits a former keeper, La Volpe has made the defensive unit hard to break down. He prefers three at the back, matching the class of Rafael Marquez with the youthful strength of Carlos Salcido and pace of Ricardo Osorio.

La Volpe, 54, still gets flack from the press, the club owners and influential former players such as Hugo Sanchez – usually over veteran striker Blanco.

Ricardo La Volpe

GROUP FIXTURES

IRAN	Sun 11 June 1700 BST
ANGOLA	Fri 16 June 2000 BST
PORTUGAL	Wed 21 June 1500 BST

Zone	North, Central America & Caribbean
Population	107,281,310
Capital	Mexico City
Language	Spanish
Top league	Primera Division
Major clubs	**Capacities**
Club America	114,500
Guadalajara	63,200
Pumas	72,500

Where likely squad players play:

In Mexico	20
In Premiership	1
In other major five European Leagues	2
Outside major European Leagues	0

Number of Mexican players playing:

In Premiership	1
In other major five European Leagues	2

World Cup record

1930 -	Group 4th	1974 -	Did not qualify
1934 -	Did not qualify	1978 -	Group 4th
1938 -	Withdrew	1982 -	Did not qualify
1950 -	Group 4th	1986 -	Quarter-finals
1954 -	Group 4th	1990 -	Disqualified
1958 -	Group 4th	1994 -	Last 16
1962 -	Group 3rd	1998 -	Last 16
1966 -	Group 3rd	2002 -	Last 16
1970 -	Quarter-finals		

KEY PLAYER

JARED BORGETTI BOLTON

It's all about nicknames in Mexico. Their number nine, Jared Borgetti is known to the fans of 'El Tricolors' – Mexico's team nickname – as El Zorro del Desierto (The Desert Fox). He top scored across the world in qualifying having formed a prolific partnership with Mexico's hottest property Francisco 'Jose' Fonseca.

Top 12 player: Rafael Marquez

Playing record	12 mths lge	wcq
Appearances:	10	12
Minutes played:	267	1004
Percentage played:	7.2%	69.7%
Goals scored:	1	10
Percentage share:	2.00	20.41
Cards:	Y0, R0	Y0, R0
Strike rate:	267	100mins
Strike rate ranking:	-	11th

AGE 32 | **STRIKER** | **WORLD RANKING 1472**

THE SQUAD

Goalkeepers	Club side	Age	QG
Jose Corona	Te Guadalajara	25	2
Moises Munoz	Monarcas Morelia	26	2
Oswaldo Sanchez	Guadalajara	32	11
Defenders			
Hector Altamirano	San Louis Potosi	29	5
Duilio Davino	America Ciudad	30	1
Joel Huiqui	Cruz Azul	23	2
Rafael Marquez	Barcelona	27	9
Mario Mendez	Monterrey	27	7
Ricardo Osorio	Cruz Azul	26	6
Francisco Rodriguez	Guadalajara	24	11
Oscar Rojas	America Ciudad	24	3
Carlos Salcido	Guadalajara	26	12
Hugo Sanchez	Monterrey	25	6
Midfielders			
Rafael Garcia	Guadalajara	23	5
Israel Lopez	Toluca	31	4
Jaime Lozano	Monterrey	26	9
Ramon Morales	Guadalajara	30	8
Antonio Naelson 'Zinha'	Toluca	30	12
Pavel Pardo	America Ciudad	29	6
Luis Perez	Monterrey	25	11
Mario Perez	Necaxa	23	3
Gonzalo Pineda	Guadalajara	23	10
Juan Pablo Rodriguez	Tecos Guadalajara	26	5
Gerardo Torrado	R Santander	27	3
Forwards			
Jesus Arellano	Monterrey	33	4
Cuauhtemoc Blanco	America Ciudad	33	5
Jared Borgetti	Bolton	32	12
Francisco Fonseca	Cruz Azul	26	11
Guillermo Franco	Villareal	29	2
Alberto Medina	Guadalajara	23	8
Sergio Santana	CD Guadalajara	26	4

■ Probable ■ Possible **QG** Qualification Games

IRAN

SEEDED 21 FIFA RANKING 18

ROUTE TO THE FINALS

Iran have qualified for two of the last three World Cup finals and have established themselves as one of the top two sides in Asia.

They are currently ranked 19th by FIFA and have been in the top 20 for the last 18 months.

Japan are the only higher-ranked Asian team and the two countries sailed through Asian Zone Group 2. Japan took maximum points off Bahrain and the Democratic Peoples Republic of Korea (previously North Korea) but lost to Iran in the 100,000 capacity Azadi Stadium.

By the time they met in Yokohama for the return, both had qualified and opted to do without their European-based players.

The veteran striker Ali Daei was Asia's top scorer with nine goals, including the consolation penalty he struck in the last game against Japan. Qualification was greeted with mass celebrations across street football-crazy Iran.

FINAL QUALIFYING TABLE
ASIA STAGE 3 – GROUP B

	P	W	D	L	GF	GA	Pts
Japan	6	5	0	1	9	4	15
Iran	6	4	1	1	7	3	13
Bahrain	6	1	1	4	4	7	4
Korea DPR	6	1	0	5	5	11	3

#	Date	Venue	Opponent	FIFA ranking	Result	Score	Scorers
1	18 Feb 04	Home	Qatar	73	W	3 1	Vahedi 8, Mahdavikia 44, Daei 62
2	31 Mar 04	Away	Laos	164	W	0 7	Daei 9, 17pen, Enayati 32, 36, Khouphachansy 54og, Taghipour 68, 83
3	09 Jun 04	Home	Jordan	59	L	0 1	
4	08 Sep 04	Away	Jordan	59	W	0 2	Vahedi 80, Daei 90
5	13 Oct 04	Away	Qatar	73	W	2 3	Hashemian 9, 89, Borhani 78
6	17 Nov 04	Home	Laos	164	W	7 0	Daei 8, 20, 28, 58, Nekoonam 63, 72, Borhani 69
7	09 Feb 05	Away	Bahrain	51	D	0 0	
8	25 Mar 05	Home	Japan	16	W	2 1	Hashemian 13, 66
9	30 Mar 05	Away	North Korea	89	W	0 2	Mahdavikia 32, Nekoonam 79
10	03 Jun 05	Home	North Korea	89	W	1 0	Rezaei 45
11	08 Jun 05	Home	Bahrain	51	W	1 0	Nosrati 47
12	17 Aug 05	Away	Japan	16	L	2 1	Daei 79
	Average FIFA ranking of opposition			67			

MAIN PLAYER PERFORMANCES IN QUALIFICATION

Match	1 2 3 4 5 6 7 8 9 10 11 12	Appearances	Started	Subbed on	Subbed off	Mins played	% played	Goals	Yellow	Red
Venue	H A H A A H A H A H H A									
Result	W W L W W W D W W W W L									
Goalkeepers										
Ebrahim Mirzapour		11	11	0	0	990	91.7	0	0	0
Seyed Rahmati		1	1	0	0	90	8.3	0	0	0
Defenders										
Ali Badavi		4	4	0	1	348	32.2	0	1	0
Hussein Kabei		12	12	0	3	1042	96.5	0	1	0
Jalal Kameli-Mofrad		3	2	1	0	184	17.0	0	0	0
Mohammed Nosrati		11	10	1	0	901	83.4	1	1	0
Rahman Rezaei		8	8	0	1	692	64.1	1	2	0
Ebrahim Taghipour		2	1	1	0	93	8.6	2	1	0
Midfielders										
Seyed Alavi		6	2	4	0	256	23.7	0	1	0
Yahya Golmohammadi		11	11	0	0	990	91.7	0	2	0
Mojtaba Jabari		1	1	0	1	45	4.2	0	0	0
Ali Karimi		11	11	0	4	961	89.0	0	1	0
Javad Kazemeyan		3	0	3	0	105	9.7	0	0	0
Mehdi Mahdavikia		8	8	0	0	720	66.7	2	2	0
Eman Mobali		5	1	4	1	174	16.1	0	0	0
Moharram Navidkia		5	1	4	0	213	19.7	0	0	0
Javad Nekoonam		12	12	0	1	1039	96.2	3	2	0
Alireza Vahedi Nikbakht		9	5	4	4	441	40.8	2	2	0
Ferydoon Zandi		5	5	0	5	315	29.2	0	1	0
Sattar Zare		4	4	0	2	288	26.7	0	2	0
Forwards										
Khodadad Azizi		2	1	1	1	73	6.8	0	0	0
Arash Borhani		5	2	3	2	173	16.0	2	1	0
Ali Daei		10	10	0	1	852	78.9	9	0	0
Gholamreza Enayati		1	1	0	0	90	8.3	2	0	0
Vahid Hashemian		7	7	0	4	622	57.6	4	0	0
Rasoul Paki Khatibi		1	0	1	0	26	2.4	0	1	0
Mehdi Rajabzadeh		2	1	1	1	61	5.6	0	0	0

FINAL PROSPECTS

Iran have a terrific record against Asian sides over the last two years alongside South Korea and Japan but will find it harder to get a result against top class opponents.

They struggle in games against quality sides, going down 2-0 to South Korea and 2-1 to Macedonia in November. Their last autumn fixture was a flukey 2-0 win over fellow finalists Togo that bodes well for the Angola game.

Iran's current hopes lie with an old guard of Bundesliga striking veterans. Ali Daei, 37, has over 100 international goals. He played for Bayern Munich and left Hertha Berlin in 2002. Mehdi Mahdavikia is out of favour at Hamburg and Vahid Hashemian barely played 250 minutes for Bayern last season before leaving for Hannover 96. Midfield star Ali Karimi was Asian footballer of the year in 2004 and covers for Michael Ballack at Bayern.

THE MANAGER

Coach Branko Ivankovic thinks Iran are ten years away from reaching 'true international level'.

Certainly, a skilful generation of street footballers is coming through but there isn't yet an infrastructure to support them.

Ivankovic, a Croatian, became Iran's team manager in 2002, having been their assistant during the World Cup 2002 qualification. He says, "Iranian players are not only quality players, but they are also full of enthusiasm." He has to tread carefully with the Iranian government who control the IFA.

Branko Ivankovic

GROUP FIXTURES

MEXICO	Sun 11 June 1700 BST
PORTUGAL	Sat 17 June 1400 BST
ANGOLA	Wed 21 June 1500 BST

Tehran

Zone	Asia
Population	68,492,793
Capital	Tehran
Language	Persian
Top league	Pro League
Major clubs	**Capacities**
Perspolis	90,000
Esteghlal	90,000
Sepahan	75,000

Where likely squad players play:

In Iran	19
In Premiership	0
In other major five European Leagues	4
Outside major European Leagues	0

Number of Iranian players playing:

In Premiership	0
In other major five European Leagues	4

World Cup record

1930 -	Did not enter	1974 -	Did not qualify
1934 -	Did not enter	1978 -	Group 4th
1938 -	Did not enter	1982 -	Withdrew
1950 -	Did not enter	1986 -	Disqualified
1954 -	Did not enter	1990 -	Did not qualify
1958 -	Did not enter	1994 -	Did not qualify
1962 -	Did not enter	1998 -	Group 3rd
1966 -	Did not enter	2002 -	Did not qualify
1970 -	Did not enter		

KEY PLAYER

MEHDI MAHDAVIKIA HAMBURG

Iran's experienced forward, Mehdi Mahdavikia has been playing for Hamburg SV since 2000. He plays right wing and striker for the club but midfield for Iran. In 2003/4, he recorded most assists in the Bundesliga and scored five goals in 32 games. The 2004/5 season was less successful and there is talk of him leaving in the summer.

Playing record	12 mths lge	wcq
Appearances:	33	8
Minutes played:	2192	720
Percentage played:	64.1%	66.7%
Goals scored:	7	2
Percentage share:	12.07	6.90
Cards:	Y3, R1	Y2, R0
Strike rate:	313mins	360mins
Strike rate ranking:	67th	56th

AGE 28 | **STRIKER** | **WORLD RANKING 355**

THE SQUAD

Goalkeepers	Club side	Age	QG
Ebrahim Mirzapour	Foolad Ahvaz	27	11
Seyed Rahmati	Sepahan Isfahan	23	1
Defenders			
Ali Badavi	Foolad Ahvaz	24	4
Hussein Kabei	Foolad Ahvaz	20	12
Jalal Kameli-Mofrad	Foolad Ahvaz	25	3
Mohammed Nosrati	Paas Tehran	24	11
Rahman Rezaei	Messina	31	8
Masoud Soleimani	Saipa	22	1
Ebrahim Taghipour	Zob Ahan	31	2
Midfielders			
Davoud Seyed Abassi	Esteghlal	29	1
Seyed Alavi	Foolad Ahvaz	23	6
Mehdi Amir	Saipa Karadj	26	1
Yahya Golmohammadi	Pirouzi Tehran	-	11
Mojtaba Jabari	Esteghlal	22	1
Ali Karimi	Bayern Munich	27	11
Javad Kazemeyan	Pirouzi Tehran	-	3
Mehdi Mahdavikia	Hamburg	28	8
Meysam Maniei	Paas Tehran	23	1
Eman Mobali	Al-Shabab Dubai	23	5
Moharram Navidkia	Sepahan	23	5
Javad Nekoonam	Al-Wahda A Dhabi	25	12
Alireza Vahedi Nikbakht	Al-Wasl Dubai	-	9
Ferydoon Zandi	Kaiserslautern	27	5
Sattar Zare	Bergh Shiraz	25	4
Forwards			
Khodadad Azizi	VFB Admira	34	2
Arash Borhani	Paas Tehran	22	5
Ali Daei	Saba Batry Tehran	37	10
Gholamreza Enayati	Esteghlal Tehran	30	1
Vahid Hashemian	Hannover 96	29	7
Rasoul Paki Khatibi	Sepahan	27	1
Mehdi Rajabzadeh	Zob Ahan	29	2

■ Probable ■ Possible **QG** Qualification Games

ANGOLA

ROUTE TO THE FINALS

One of the poorest and most politically unstable nations on earth, with a life expectancy of only 37 years, Angola have surprised everyone by qualifying for the finals.

Mostly, they surprised Nigeria, one of the super powers of African football who would have expected to qualify comfortably from Africa Group 4.

Angola began by struggling in the preliminary round ahead of Chad, only squeezing through on away goals.

Like most of the unexpected African finalists, they did their damage against the group favourites. Captain Fabrice Akwa scored the goal that beat Nigeria at home in their second game. That gave the Angolans the confidence they needed to ratchet up five home wins.

A 1-1 draw in Nigeria, an early Jay-Jay Okocha goal answered by Figueiredo, proved crucial as it gave the Angolans the head-to-head advantage over Nigeria when both teams finished on 21 points.

A settled defence in front of keeper Pereira must take most of the credit for taking the Angolans to their first World Cup finals.

FINAL QUALIFYING TABLE
AFRICA GROUP 4

	P	W	D	L	GF	GA	Pts
Angola	10	6	3	1	12	6	21
Nigeria	10	6	3	1	21	7	21
Zimbabwe	10	4	3	3	13	14	15
Gabon	10	2	4	4	11	13	10
Algeria	10	1	5	4	8	15	8
Rwanda	10	1	2	7	6	16	5

#	Date	Venue	Opponent	FIFA ranking	Result	Score	Scorers
1	05 Jun 04	Away	Algeria	78	D	0 0	
2	20 Jun 04	Home	Nigeria	25	W	1 0	Akwa 84
3	03 Jul 04	Away	Gabon	104	D	2 2	Akwa 19, Marco Paulo 81
4	05 Sep 04	Home	Rwanda	100	W	1 0	Freddy 52
5	10 Oct 04	Home	Zimbabwe	55	W	1 0	Flavio 53
6	27 Mar 05	Away	Zimbabwe	55	L	2 0	
7	05 Jun 05	Home	Algeria	78	W	2 1	Flavio 50, Akwa 58
8	18 Jun 05	Away	Nigeria	25	D	1 1	Figueiredo 60
9	04 Sep 05	Home	Gabon	104	W	3 0	Isakunia 25og, Mantorras 44, Ze Kalanga 89
10	08 Oct 05	Away	Rwanda	100	W	0 1	Akwa 79
	Average FIFA ranking of opposition			72			

Not including pre-qualifying games

MAIN PLAYER PERFORMANCES IN QUALIFICATION

Match	1 2 3 4 5 6 7 8 9 10	Appearances	Started	Subbed on	Subbed off	Mins played	% played	Goals	Yellow	Red
Venue	A H A H H A H A H A									
Result	D W D W W L W D W W									
Goalkeepers										
Joao Pereira		10	10	0	0	900	100.0	0	1	0
Defenders										
Jamba		10	10	0	0	900	100.0	0	0	0
Kali		7	7	0	0	630	70.0	0	0	0
Lebo Lebo		3	3	0	0	270	30.0	0	0	0
Loco		3	2	1	0	186	20.7	0	0	0
Pedro Manuel		1	1	0	0	90	10.0	0	0	0
Jacinto Pereira		7	7	0	0	630	70.0	0	2	0
Yamba Asha		10	10	0	0	900	100.0	0	1	0
Midfielders										
Andre		7	7	0	0	630	70.0	0	1	0
Chinho		2	0	2	0	28	3.1	0	0	0
Figueiredo		8	8	0	8	522	58.0	1	2	0
Freddy		7	6	1	4	480	53.3	1	0	0
Gilberto		9	8	1	1	726	80.7	0	1	0
Joaquin		1	1	0	1	84	9.3	0	0	0
Andre Macanga		2	2	0	0	180	20.0	0	0	0
Antonio Viana Mendonca		4	4	0	1	324	36.0	0	0	0
Paulo		1	0	1	0	14	1.6	0	0	0
Rats		1	0	1	0	2	0.2	0	0	0
Ze Kalanga		8	0	8	0	233	25.9	1	0	0
Forwards										
Fabrice Akwa		7	7	0	1	617	68.6	4	2	0
Bruno Mauro		2	2	0	2	162	18.0	0	0	0
Flavio		8	6	2	5	452	50.2	2	0	0
Love		6	1	5	1	185	20.6	0	1	0
Mantorras		3	1	2	1	131	14.6	1	0	0
Marco Paulo		3	1	2	1	96	10.7	1	0	0
Maurito		8	6	2	4	518	57.6	0	0	0

FINAL PROSPECTS

Angola are the least known of the World Cup finalists and also lowliest rated – 68th on the FIFA Rankings.

They are very solid defensively, only conceding six goals in the qualifiers and the team spirit makes them more than the sum of their parts. The bulk of the squad still play in Angola but with a sprinkling of lesser lights from the Portuguese league. The exception is Benfica forward Pedro Mantorras, who will be the best hope of adding to a poor scoring record.

Captain Akwa plays his football in Qatar and is the backbone of the side. His comments on qualifying summed up what it meant to the country. "We have proved that Angola is not just about oil, war and poverty," he said.

Angola will revel in their opening Group D game against former colonial masters Portugal, but they will struggle to contain Portugal or Mexico.

THE MANAGER

The Palancas Negras (the Black Impalas) found the best possible coach in Luis De Oliveira Goncalves. Former manager, Brazilian Ismail Kurtz was dismissed after Angola suffered a surprise 3-1 defeat in Chad.

The 2-0 home win in the return smoothed the way through to qualifying Group 4 and gained Goncalves, 45, the time to construct a formidable defensive shield. He put his belief in burly Qatar-based striker Akwa, who has scored 29 goals for Angola since 1995, as captain. Goncalves has made little use of Benfica star and local hero Mantorras, who accused the coach of a lack of respect during the African Cup.

Luis De Oliveira Goncalves

GROUP FIXTURES

PORTUGAL	Sun 11 June 2000 BST
MEXICO	Fri 16 June 2000 BST
IRAN	Wed 21 June 1500 BST

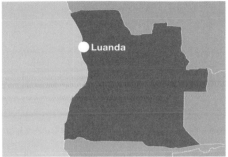

Luanda

Zone	Africa
Population	11,992,115
Capital	Luanda
Language	Portuguese
Top league	Girabola
Major clubs	**Capacities**
Petro Atlético	60,000
Primeiro de Agosto	60,000
Aviacao	10,000
Where likely squad players play:	
In Angola	19
In Premiership	0
In other major five European Leagues	0
Outside major European Leagues	4
Number of Angolan players playing:	
In Premiership	0
In other major five European Leagues	1

World Cup record

1930 -	Did not enter	1974 -	Did not enter
1934 -	Did not enter	1978 -	Did not enter
1938 -	Did not enter	1982 -	Did not enter
1950 -	Did not enter	1986 -	Did not qualify
1954 -	Did not enter	1990 -	Did not qualify
1958 -	Did not enter	1994 -	Did not qualify
1962 -	Did not enter	1998 -	Did not qualify
1966 -	Did not enter	2002 -	Did not qualify
1970 -	Did not enter		

THE SQUAD

	Club side	Age	QG
Goalkeepers			
Joao Ricardo	Unattached	36	10
Goliath	Esperance	33	0
Lama	Petrow Atletico	25	0
Defenders			
Jamba	AS Aviacao	28	10
Kali	Santa Clara	27	7
Lebo Lebo	Esperance	29	3
Loco	Benfica Luanda	-	3
Pedro Manuel	AS Aviacao	24	1
Mateus	AS Aviacao	23	1
Jacinto Pereira	AS Aviacao	33	7
Yamba Asha	AS Aviacao	27	10
Midfielders			
Andre	Kuwait SC	28	7
Chinho	Esperance	23	2
Figueiredo	Varzim	33	8
Freddy	Moreirense	26	7
Gilberto	Al Ahly	23	9
Joaquin	-	25	1
Andre Macanga	-	-	2
Antonio Mendonca	Varzim	24	4
Paulo	-	31	1
Rats	AS Aviacao	29	1
Simao	AS Aviacao	-	1
Ze Kalanga	Petrow Atletico	22	8
Forwards			
Fabrice Akwa	Al Wakra	29	7
Bruno Mauro	Belenenses Lisboa	32	2
Flavio	Al Ahli	26	8
Love	AS Aviacao	24	6
Mantorras	Benfica	24	3
Marco Paulo	Stade Laval	30	3
Maurito	Al Wahda	24	8

■ Probable ■ Possible **QG** Qualification Games

KEY PLAYER

PEDRO MANTORRAS BENFICA

Angola's only high profile player is Pedro Mantorras, a Benfica striker who starred in their Under-20 side in 2002.
He comes from the slums of Sambizanga in Luanda. Portuguese side Alverca developed his talents and sold him on to national giants Benfica for £3.5m in 2001. He played a key role in Benfica's Portuguese championship last season scoring crucial goals after coming back from long-term injury.
He was barely used in qualifying, initially due to injury and ultimately because manager Goncalves decided not to disrupt his squad. When he was left out for all but half a game of a poor African Cup of Nations, Mantorras accused Goncalves of a lack of respect and said he would retire after the World Cup.

AGE 24   **STRIKER**   **WORLD RANKING** –

PORTUGAL

ROUTE TO THE FINALS

Thirty points from 12 games is a Chelsea-esque qualifying display from Portugal. They hit 35 goals with an excellent goal difference of +30.

Qualifying began after the Euro 2004 defeat against Greece but Portugal showed they had put it behind them with wins against Latvia and Estonia. A draw with Liechtenstein was followed by the 7-1 humiliation of Russia and a 5-0 win over Luxembourg.

After five games, both Slovakia and Portugal were on 13 points and Group 3 was between these two. Former Spurs star Helder Postiga made his usual scoring appearance from the subs bench in Slovakia to earn a draw.

Luis Figo came out of international retirement for the return against the Slovakians, who had Bundesliga scoring sensation Marek Mintel 'the Phantom' in midfield. Portugal began with Fernando Meira poking home a corner before Cristiano Ronaldo's 25-metre free kick sealed the win. A goalless draw away in Russia was the only hiccup on the run in.

FINAL QUALIFYING TABLE
EUROPE GROUP 3

	P	W	D	L	GF	GA	Pts
Portugal	12	9	3	0	35	5	30
Slovakia	12	6	5	1	24	8	23
Russia	12	6	5	1	23	12	23
Estonia	12	5	2	5	16	17	17
Latvia	12	4	3	5	18	21	15
Liechtenstein	12	2	2	8	13	23	8
Luxembourg	12	0	0	12	5	48	0

					FIFA ranking			
1	04 Sep 04	Away	Latvia	65	W	0 2	Ronaldo 57, Pauleta 58
2	08 Sep 04	Home	Estonia	80	W	4 0	Ronaldo 75, Postiga 83, 90, Pauleta 86
3	09 Oct 04	Away	Liechtenstein	135	D	2 2	Pauleta 23, D.Hasler 39og
4	13 Oct 04	Home	Russia	31	W	7 1	Pauleta 26, Ronaldo 39, 69, Deco 45, Simao Sabrosa 83, Petit 90, 90
5	17 Nov 04	Away	Luxembourg	154	W	0 5	Federspiel 11og, Ronaldo 28, Maniche 52, Pauleta 67, 82
6	30 Mar 05	Away	Slovakia	47	D	1 1	Postiga 62
7	04 Jun 05	Home	Slovakia	47	W	2 0	Meira 21, Ronaldo 42
8	08 Jun 05	Away	Estonia	80	W	0 1	Ronaldo 33
9	03 Sep 05	Home	Luxembourg	154	W	6 0	Andrade 22, Ricardo 30, Pauleta 36, 56, Simao Sabrosa 78, 84
10	07 Sep 05	Away	Russia	31	D	0 0	
11	08 Oct 05	Home	Liechtenstein	135	W	2 1	Pauleta 49, Nuno Gomes 86
12	12 Oct 05	Home	Latvia	65	W	3 0	Pauleta 19, 21, Viana 85
	Average FIFA ranking of opposition			85			

MAIN PLAYER PERFORMANCES IN QUALIFICATION

Match	1 2 3 4 5 6 7 8 9 10 11 12	Appearances	Started	Subbed on	Subbed off	Mins played	% played	Goals	Yellow	Red
Venue	A H A H A A H A H A H H									
Result	W W D W W D W W W D W W									
Goalkeepers										
Joaquim Manuel Sampaio		1	1	0	0	90	8.3	0	0	0
Pereira Ricardo		11	11	0	0	990	91.7	1	0	0
Defenders										
Jorge Andrade		12	12	0	0	1080	100.0	1	1	0
Marco Caneira		4	3	1	0	288	26.7	0	0	0
Ricardo Carvalho		9	9	0	0	810	75.0	0	1	0
Paulo Ferreira		8	8	0	1	693	64.2	0	0	0
Miguel Jorge Ribeiro		2	2	0	0	180	16.7	0	0	0
Fernando Meira		2	2	0	0	180	16.7	1	0	0
Luis Garcia Miguel		4	2	2	0	243	22.5	0	1	0
Nuno Valente		5	5	0	1	432	40.0	0	1	0
Midfielders										
Francisco Costinha		9	8	1	1	732	67.8	0	2	0
Anderson Deco		11	11	0	4	927	85.8	1	2	0
Luis Madeira Caeira Figo		6	6	0	1	528	48.9	0	1	0
Maniche		12	12	0	6	926	85.7	1	1	0
Armando Teixeira Petit		7	3	4	1	314	29.1	2	0	0
Cristiano Ronaldo		12	11	1	7	907	84.0	7	1	0
Simao Sabrosa		6	4	2	3	351	32.5	1	0	0
Cardoso Tiago		6	2	4	1	180	16.7	0	2	0
Hugo Viana		3	0	3	0	29	2.7	1	0	0
Forwards										
Luis Boa Morte		4	1	3	0	94	8.7	0	0	0
Ricardo Quarasma		2	2	0	0	180	16.7	0	0	0
Nuno Gomes		3	0	3	0	76	7.0	1	0	0
Pauleta		12	12	0	6	926	85.7	11	1	0
Helder Postiga		8	1	7	1	259	24.0	3	0	0

FINAL PROSPECTS

Portugal have the look of a team capable of winning the 2006 World Cup. They are the form side of the European qualifying tournament with nine wins and three draws and boast an impressive array of midfield talent.

All the current squad gained valuable experience in the Euro 2004 tournament and the memory and hurt of their final defeat by outsiders Greece will be a fresh stimulus.

There is a note of experience and quality with former Real Madrid 'Galactico' Luis Figo back in form at Inter Milan and out of international retirement to captain the side.

On the other wing there is the youthful bedazzlement and pace of Cristiano Ronaldo, hitting swerving goals from distance.

However, the real power of the side comes from the recent strength of Portuguese club sides in the European cups. Porto's Champions League-winning contingent are dispersed around other top clubs. Ricardo Carvalho and Paulo Ferreira have been joined by Maniche at Chelsea. Costinha is at Dinamo Moscow and Deco has emerged as one of the best creative midfielders around since his move to Barcelona.

> **"I expect Cristiano Ronaldo to be one of the best and most exciting players of the World Cup."**
> Martin Jol

The strengths of the side in 2004 were a sturdy defence and a combative midfield, with Deco, Figo and Ronaldo sparking or misfiring around the edges. The real difference comes in adding a cutting edge to their 4-2-3-1 formation. Striker Pauleta is now finally reproducing on the international stage the scoring form he displays for Paris St Germain - currently the top-scorer in the France league - and has ignited the Portuguese attack.

They will sail through their group and will probably have the luxury of a meaningless final Group D game against Mexico.

The last 16 game will be a tough match no matter who they meet from Group C but they showed in Euro 2004, against Holland and England, they could beat top teams.

GROUP FIXTURES

ANGOLA	Sun 11 June 2000 BST
IRAN	Sat 17 June 1400 BST
MEXICO	Wed 21 June 1500 BST

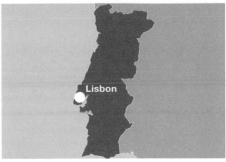

Lisbon

Zone	Europe
Population	10,500,000
Capital	Lisbon
Language	Portuguese
Top league	Betandwin Liga
Major clubs	**Capacities**
FC Porto	51,000
Sporting Lisbon	52,500
Benfica	65,600

Where likely squad players play:

In Premiership	6	In Spain	5
In Holland	-	In France	3
In Italy	1	In Germany	1

Number of Portuguese players playing:

In Premiership	12	In Spain	11
In Holland	3	In France	7
In Italy	6	In Germany	6

World Cup record

1930 -	Did not enter	1974 -	Did not qualify
1934 -	Did not qualify	1978 -	Did not qualify
1938 -	Did not qualify	1982 -	Did not qualify
1950 -	Did not qualify	1986 -	Group 4tth
1954 -	Did not qualify	1990 -	Did not qualify
1958 -	Did not qualify	1994 -	Did not qualify
1962 -	Did not qualify	1998 -	Did not qualify
1966 -	Third place	2002 -	Group 3rd
1970 -	Did not qualify		

KEY PLAYER

LUIS FIGO INTER MILAN

Rated the best winger of his generation and FIFA's World Player of the Year in 2001, Luis Figo hoped to win a major trophy for Portugal. Captaining the side in Euro 2004, he looked past his best. However, as Portugal swept through qualification and Figo's form revived at Inter, he returned for one final attempt.

Top 12 players: Deco, Paulo Ferreira

Playing record	12 mths lge	wcq
Appearances:	42	6
Minutes played:	2853	528
Percentage played:	70.4%	48.9%
Goals scored:	4	0
Goals conceded:	25	1
Cards:	Y4, R0	Y1, R0
Power rating:	52mins	41mins
Power ranking:	55th	31st

AGE 33   **MIDFIELDER**   **WORLD RANKING 648**

THE SQUAD

Goalkeepers	Club side	Age	QG
Joaquim Sampaio	Benfica	30	1
Pereira Ricardo	Sporting Lisbon	30	11
Defenders			
Jorge Andrade	Deportivo	28	12
Marco Caneira	Sporting Lisbon	27	4
Ricardo Carvalho	Chelsea	28	9
Paulo Ferreira	Chelsea	27	9
Fernando Meira	Stuttgart	28	3
Luis Garcia Miguel	Valencia	26	4
Nuno Valente	Everton	31	5
Jorge Ribeiro	Malaga	24	2
Rui Jorge	Sp Lisbon	33	1
Midfielders			
Alex	Wolfsburg	26	2
Francisco Costinha	Dinamo Moscow	31	9
Anderson Deco	Barcelona	28	11
Luis Figo	Inter Milan	33	6
Maniche	Chelsea	28	12
Joao Moutinho	Sp Lisbon	19	2
Armando Teixeira Petit	Benfica	29	7
Cristiano Ronaldo	Man Utd	21	12
Simao Sabrosa	Benfica	26	6
Cardoso Tiago	Lyon	25	6
Hugo Viana	Valencia	23	3
Forwards			
Luis Boa Morte	Fulham	28	4
Nuno Gomes	Benfica	29	3
Pauleta	Paris SG	33	12
Helder Postiga	St Etienne	23	8
Ricardo Quaresma	Porto	22	2

■ Probable ■ Possible **QG** Qualification Games

KEY GOALKEEPER

PEREIRA RICARDO
SPORTING LISBON

Ricardo is the Portuguese keeper who broke England fans' hearts in Euro 2004.

First he saved Darius Vassell's spot kick in the penalty shoot-out and then the confident keeper took the final kick himself. When his shot hit the back of David James' net, Portugal celebrated.

The Sporting Lisbon keeper made his national debut in June 2000 and spent the next few years tussling over the No. 1 shirt with the experienced Vitor Baia. 'Big Phil' Scolari made the former Boavista youngster a fixture.

AGE 30	WORLD RANKING –

THE MANAGER

'Big Phil' Scolari had a reputation as the tough man of club management in South America. So when Brazil's World Cup qualification was stuttering badly before the 2002 finals, the nation turned to Luiz Felipe in desperation to sort them out.

He did, but amid accusations that he had sacrificed 'the beautiful game' to do it with ball-winners such as Kleberson and current Arsenal star Gilberto Silva in midfield,

'Big Phil', 57, was true to his reputation; he stuck to his guns and with a rejuvenated Ronaldo, they beat Germany to win the tournament.

He looked a shrewd appointment by the Portuguese when he pulled them up from a poor start to reach the finals of their own tournament, Euro 2004.

He has the national side playing better than ever but says he will leave Portugal after the World Cup finals, whatever the result.

He is one of two top foreign manager names being spoken about for the England manager's job.

KEY DEFENDERS

RICARDO CARVALHO
CHELSEA

Porto won both the Uefa Cup and the Champions League trophy in consecutive seasons on the back of defiant defending. At the centre of it was Ricardo Carvalho.

Jose Mourinho ignored Deco and Costinha but paid £19.8m to take him to Chelsea. Two good seasons alongside John Terry in the tightest defence in Europe have shown why.

Playing record	12 mths lge	wcq
Appearances:	26	9
Minutes played:	2207	810
Percentage played:	58.4%	75.0%
Goals conceded:	17	5
Clean sheets:	12	5
Cards:	Y5, R1	Y1, R0
Defensive rating:	130mins	162mins
Defensive ranking:	10th	42nd

AGE 28	WORLD RANKING 164

JORGE ANDRADE
DEPORTIVO

Playing record	12 mths lge	wcq
Appearances:	33	12
Minutes played:	2913	1080
Percentage played:	77.1%	100.0%
Goals conceded:	31	5
Clean sheets:	13	8
Cards:	Y13, R0	Y1, R0
Defensive rating:	94mins	216mins
Defensive ranking:	46th	26th

AGE 28	WORLD RANKING 320

KEY MIDFIELDERS

CARDOSO TIAGO
LYON

Tiago is the pick of a group of three top competitive ball-winning midfielders battling for two spots protecting the Portuguese defence.

He uses the ball well, holds onto possession, and plays in the highest standard of club football.

Tiago made 51 appearances for Chelsea last season before making way for the arrival of Michael Essien. He moved to Lyon (effectively swapping clubs with Essien) and has become a key player in the French champions' defence of their title and dominating group form in the Champions League.

Costinha and Maniche have played most of qualifying but Tiago's club form is stronger.

Playing record	12 mths lge	wcq
Appearances:	34	6
Minutes played:	2396	180
Percentage played:	61.9%	16.7%
Goals scored:	4	0
Goals conceded:	19	2
Cards:	Y9, R0	Y2, R0
Power rating:	56mins	-
Power ranking:	68th	-

AGE 25	WORLD RANKING 705

MANICHE
CHELSEA

The ex-Porto midfielder rejoined Jose Mourinho at Chelsea after a frustrating spell with Dynamo Moscow.

He had moved to Russia with Costinha – also ex-Porto – the third of Portugal's trio of top midfield ball winners.

AGE 28	WORLD RANKING –

HUGO VIANA
VALENCIA

The former Newcastle reserve played well for Sporting Lisbon before joining Valencia.

Playing record	12 mths lge	wcq
Appearances:	13	3
Minutes played:	563	29
Percentage played:	14.9%	2.7%
Goals scored:	0	1
Goals conceded:	5	0
Cards:	Y0, R0	Y0, R0
Power rating:	-	-
Power ranking:	-	-

AGE 23	WORLD RANKING –

KEY STRIKER

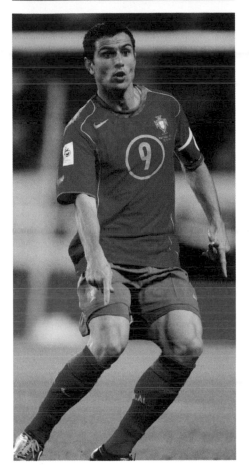

PAULETA
PARIS SG

Pauleta finished the World Cup qualifying tournament as Europe's most prolific striker, hitting the net 11 times.

His brace, in the last qualification game against Latvia, also made him Portugal's highest-ever scorer, beating the 41 scored by the legendary 1966 World Cup star Eusebio.

Born in the Azores and nicknamed 'Pedro', Pauletta was regularly one of the French league's top scorers and is having another fine season for Paris St Germain again, surpassing last season's total of 13 by the end of January.

He took a while to adjust to the international game, now his Portuguese strike rate is better than a goal every two games.

Playing record	12 mths lge	wcq
Appearances:	38	12
Minutes played:	3213	926
Percentage played:	85.0%	85.7%
Goals scored:	18	11
Percentage share:	40.00	31.43
Cards:	Y5, R0	Y1, R0
Strike rate:	178mins	84mins
Strike rate ranking:	30th	7th

AGE 33   **WORLD RANKING 125**

ONE TO WATCH

CRISTIANO RONALDO MAN UTD

Cristiano Ronaldo has speed, more tricks than a pack of cards and can flummox football commentators, as much as defenders, as they try to guess how he did what he just did.

He is widely criticised at Manchester United for not producing an 'end product' to his stunning wing-play, but he is far more effective for Portugal.

Playing record	12 mths lge	wcq
Appearances:	33	12
Minutes played:	2222	939
Percentage played:	60.2%	86.9%
Goals scored:	10	7
Goals conceded:	27	4
Cards:	Y8, R1	Y1, R0
Power rating:	52mins	32mins
Power ranking:	54th	15th

AGE 21   **MIDFIELDER**   **WORLD RANKING 70**

WORLD CUP SCHEDULE GERMANY 2006

GROUP STAGE

MARTIN JOL'S PREDICTIONS IN YELLOW

Match	Group	Home		V		Away
MATCH 1 – MUNICH 1700 BST	A	GERMANY		V		COSTA RICA
MATCH 2 – GELSENKIRCHEN 2000 BST	A	POLAND		V		ECUADOR
MATCH 3 – FRANKFURT 1400 BST	B	ENGLAND		V		PARAGUAY
MATCH 4 – DORTMUND 1700 BST	B	TRIN & TOBAG		V		SWEDEN
MATCH 6 – LEIPZIG 1400 BST	C	SERB & MONT		V		HOLLAND
MATCH 7 – NUREMBURG 1700 BST	D	MEXICO		V		IRAN
MATCH 12 – KAISERSLAUTERN 1400 BST	F	AUSTRALIA		V		JAPAN
MATCH 10 – GELSENKIRCHEN 1700 BST	E	USA		V		CZECH REP
MATCH 14 – FRANKFURT 1400 BST	G	SOUTH KOREA		V		TOGO
MATCH 13 – STUTTGART 1700 BST	G	FRANCE		V		SWITZERLAND
MATCH 15 – LEIPZIG 1400 BST	H	SPAIN		V		UKRAINE
MATCH 16 – MUNICH 1700 BST	H	TUNISIA		V		SAUDI ARABIA
MATCH 18 – HAMBURG 1400 BST	A	ECUADOR		V		COSTA RICA
MATCH 19 – NUREMBURG 1700 BST	B	ENGLAND		V		TRIN & TOBAG
MATCH 21 – GELSENKIRCHEN 1400 BST	C	ARGENTINA		V		SERB & MONT
MATCH 22 – STUTTGART 1700 BST	C	HOLLAND		V		IVORY COAST
MATCH 24 – FRANKFURT 1400 BST	D	PORTUGAL		V		IRAN
MATCH 26 – COLOGNE 1700 BST	E	CZECH REP		V		GHANA
MATCH 28 – NUREMBURG 1400 BST	F	JAPAN		V		CROATIA
MATCH 27 – MUNICH 1700 BST	F	BRAZIL		V		AUSTRALIA
MATCH 30 – DORTMUND 1400 BST	G	TOGO		V		SWITZERLAND
MATCH 32 – HAMBURG 1700 BST	H	SAUDI ARABIA		V		UKRAINE
MATCH 33 – BERLIN 1500 BST	A	ECUADOR		V		GERMANY
MATCH 34 – HANOVER 1500 BST	A	COSTA RICA		V		POLAND
MATCH 39 – GELSENKIRCHEN 1500 BST	D	PORTUGAL		V		MEXICO
MATCH 40 – LEIPZIG 1500 BST	D	IRAN		V		ANGOLA
MATCH 41 – HAMBURG 1500 BST	E	CZECH REP		V		ITALY
MATCH 42 – NUREMBURG 1500 BST	E	GHANA		V		USA
MATCH 47 – KAISERSLAUTERN 1500 BST	H	SAUDI ARABIA		V		SPAIN
MATCH 48 – BERLIN 1500 BST	H	UKRAINE		V		TUNISIA

SECOND ROUND

MARTIN JOL'S PREDICTIONS IN BRACKETS

MATCH 49 – MUNICH 1600 BST						
49	1ST A (GER)		V		(SWE) 2ND B	JUNE 24TH
MATCH 50 – LEIPZIG 2000 BST						
50	1ST C (ARG)		V		(MEX) 2ND D	
MATCH 51 – STUTTGART 1600 BST						
51	1ST B (ENG)		V		(POL) 2ND A	JUNE 25TH
MATCH 52 – NUREMBURG 2000 BST						
52	1ST D (POR)		V		(HOL) 2ND C	
MATCH 53 – KAISERSLAUTERN 1600 BST						
53	1ST E (ITA)		V		(AUS) 2ND F	JUNE 26TH
MATCH 54 – COLOGNE 2000 BST						
54	1ST G (FRA)		V		(SPA) 2ND H	
MATCH 55 – DORTMUND 1600 BST						
55	1ST F (BRA)		V		(CZE) 2ND E	JUNE 27TH
MATCH 56 – HANOVER 2000 BST						
56	1ST H (UKR)		V		(SWI) 2ND G	

							JUNE 9TH
MATCH 5 – HAMBURG 2000 BST							**JUNE 10TH**
C	ARGENTINA	V	IVORY COAST				
MATCH 8 – COLOGNE 2000 BST							**JUNE 11TH**
D	ANGOLA	V	PORTUGAL				
MATCH 9 – HANOVER 2000 BST							**JUNE 12TH**
E	ITALY	V	GHANA				
MATCH 11 – BERLIN 2000 BST							**JUNE 13TH**
F	BRAZIL	V	CROATIA				
MATCH 17 – DORTMUND 2000 BST							**JUNE 14TH**
A	GERMANY	V	POLAND				
MATCH 20 – BERLIN 2000 BST							**JUNE 16TH**
B	SWEDEN	V	PARAGUAY				
MATCH 23 – HANOVER 2000 BST							**JUNE 16TH**
D	MEXICO	V	ANGOLA				
MATCH 25 – KAISERSLAUTERN 2000 BST							**JUNE 17TH**
E	ITALY	V	USA				
MATCH 29 – LEIPZIG 2000 BST							**JUNE 18TH**
G	FRANCE	V	SOUTH KOREA				
MATCH 31 – STUTTGART 2000 BST							**JUNE 19TH**
H	SPAIN	V	TUNISIA				

MATCH 35 – COLOGNE 2000 BST			MATCH 36 – KAISERSLAUTERN 2000 BST			
B SWEDEN V ENGLAND		**B** PARAGUAY V TRIN & TOBAG				**JUNE 20TH**
MATCH 37 – FRANKFURT 2000 BST		MATCH 38 – MUNICH 2000 BST				
C HOLLAND V ARGENTINA		**C** IVORY COAST V SERB & MONT				**JUNE 21ST**
MATCH 43 – DORTMUND 2000 BST		MATCH 44 – STUTTGART 2000 BST				
F JAPAN V BRAZIL		**F** CROATIA V AUSTRALIA				**JUNE 22ND**
MATCH 45 – COLOGNE 2000 BST		MATCH 46 – HANOVER 2000 BST				
G TOGO V FRANCE		**G** SWITZERLAND V SOUTH KOREA				**JUNE 23RD**

QUARTER FINALS	**57**	W49 (GER)	V (ARG) W50	MATCH 57 – BERLIN 1600 BST	**JUNE 30TH**
	58	W53 (ITA)	V (FRA) W54	MATCH 58 – HAMBURG 2000 BST	
	59	W51 (ENG)	V (POR) W52	MATCH 59 – GELSENKIRCHEN 1600 BST	**JULY 1ST**
	60	W55 (BRA)	V (UKR) W56	MATCH 60 – FRANKFURT 2000 BST	
SEMI FINALS	**61**	W57 (ARG)	V (ITA) W58	MATCH 61 – DORTMUND 2000 BST	**JULY 4TH**
	62	W59 (ENG)	V (BRA) W60	MATCH 62 – MUNICH 2000 BST	**JULY 5TH**
THIRD PLACE	**63**	L61(ITA)	V (ENG) L62	MATCH 63 – STUTTGART 2000 BST	**JULY 8TH**
FINAL	**64**	W61 (ARG)	V (BRA) W62	MATCH 64 – BERLIN 1900 BST	**JULY 9TH**

12th RAFAEL MARQUEZ
BARCELONA

Rafael Marquez is one of the very few Mexicans to play in European football. He made his international debut at the age of just 17 and now captains the side.

A powerful and aggressive central defender, Marquez can also play a holding role in midfield. Monaco brought him to Europe and Barcelona signed him in 2003. He had the second-best Defensive Rating in Spain's Primera Liga in 2004/5 and in the current season, only Carlos Puyol is playing more games in the Barca defence.

Playing record	12 mths lge	wcq
Appearances:	35	9
Minutes played:	2715	760
Percentage played:	71.8%	52.8%
Goals conceded:	23	5
Clean sheets:	20	5
Cards:	Y10, R2	Y2, R0
Defensive rating:	118mins	152mins
Defensive ranking:	19th	46th

AGE 27 **WORLD RANKING 75**

11th HABIB KOLO TOURE
ARSENAL

The athleticism of Kolo Toure is widely admired in the Premiership and is at the heart of one of the meanest defences in the African qualifying groups – only Ghana and Angola conceded less goals.

Toure was vital to Arsenal's record-breaking 'Untouchables' season in 2003/4, conceding just 26 league goals in 36 games. Since then his consistency and fitness have made him more vital to Arsenal than Cole or Campbell. He was crucial to the Ivory Coast's run to the finals of the African Cup of Nations.

Playing record	12 mths lge	wcq
Appearances:	33	10
Minutes played:	2954	855
Percentage played:	80.1%	95.0%
Goals conceded:	23	7
Clean sheets:	16	6
Cards:	Y2, R0	Y0, R0
Defensive rating:	128mins	122mins
Defensive ranking:	12th	58th

AGE 25 **WORLD RANKING 66**

10th ROBERT KOVAC
JUVENTUS

Robert Kovac's reputation as one of the game's top man-markers has taken him to some of the top side's in Europe, including Bayer Leverkusen, Bayern Munich and more recently Italian giants Juventus.

He was born in Berlin but retained Croatian nationality despite playing all his early club football in Germany. He has won the Bundesliga title with Bayern.

The solid and dependable Kovac, whose brother Nico also plays for Croatia, will be appearing in his third World Cup.

Playing record	12 mths lge	wcq
Appearances:	10	8
Minutes played:	788	692
Percentage played:	19.5%	76.9%
Goals conceded:	7	2
Clean sheets:	4	6
Cards:	Y1, R0	Y4, R0
Defensive rating:	-	346mins
Defensive ranking:	-	16th

AGE 32 **WORLD RANKING 65**

9th MARCO MATERAZZI
INTER MILAN

A tall, imposing and aggressive central defender, Marco Materazzi is a regular in the Italian national squad and a reliable presence at the back for Inter Milan.

A late developer in football terms – he made his full international debut in 2001 at the age of 27 - Materazzi played for a number of lower league Italian clubs and even spent the 1998/99 season at Everton before moving back to the San Siro. His 27 appearances for Milan last season saw ten clean sheets and just 23 goals conceded.

Playing record	12 mths lge	wcq
Appearances:	25	6
Minutes played:	1979	527
Percentage played:	48.9%	58.6%
Goals conceded:	13	6
Clean sheets:	18	3
Cards:	Y9, R1	Y1, R0
Defensive rating:	152mins	88mins
Defensive ranking:	6th	73rd

AGE 32 **WORLD RANKING 63**

8th YOUNG-PYO LEE
TOTTENHAM

Already with one impressive World Cup campaign behind him, Young-Pyo Lee has far more experience to bring to South Korea in Germany.

Playing for Guus Hiddink's PSV Eindhoven side, Lee was hailed as 'the best left back in Holland' as he earned a league-winners' medal and impressed in a Champions League run to the semi-final.

Now at Spurs, Lee is a great tackler, tireless in support of the attack down his flank and makes defending look simple.

Playing record	12 mths lge	wcq
Appearances:	20	11
Minutes played:	1754	990
Percentage played:	46.4%	91.7%
Goals conceded:	18	7
Clean sheets:	7	5
Cards:	Y1, R0	Y1, R0
Defensive rating:	97mins	141mins
Defensive ranking:	41st	47th

AGE 29 | **WORLD RANKING 44**

7th CARLOS PUYOL
BARCELONA

Catalan-born Carlos Puyol rose through the ranks at Barcelona to become the defensive linchpin of the new Spanish champions.

The Barca fans worship their skipper for his rock solid performances and high-energy game. He returned home from the 2002 World Cup finals as one Spain's few successes in the tournament.

Puyol has recently moved from right back to centre back at the Nou Camp and looks even more influential.

Playing record	12 mths lge	wcq
Appearances:	40	11
Minutes played:	3594	862
Percentage played:	95.1%	79.8%
Goals conceded:	32	4
Clean sheets:	21	7
Cards:	Y8, R0	Y1, R0
Defensive rating:	112mins	215mins
Defensive ranking:	27th	28th

AGE 28 | **WORLD RANKING 33**

6th ANDRE OOIJER
PSV EINDHOVEN

Andre Ooijer is a vastly under-rated Dutch defender who can play at full back or in the middle of a back four.

His promising early career was held back when he suffered a broken leg shortly after winning his first cap for Holland in a friendly against Brazil in July 1999. Rock solid in defence, he was a key figure in PSV Eindhoven's league and cup winning side in 2004/5 and has fought his way back into the Dutch squad. His 24 appearances for PSV last year saw just 14 goals conceded.

Playing record	12 mths lge	wcq
Appearances:	33	2
Minutes played:	2864	180
Percentage played:	75.8%	16.7%
Goals conceded:	15	0
Clean sheets:	23	2
Cards:	Y7, R0	Y0, R0
Defensive rating:	191mins	-
Defensive ranking:	2nd	-

AGE 31 | **WORLD RANKING 29**

5th LUCIO
BAYERN MUNICH

Lucio is rated one of the best central defenders to have played for Brazil – and he also scores crucial goals.

He was outstanding during the 2002 World Cup finals, and although Ronaldinho and Ronaldo took the headlines, Lucio's inspired defending did as much as anyone to help Brazil win the trophy.

Bayern Munich signed him from Bayer Leverkusen for £8m in 2004 and, in his first season, the Bavarian club clinched a German league and cup double.

Playing record	12 mths lge	wcq
Appearances:	36	10
Minutes played:	3218	888
Percentage played:	94.1%	54.8%
Goals conceded:	29	7
Clean sheets:	15	5
Cards:	Y4, R0	Y1, R1
Defensive rating:	111mins	127mins
Defensive ranking:	29th	55th

AGE 28 | **WORLD RANKING 28**

4th

FABIO CANNAVARO
JUVENTUS

The captain of the Azzurri is the tenacious Fabio Cannavaro. Along with the elegant Nesta, and Juve team-mates Buffon and Zambrotta, he forms part of the best central defence in international football.

Only 1.76m tall, he is still powerful in the air, times his tackles well and man-marks fiercely. Inter paid around £16m for him in 2002 but their crowd never took to him. His move to Juventus in 2004 was a mutual success, Juve won the title and Cannavaro regained the respect of Italian fans.

Playing record	12 mths lge	wcq
Appearances:	43	7
Minutes played:	3747	563
Percentage played:	92.5%	62.6%
Goals conceded:	28	5
Clean sheets:	21	3
Cards:	Y5, R1	Y1, R0
Defensive rating:	134mins	113mins
Defensive ranking:	9th	60th

AGE 32	WORLD RANKING 21

3rd

PAULO FERREIRA
CHELSEA

Portugal's Paulo Ferreira is a well-balanced and dependable full back.

He is equally adept at defending or joining in with his attack. He played in every minute of FC Porto's triumphant Champions League campaign in 2004 under their then coach Jose Mourinho. After taking over at Chelsea, Mourinho's first move in the transfer market was the £13m acquisition of Ferreira. He won the Premiership in his first season with Chelsea conceding just ten goals in the 2600 minutes Ferreira was on the pitch.

Playing record	12 mths lge	wcq
Appearances:	19	9
Minutes played:	1570	783
Percentage played:	41.5%	72.5%
Goals conceded:	6	5
Clean sheets:	14	5
Cards:	Y1, R0	Y0, R0
Defensive rating:	262mins	157mins
Defensive ranking:	1st	45th

AGE 27	WORLD RANKING 10

2nd

JOHN TERRY
CHELSEA

A fiercely competitive centre half, John Terry is now regarded as one of the best defenders in the world.

Having risen through the ranks at Stamford Bridge, he became club captain in the 2003/4 season and has been the heartbeat of the Chelsea side ever since. Last season he lifted the Premiership and Carling Cup and was voted the PFA Player of the Season. He leads by example and is seen by many as a future England captain. Not the fastest but his positional sense more than makes up for it.

Playing record	12 mths lge	wcq
Appearances:	39	6
Minutes played:	3510	540
Percentage played:	92.9%	60.0%
Goals conceded:	21	4
Clean sheets:	22	3
Cards:	Y8, R0	Y0, R0
Defensive rating:	167mins	135mins
Defensive ranking:	5th	51st

AGE 25	WORLD RANKING 4

THE TOP DEFENDER

FRANCE WILLIAM GALLAS

William Gallas's strength in the tackle, speed over the ground and unfailing consistency are qualities that mark him out as a defender of the highest calibre.

The France and Chelsea star says he prefers to play as a central defender but has demonstrated his versatility at full back for both club and country. He is probably the Chelsea player other managers most envy.

Playing record	12 mths lge	wcq
Appearances:	35	10
Minutes played:	3017	900
Percentage played:	79.8%	100.0%
Goals conceded:	16	2
Clean sheets:	21	8
Cards:	Y4, R0	Y0, R0
Defensive rating:	189mins	450mins
Defensive ranking:	3rd	10th

AGE 28 | CHELSEA | WORLD RANKING 3

1st

Position	1st	2nd	3rd	4th	5th	6th	7th	8th
Group	E	F	C	A	D	H	B	G
Total FIFA ranking	89	93	95	96	101	109	117	138

USA V CZECH REPUBLIC
CZEW CZEW — Gelsenkirchen, Monday 12 June 1700 BST

The USA mugged Portugal in their first game in 2002 but the Czechs are a settled team who know how to get the best out of their resources. If Koller is match fit the USA defence will struggle. Both coaches will have their sides well prepared but Bruckner is sneakier. Landon Donovan is back to his best according to Bruce Arena and if he can provide the ammunition for McBride, the Czech defence could come under pressure.

ITALY V GHANA
ITAW ITAW — Hanover, Monday 12 June 2000 BST

Italy have had dreadful group phases in their last two tournaments and coach Marcello Lippi seems unsure of his best team – although the Italian press seem to know it! Ghana will be pressing and tackling fiercely in midfield, striving to prevent the Azzurri getting a good start.

Michael Essien will be determined not to give Italy time on the ball and he also has the pace to power through their midfield.
However, Italy have hardened Serie A ball-winners enough to battle through and their sharp new strikers will earn three points.

CZECH REPUBLIC V GHANA
CZEW CZEW — Cologne, Saturday 17 June 1700 BST

The Czechs were kept goalless by Greece in their semi-final at Euro 2004. It's hard to believe that Ghana's defence can muster the same resistance but they are strong through the centre and that's usually where the Czechs do most damage. If Sammy Kuffour returns alongside John Mensah, he will be a powerful barrier for Koller to work around.

Ghana's John Mensah

USA V ITALY
DRAW DRAW — K'slautern, Saturday 17 June 2000 BST

A real test of the FIFA Rankings this. Much depends on the relative confidence of the sides following their first games. The Rankings would suggest the USA should win while any player form guide says Italy hands down. The USA will strain every sinew to get a point out of this one. It's hard to see them scoring but McBride will throw himself at every cross. If Italy get frustrated they could be held to an unlikely draw.

CZECH REPUBLIC V ITALY
ITAW DRAW — Hamburg, Thursday 22 June 1500 BST

There are no excuses for this being played at half pace, no matter what the state of the group. Brazil lie in wait for the runners-up and there ought to be goals in it. Pavel Nedved will be determined to use his Serie A insight to gain an advantage and the Czech midfield are a tight unit, who will work extra hard to protect their defence. There's also a battle of giants up front with Luca Toni every bit as tall and predatory as Jan Koller.
Koller will be key to the whole Czech campaign. He was missing when the Dutch won in Prague and the entire team works around him and plays off him. Not just Czech fans are praying he's fully recovered from his cruciate ligament tear in time to get match fit.

GHANA V USA
USAW USAW — Nuremberg, Thursday 22 June 1500 BST

The USA may have garnered a point from their previous two games, but even if they are just playing for pride, they should win the final game. Steve Ralston will be a handful from set pieces and you can guarantee that Arena will have something up his sleeve.
The Ghanaian full backs will struggle to cut out crosses from the American speed merchants on the flanks.
Expect to see Freddy Adu given a start in this match. Ghana have been trying to tempt him to play for the land of his birth, but he is set on playing for the US and this would be an interesting debut.

KEY MATCH

MARTIN JOL'S VIEW

Italy, are in with a chance of winning in Germany. They always look strong for tournaments – it sounds like a cliché, but it's true.

More unusual for Italy is the wide range of strikers they have developed lately. This is the reason they will have to play with two up front. I mention Iaquinta, Gilardino and Luca Toni from Fiorentina – the only one who must be sure of playing. In Serie A, he has a goal average that is unheard of. His goal-tally had reached 16 half way through the league season.

I must not forget Christian Vieri, who until two seasons ago, was Europe's best striker.

He hopes to have the chance to get himself back into contention by scoring goals for Monaco. I wanted him at Tottenham, but he demanded a place in the first team. He said to me he wanted it guaranteed, even if he didn't score for Spurs. I couldn't agree, but apparently Monaco did.

"Italy are normally good enough for a place in the last four, but this time they look likely to be the biggest threat to Argentina and Brazil"

Toldo and Buffon are both world-class goalkeepers. Fabio Cannavaro and Alessandro Nesta are tremendous and they have a fine attacking fullback in Zambrotta.

Their midfield with Pirlo, Cameronesi, Gattuso and Antonio Cassano (now at Real Madrid) are all excellent but Francesco Totti is my favourite and I expect much of him in June. He has played in Roma's first team since he was 16 and I've always admired him.

Italy are normally good enough for a place in the last four, but this time they look likely to be the biggest threat to Brazil and Argentina.

When the Czech Republic have everybody fit, they are a country to be reckoned with. They reached the semi finals in Euro 2004 but lost surprisingly to Greece.

However, when a striker like Jan Koller, who was injured for a long period this season, is missing, they cannot replace him easily. Of course, the same is true for Nedved.

Rosicky and Nedved (and even Poborsky who is 34) will be influential in their midfield.

Goalkeeper Petr Cech is regarded as the best in the Premier League. The defence in front of him, with Tomas Ujfalusi as leader, is strong. I hope Marek Jankulovski will be able to show that he is one of Europe's better attacking left-sided defenders.

I was not impressed with Ghana during the recent African Cup.

In Chelsea's Essien they have Africa's most expensive player in their ranks.

Sammy Kuffour and John Mensah play an important role in the team, as does Matthew Amoah. But, I don't expect much of them this time.

Every time we think the United States are not a real football team – since they don't have a football culture – but they usually prove to be a good tournament team. They have no real stars, but good players in Claudio Reyna, while Kasey Keller is an experienced and capable goalkeeper.

They have mastery of the air in Fulham's Brian McBride, who will probably be the best header of a ball at this World Cup.

Their main asset is their character, but I cannot see them going very far this time.

There is a chance that Freddy Adu will make the team, becoming the youngest World Cup player ever, but I doubt he will impress at this stage.

Gilardino – the leading canditate to start up front alongside Luca Toni – celebrates a goal

MARTIN JOL'S PREDICTIONS FOR THE TOP TWO TEAMS FROM THIS GROUP

Schedule of play is on page 80

GROUP STAGE

FIRST GROUP E

> ITALY

LAST SIXTEEN

v SECOND GROUP F

> ITALY v AUSTRALIA

QUARTER-FINALS

v FIRST GROUP G or SECOND GROUP H

> ITALY v FRANCE

SECOND GROUP E

> CZECH REPUBLIC

v FIRST GROUP F

> CZECH REPUBLIC v BRAZIL

v FIRST GROUP H or SECOND GROUP G

> BRAZIL v UKRAINE

GROUP E
ITALY, GHANA, USA, CZECH REPUBLIC

GROUP F
BRAZIL, CROATIA, AUSTRALIA, JAPAN

GROUP G
FRANCE, SWITZERLAND, SOUTH KOREA, TOGO

GROUP H
SPAIN, UKRAINE, TUNISIA, SAUDI ARABIA

The fascination here is finding out Brazil's opponents in the last 16. A stubborn fired up Italy could damage the favourites if they come second in this Group.

ROUTE TO THE FINALS

The Italian public expect to get into a state of national anxiety about their football team. So it was no surprise that their third game in little Slovenia gave them something to fret about.

Ranked about 40 places behind Italy, Slovenia fielded a team of unknown names, were minus their injured captain and their headed winner came courtesy of substitute Bostian Cesar.

After the game, the expensive thoroughbreds from Roma, Juventus and the Milans were staring up the Group Five table at tiny neighbours Slovenia with players from Gorica, Domzale and Nafta – says it all really!

The next game was crucial for Italian pride and it was a best of seven-goal tussle with unfancied Belarus. Roma's Francesco Totti capped a fine individual performance with two goals and they withstood a late fight-back by the visitors to hang onto a 4-3 win.

Draws in Norway and Glasgow before three final wins saw Italy through.

During the course of qualification, the new generation of Italian striking stars started to be bedded in. Seven starts for Gilardino, (who looked in stunning form against Germany in March) and two each for Iaquinta and Toni.

EUROPE GROUP 5

	P	W	D	L	GF	GA	Pts
Italy	10	7	2	1	17	8	23
Norway	10	5	3	2	12	7	18
Scotland	10	3	4	3	9	7	13
Slovenia	10	3	3	4	10	13	12
Belarus	10	2	4	4	12	14	10
Moldova	10	1	2	7	5	16	5

#	Date		Opponent	FIFA ranking		Result	Scorers
1	04 Sep 04	Home	Norway	36	W	2 1	de Rossi 4, 4, Toni 80, 80
2	08 Sep 04	Away	Moldova	112	W	0 1	Del Piero 32
3	09 Oct 04	Away	Slovenia	50	L	1 0	
4	13 Oct 04	Home	Belarus	64	W	4 3	Totti 27pen, 75, de Rossi 33, Gilardino 86
5	26 Mar 05	Home	Scotland	78	W	2 0	Pirlo 35, 85
6	04 Jun 05	Away	Norway	36	D	0 0	
7	03 Sep 05	Away	Scotland	78	D	1 1	Grosso 76
8	07 Sep 05	Away	Belarus	64	W	1 4	Toni 6, 14, 55, Camoranesi 45
9	08 Oct 05	Home	Slovenia	50	W	1 0	Zaccardo 77
10	12 Oct 05	Home	Moldova	112	W	2 1	Vieri 70, Gilardino 85
	Average FIFA ranking of opposition			68			

MAIN PLAYER PERFORMANCES IN QUALIFICATION

Match	1 2 3 4 5 6 7 8 9 10	Appearances	Started	Subbed on	Subbed off	Mins played	% played	Goals	Yellow	Red
Venue	H A A H H A A A H H									
Result	W W L W W D D W W W									
Goalkeepers										
Gianluigi Buffon		6	6	0	0	540	60.0	0	0	0
Morgan De Sanctis		1	1	0	0	90	10.0	0	0	0
Angelo Peruzzi		3	3	0	0	270	30.0	0	0	0
Defenders										
Daniele Bonera		6	6	0	2	488	54.2	0	3	0
Fabio Cannavaro		7	6	1	0	563	62.6	0	1	0
Stefano Aimo Diana		5	3	2	1	277	30.8	0	1	0
Marco Materazzi		6	6	0	1	527	58.6	0	1	0
Alessandro Nesta		7	7	0	0	630	70.0	0	1	0
Guiseppe Pancaro		1	1	0	0	90	10.0	0	0	0
Cristian Zaccardo		4	3	1	1	257	28.6	1	1	0
Gianluca Zambrotta		8	7	1	0	659	73.2	0	4	0
Midfielders										
Massimo Ambrosini		1	1	0	1	73	8.1	0	0	0
Simone Barone		2	1	1	0	124	13.8	0	0	0
Manuele Blasi		3	0	3	0	69	7.7	0	0	0
Mauro Camoranesi		6	5	1	2	467	51.9	1	1	0
Daniele De Rossi		8	6	2	2	521	57.9	1	1	0
Stefano Fiore		2	1	1	0	111	12.3	0	0	0
Gennaro Gattuso		8	8	0	0	720	80.0	0	3	0
Fabio Grosso		5	4	1	1	376	41.8	1	0	0
Andrea Pirlo		6	6	0	1	530	58.9	2	0	0
Forwards										
Antonio Cassano		2	2	0	2	149	16.6	0	0	0
Alessandro Del Piero		2	2	0	0	180	20.0	1	1	0
Alberto Gilardino		8	7	1	5	524	58.2	2	0	0
Vincenzo Iaquinta		4	2	2	2	184	20.4	0	0	0
Luca Toni		8	2	6	2	264	29.3	5	0	0
Francesco Totti		6	6	0	1	521	57.9	2	2	0
Christian Vieri		4	3	1	1	238	26.4	1	0	0

FINAL PROSPECTS

Italy must have cursed their way through the World Cup draw. The Czechs will be Group E formbook favourites, Ghana are the second strongest of the African qualifiers and the USA were quarter-finalists in 2002 and arguably stronger now.

Italy's nerves didn't survive the group stages of Euro 2004 where they were third behind Sweden and Denmark. They barely escaped a feeble group in Japan/Korea 2002, qualifying on just four points after losing to Croatia and were then humiliated by their defeat to hosts South Korea in the last 16 stage.

A glance through the host of Italian stars playing well at big clubs in Serie A suggests Italy should be a threat, a long hard look at the Azzurri nearly stalling in the weakest European qualifying group, doesn't inspire confidence.

The press are pillorying manager, Marcello Lippi and when you look at the talent he has available, you can see why.

Only Spain are blessed with better goalkeeping options than Italy, who have Gianluigi Buffon and Morgan de Sanctis of Udinese. The defence is settled with household names in Alessandro Nesta and Fabio Cannavaro at the centre and Gianluca Zambrotta at right back. Inter's

> **"Italy are in with a chance of winning in Germany. They always look strong for tournaments – it sounds like a cliché but it's true."**
> Martin Jol

Marco Materazzi and Palermo's full back Cristian Zaccardo are both in good club form.

Midfield hinges on AC Milan pair Andrea Pirlo and Gennaro Gattuso with Juve's Mauro Cameronesi and one of Antonio Cassano, Fabio Grosso or Daniele de Rossi.

Francesco Totti is striving to recover from injury and, if fit, will probably play behind one of the current young hotshots of Serie A, Milan's Alberto Gilardino or Fiorentina's Luca Toni.

Lippi rang the changes to poor effect in qualifying and didn't seem to know his best XI. Friendly wins against Holland and Germany suggest he may be finding the right combinations and his squad has the depth to overcome injuries .

GROUP FIXTURES

GHANA	Mon 12 June 2000 BST
USA	Sat 17 June 2000 BST
CZECH REPUBLIC	Thur 22 June 1500 BST

KEY PLAYER

ANDREA PIRLO AC MILAN

Andrea Pirlo sets the pace of Italy's attacking play. The AC Milan midfielder sits deep in the diamond and uses his vision and passing ability to prompt the attack. He had an unsuccessful spell with Inter, before AC Milan moved for him in 2001. Now he is the key component in their midfield.

Top 12 players: Cannavaro, Materazzi, Toni

Playing record	12 mths lge	wcq
Appearances:	35	6
Minutes played:	2908	530
Percentage played:	71.8%	58.9%
Goals scored:	6	2
Goals conceded:	27	2
Cards:	Y3, R0	Y0, R0
Power rating:	44mins	59mins
Power ranking:	24th	89th

AGE 27	MIDFIELDER	WORLD RANKING 55

Zone	Europe
Population	58,066,128
Capital	Rome
Language	Italian
Top league	Serie A
Major clubs	**Capacities**
Juventus	69,000
Inter Milan	85,700
AC Milan	85,000

Where likely squad players play:

In Italy			21
In Premiership			-
In Holland	-	In France	1
In Spain	1	In Germany	-

Number of Italian players playing:

In Italy			475
In Premiership			8
In Holland	1	In France	4
In Spain	10	In Germany	2

World Cup record

1930 -	Did not enter	1974 -	Group 3rd
1934 -	Champions	1978 -	Fourth place
1938 -	Champions	1982 -	Champions
1950 -	Group 2nd	1986 -	Last 16
1954 -	Group 3rd	1990 -	Third place
1958 -	Did not qualify	1994 -	Runners-up
1962 -	Group 4th	1998 -	Quarter-finals
1966 -	Group 3rd	2002 -	Last 16
1970 -	Runners-up		

THE SQUAD

Goalkeepers	Club side	Age	QG
Gianluigi Buffon	Juventus	28	6
Morgan De Sanctis	Udinese	29	1
Angelo Peruzzi	Lazio	36	3
Defenders			
Andrea Barzagli	Palermo	25	1
Daniele Bonera	Parma	25	6
Fabio Cannavaro	Juventus	32	7
Giorgio Chiellini	Juventus	21	1
Stefano Aimo Diana	Sampdoria	28	5
Giuseppe Favalli	Inter Milan	34	1
Marco Materazzi	Inter Milan	32	6
Alessandro Nesta	AC Milan	30	7
Massimo Oddo	Lazio	29	2
Giuseppe Pancaro	Fiorentina	34	1
Cristian Zaccardo	Palermo	24	4
Gianluca Zambrotta	Juventus	29	8
Midfielders			
Simone Barone	Palermo	28	2
Manuele Blasi	Juventus	25	3
Mauro Camoranesi	Juventus	29	6
Daniele De Rossi	Roma	21	8
Stefano Fiore	Fiorentina	31	2
Gennaro Gattuso	AC Milan	28	8
Fabio Grosso	Palermo	28	5
Andrea Pirlo	AC Milan	27	6
Forwards			
Antonio Cassano	Real Madrid	23	2
Bernardo Corradi	Parma	30	1
Alessandro Del Piero	Juventus	31	2
Alberto Gilardino	AC Milan	23	8
Vincenzo Iaquinta	Udinese	26	4
Luca Toni	Fiorentina	29	8
Francesco Totti	Roma	29	6
Christian Vieri	AS Monaco	32	4

■ Probable ■ Possible **QG** Qualification Games

KEY GOALKEEPER

GIANLUIGI BUFFON
JUVENTUS

Italy takes its defending seriously. The last time they won the World Cup they had the legendary Dino Zoff in goal.

This time they have another Juventus keeper and the world's most expensive, Gianluigi Buffon. Justifying a price tag of £32m, 'Gigi' has been Italy's number one since his first cap in 1997 at the age of 20. A broken thumb kept him out of Euro 2000 and has suffered a long injury from the start of this season until a comeback in December.

Italy has a rich seam of keepers with Udinese's Morgan De Sanctis and Lazio's Angelo Peruzzi as backup.

Playing record	12 mths lge	wcq
Appearances:	25	6
Minutes played:	2205	540
Percentage played:	54.4%	60.0%
Goals conceded:	19	6
Clean sheets:	10	3
Cards:	Y1, R0	Y0, R0
Defensive rating:	116mins	90mins
Defensive ranking:	4th	15th

AGE 28	WORLD RANKING 252

KEY DEFENDERS

GIANLUCA ZAMBROTTA
JUVENTUS

Gianluca Zambrotta has won three Italian league titles in his six years at Juventus and is well on his way to a seventh.

He can play on either flank and as a wing back, he's at home in midfield or in defence. He started his Serie A career with Bari in 1997 and moved to Juve in 1999. He mainly plays left back for club and country now and has extended his contract in Turin until 2010.

Playing record	12 mths lge	wcq
Appearances:	39	8
Minutes played:	3469	659
Percentage played:	85.7%	73.2%
Goals scored:	0	0
Goals conceded:	27	8
Cards:	Y3, R0	Y4, R0
Power rating:	47mins	51mins
Power ranking:	33rd	77th

AGE 29	WORLD RANKING 35

MARCO MATERAZZI
INTER MILAN

Marco Materazzi is a tough central defender who has played well for Italy when he's been given the chance.

He is likely to go to Germany as cover for Nesta and Cannavaro. He holds the Serie A record for a goal-scoring defender with 12 in the 2000/1 season.

He is a Top 12 Defender.

AGE 32	WORLD RANKING 63

CRISTIAN ZACCARDO
PALERMO

Palermo right back Cristian Zaccardo played 33 times in his club's sixth-place finish last season and picked up four caps.

Palermo's strong finish brought a number of their players to the Azzurri's attention.

Zaccardo featured late in the qualifying campaign but showed to good effect against Slovenia, coming on to score the winning goal 13 minutes from time.

Playing record	12 mths lge	wcq
Appearances:	40	4
Minutes played:	3475	257
Percentage played:	85.8%	28.6%
Goals conceded:	57	3
Clean sheets:	9	1
Cards:	Y10, R1	Y1, R0
Defensive rating:	61mins	86mins
Defensive ranking:	103rd	73rd

AGE 24	WORLD RANKING 620

FABIO CANNAVARO
JUVENTUS

Fabio Cannavaro was a youth player watching Diego Maradona at Naples before making his Serie A debut, aged 20 in 1993/4.

He became a full international in 1997 and has been one of the most in demand Serie A defenders ever since.

He is a Top 12 Defender.

AGE 32	WORLD RANKING 21

THE MANAGER

Marcello Lippi has fulfilled his dream to manage the Azzurri.

His chance came after the nightmare of Euro 2004 where Totti was banned for spitting at a Danish player and Italy battled to a last minute group win over Bulgaria, only to find it wasn't enough. Giovanni Trapattoni ended his unhappy spell in charge and Lippi, having won five Serie A league titles, was seen as the right candidate by the Italian press.

However, Italy's stuttering progress through a weak qualifying group and a frantic confusion of selections changed the headlines.

Lippi, 58, has to combine the old guard of Italian football with the new batch of strikers that emerged at club level last season. Vincenzo Iaquinta is a withdrawn striker in the Totti or Del Piero mould, Luca Toni is currently leading scorer at Fiorentina and Alberto Gilardino is netting for AC Milan. Elsewhere Lippi's experiments have floundered and he returned to established stars for the friendly wins over Holland and Germany.

KEY DEFENDER

ALESSANDRO NESTA AC MILAN

Alessandro Nesta is appearing in his third World Cup, having made his debut for Italy in 1996, aged just 20.

The Azzurri blood top defenders young and play them for a long time. Nesta has played all bar one of AC Milan's games this season. Since leading Lazio to the Italian title in 1999/2000, he has won another Scudetto and a Champions League trophy with Milan.

Playing record	12 mths lge	wcq
Appearances:	34	7
Minutes played:	2898	630
Percentage played:	71.6%	70.0%
Goals conceded:	25	8
Clean sheets:	14	2
Cards:	Y9, R0	Y1, R0
Defensive rating:	116mins	79mins
Defensive ranking:	22nd	75th

AGE 30 | **DEFENDER** | **WORLD RANKING 200**

KEY MIDFIELDERS

KEY STRIKERS

MAURO GERMAN CAMORANESI
JUVENTUS

Mauro German Camoranesi is the Argentinian who controls the right flank for Italy's national team. Camoranesi played his club football mostly in Mexico before moving to Italy and ultimately, Juventus.

He's a creative winger who takes his defensive duties seriously but always contributes goals. Overlooked by Argentina, Camoranesi took the chance to represent the Azzurri in 2003 and was a regular in Italy's 2006 World Cup qualifying campaign. He says, "I'm not a traitor, I still feel one 100% Argentine and have done nothing to find myself in this situation. It's only football."

Playing record	12 mths lge	wcq
Appearances:	41	6
Minutes played:	2945	467
Percentage played:	72.7%	51.9%
Goals scored:	4	1
Goals conceded:	28	2
Cards:	Y8, R0	Y1, R0
Power rating:	47mins	58mins
Power ranking:	30th	88th

AGE 29   **WORLD RANKING 49**

ALESSANDRO DEL PIERO
JUVENTUS

Alessandro del Piero has played himself back into contention for the national side.

He's scoring freely for Juventus – outscoring Zlatan Ibrahimovic – and even netted against Germany in the March friendly.

Playing record	12 mths lge	wcq
Appearances:	38	2
Minutes played:	2280	180
Percentage played:	56.3%	20.0%
Goals scored:	16	1
Percentage share:	18.82	5.26
Cards:	Y1, R0	Y1, R0
Strike rate:	142mins	-
Strike rate ranking:	15th	-

AGE 31   **WORLD RANKING 57**

LUCA TONI
FIORENTINA

Luca Toni is one of our Top 12 Strikers.

AGE 29   **WORLD RANKING 34**

GENNARO GATTUSO
AC MILAN

Gennaro Gattuso is one of the world's most tenacious ball-winners. He drives the midfield for AC Milan and Italy and his energy and hunger ensures he is always in the thick of the action.

He was most people's man-of-the-match in the 2002/3 Champions League final between Milan and their Serie A rivals Juventus, which Milan won on penalties.

His career initially blossomed under Walter Smith at Glasgow Rangers but now Gattuso provides the steel for Italy. He will probably play alongside his club-mate Andrea Pirlo and the two complement each other.

Playing record	12 mths lge	wcq
Appearances:	39	8
Minutes played:	3049	720
Percentage played:	75.3%	80.0%
Goals scored:	1	0
Goals conceded:	27	8
Cards:	Y4, R0	Y3, R0
Power rating:	46mins	42mins
Power ranking:	30th	37th

AGE 28   **WORLD RANKING 118**

DANIELE DE ROSSI
ROMA

Daniele De Rossi is a Roma Youth player who has broken into the Italian midfield.

He made his Serie A debut in 2003 and won the Under 21 European Cup with Italy in 2004 plus a bronze at the Olympics.

Playing record	12 mths lge	wcq
Appearances:	39	8
Minutes played:	3250	521
Percentage played:	80.2%	57.9%
Goals scored:	5	1
Goals conceded:	41	6
Cards:	Y13, R1	Y1, R0
Power rating:	60mins	58mins
Power ranking:	86th	87th

AGE 21   **WORLD RANKING 383**

ANDREA PIRLO
AC MILAN

Andrea Pirlo is our choice as Key Player

AGE 27   **WORLD RANKING 55**

ONE TO WATCH

FRANCESCO TOTTI ROMA

Francesco Totti has left the last two international tournaments in disgrace; sent off against South Korea and banned for spitting in Euro 2004. This time he 's hoping just to get there after an injury in February. He is still a vital player and can play as an advanced midfielder, lead the line or play in the hole behind a target-man striker. Lippi will find room for him if he's fit.

Playing record	12 mths lge	wcq
Appearances:	33	6
Minutes played:	2853	521
Percentage played:	70.4%	57.9%
Goals scored:	16	2
Percentage share:	24.24	10.53
Cards:	Y7, R3	Y2, R0
Strike rate:	178mins	260mins
Strike rate ranking:	29th	47th

AGE 29 | **STRIKER** | **WORLD RANKING 301**

GHANA

ROUTE TO THE FINALS

Ghana have finally reached the World Cup Finals at their 11th attempt. During that time, they have won four African Cup titles with some of the top stars to hail from Africa in Osei Koffi, and Abedi Pele.

When African Group 2 was drawn, the hot favourites were South Africa – then ranked in the mid-30s by FIFA International Rankings – while Ghana, the Democratic Republic of Congo and Burkina Faso were viewed as battling for the runners-up spot.

Two easy preliminary wins over Somalia followed by a Group 2 defeat to Burkina Faso didn't change anyone's opinion but, in their third game, Ghana announced their intentions. At home to South Africa, Sulley Ali Muntari scored after 13 minutes and captain Stephen Appiah added two more in the second half.

Coach Mariano Barreto resigned for another job offer in Portugal but South Africa were beaten again in the return - this time in a side managed by Ghana's new Serbian coach Ratomir Dujkovic.

The Black Stars had found the confidence and form to run out convincing winners in their final two games against Uganda and Cape Verde Islands and qualify with points to spare.

AFRICA GROUP 2

	P	W	D	L	GF	GA	Pts
Ghana	10	6	3	1	17	4	21
Congo DR	10	4	4	2	14	10	16
South Africa	10	5	1	4	12	14	16
Burkina Faso	10	4	1	5	14	13	13
Cape Verde	10	3	1	6	8	15	10
Uganda	10	2	2	6	6	15	8

#	Date	Venue	Opponent	FIFA ranking	Result	Score	Scorers
1	05 Jun 04	Away	Burkina Faso	87	L	1 0	
2	20 Jun 04	Home	South Africa	41	W	3 0	Muntari 13, Appiah 55, 78
3	03 Jul 04	Away	Uganda	109	D	1 1	A.Gyan 88
4	05 Sep 04	Home	Cape Verde Islands	122	W	2 0	Essien 24pen, Veiga 62og
5	10 Oct 04	Home	Congo DR	75	D	0 0	
6	27 Mar 05	Away	Congo DR	75	D	1 1	A.Gyan 30
7	05 Jun 05	Home	Burkina Faso	87	W	2 1	Appiah 66, M.Amoah 83
8	18 Jun 05	Away	South Africa	41	W	0 2	M.Amoah 59, Essien 90
9	04 Sep 05	Home	Uganda	109	W	2 0	Essien 10, M.Amoah 15
10	08 Oct 05	Away	Cape Verde Islands	122	W	0 4	Asamoah 5, Muntari 35, A.Gyan 75, Attram 87
	Average FIFA ranking of opposition			83			

Not including pre-qualifying games

MAIN PLAYER PERFORMANCES IN QUALIFICATION

Match	Appearances	Started	Subbed on	Subbed off	Mins played	% played	Goals	Yellow	Red
Goalkeepers									
Sam Adjei	8	8	0	0	720	80.0	0	0	0
Richard Kingston	2	2	0	1	149	16.6	0	0	0
George Owu	1	1	0	0	90	10.0	0	0	0
Defenders									
Yaw Amankwa Mireku	2	1	1	0	116	12.9	0	0	0
Kofi Amponsah	3	3	0	2	189	21.0	0	0	0
Daniel Edusei	4	3	1	0	278	30.9	0	0	0
Gabriel Issah	4	3	1	0	325	36.1	0	0	0
Samuel Osei Kuffour	5	5	0	0	450	50.0	0	0	0
John Mensah	9	9	0	0	810	90.0	0	3	0
John Pantsil	4	4	0	0	360	40.0	0	1	0
Emmanuel Pappoe	8	8	0	0	720	80.0	0	2	0
Daniel Quaye	3	3	0	1	254	28.2	0	0	0
Abukari Yakubu	2	1	1	0	103	11.4	0	0	0
Midfielders									
Stephen Appiah	9	9	0	1	805	89.4	3	1	0
Godwin Attram	3	1	2	1	87	9.7	1	0	0
Yussif Chibsah	1	1	0	0	90	10.0	0	0	0
Michael Essien	8	8	0	2	658	73.1	3	3	0
Kingston Laryea	3	3	0	2	211	23.4	0	2	0
Sulley Muntari	7	7	0	6	504	56.0	2	3	0
Ibrahim Tanko	3	3	0	3	177	19.7	0	0	0
Forwards									
Matthew Amoah	5	5	0	2	441	49.0	3	0	0
Frimpong Asamoah	4	3	1	2	234	26.0	1	0	0
Asamoah Gyan	5	3	2	1	296	32.9	3	0	0
Baffour Gyan	4	4	0	2	327	36.3	0	2	0
Kwadwo Poku	4	1	3	1	108	12.0	0	0	0
William Tiero	3	3	0	0	270	30.0	0	1	0

Match: 1 2 3 4 5 6 7 8 9 10
Venue: A H A H H A H A H A
Result: L W D W D D W W W W

FINAL PROSPECTS

The young Ghanaian side has the strongest midfield of the African finalists. Michael Essien – the most expensive African player ever – is the powerhouse at its centre alongside Udinese's talented youngster Sulley Ali Muntari and captain Stephen Appiah of Fenerbahce.

The attack looked lightweight until the international return of Matthew Amoah then at Dutch side Vitesse Arnhem halfway through qualifying. A January transfer window signing for German Bundesliga side Borussia Dortmund, Amoah is a fine poacher. He hit 70 goals in 189 games for Vitesse.

Hugely experienced but out-of-favour Samuel Kuffour was brought back into the squad for the African Cup of Nations. The former Bayern Munich Champions League winner is still playing at the highest standard for Roma and would bolster the defence.

THE MANAGER

Ratomir Dujkovic, 59, came into the Ghanaian camp halfway through the qualification process when Portuguese coach Mariano Barreto quit the job to return home and manage Maritimo.

The experienced Serbian is the Black Stars' fifth coach in two years. He caught the eye when he led Rwanda to their first African Cup of Nations finals in Tunisia, ironically at the expense of Ghana.

He immediately showed his metal by excluding Ghana's most high-profile defender Samuel Kuffour, for critical comments about the his appointment. Now Kuffour has apologised.

Ratomir Dujkovic

GROUP FIXTURES

ITALY	Mon 12 June 2000 BST
CZECH REPUBLIC	Sat 17 June 1700 BST
USA	Thur 22 June 1500 BST

Accra

Zone	Africa
Population	22,238,459
Capital	Accra
Language	English
Top league	Telecom Premier
Major clubs	**Capacities**
Accra Hearts of Oak	35,000
Asante Kotoko	51,500
Goldfields	30,000

Where likely squad players play:

In Premiership	1
In other major five European Leagues	5
Outside major European Leagues	17

Number of Ghanaian players playing:

In Premiership	1
In other major five European Leagues	13

World Cup record

1930 -	Did not enter	1974 -	Did not qualify
1934 -	Did not enter	1978 -	Did not qualify
1938 -	Did not enter	1982 -	Withdrew
1950 -	Did not enter	1986 -	Did not qualify
1954 -	Did not enter	1990 -	Did not qualify
1958 -	Did not enter	1994 -	Did not qualify
1962 -	Did not qualify	1998 -	Did not qualify
1966 -	Withdrew	2002 -	Did not qualify
1970 -	Did not qualify		

ONE TO WATCH

SULLEY ALI MUNTARI UDINESE

The youngest of Ghana's midfield trio is Sulley Ali Muntari. He has already made an impact in Serie A, with 33 appearances in Udinese's run to fourth place in 2004/5 and qualification for their first-ever Champions League.

He combines great touch, with tireless work and a strong competitive instinct.

Michael Essien is a Top 12 Midfielder.

Playing record	12 mths lge	wcq
Appearances:	33	7
Minutes played:	2504	504
Percentage played:	61.8%	56.0%
Goals scored:	5	2
Goals conceded:	36	2
Cards:	Y11, R1	Y3, R0
Power rating:	74mins	72mins
Power ranking:	116th	105th

AGE 21 MIDFIELDER WORLD RANKING 399

THE SQUAD

	Club side	Age	QG
Goalkeepers			
Sam Adjei	Ashdod	25	8
Richard Kingston	Ankaraspor	30	1
George Owu	Ashanti Gold	23	1
Defenders			
Yaw Amankwa Mireku	Hearts Accra	26	2
Kofi Amponsah	Apollon	30	3
Daniel Edusei	Aigaleo	25	4
Gabriel Issah	Asante Kotoko	24	4
Samuel Osei Kuffour	Roma	29	5
John Mensah	Rennes	23	9
John Pantsil	Hapoel Tel-Aviv	24	4
Emmanuel Pappoe	Kfar-Saba	25	8
Daniel Quaye	Hearts Accra	25	3
Hans Sarpei	Wolfsburg	29	1
Abukari Yakubu	Vitesse Arnhem	24	2
Midfielders			
Stephen Appiah	Fenerbahce	25	9
Charles Taylor	Asante Kumasi	24	2
Godwin Attram	Al Shabab	25	3
Mark Edusei	Torino	29	1
Michael Essien	Chelsea	23	8
Laryea Kingston	Lokomotiv Moscow	25	1
Kingston Laryea	Lokomotiv Moscow	25	3
Hamza Mohamed	RTU	25	6
Ablade Morgan	Hearts of Oak	25	1
Sulley Muntari	Udinese	21	7
Ibrahim Tanko	Freiburg	28	3
Forwards			
Matthew Amoah	B Dortmund	25	5
Frimpong Asamoah	Enyimba	24	4
Derek Boateng	AIK Stockholm	23	1
Asamoah Gyan	Modena	20	5
Baffour Gyan	Dinamo Moscow	25	4
Kwadwo Poku	Midtjylland	21	4
William Tiero	Vitoria Guimaraes	25	3
Abubakar Yahuza	King Faisal Babies	22	2

■ Probable ■ Possible **QG** Qualification Games

USA

ROUTE TO THE FINALS

America's status, along with Mexico, atop of the CONCACAF region has been assured by what will be their fifth consecutive appearance on this stage.
The US were comfortable all the way through the qualification campaign, and secured their berth with three matches remaining. Defeat away to Mexico was the only instance of points dropped before qualification was assured. The match that clinched it was also the undoubted highlight, a fantastic 2-0 revenge over the Mexicans in Columbus, Ohio. The atmosphere was electric, debunking the myth that soccer is of little interest Stateside. The increase in the standard and amount of the available talent is a result of the ever-improving MLS and the increasing success of American players in the major European leagues.

FINAL QUALIFYING TABLE
N/C AMERICA & CAR. STAGE 3

	P	W	D	L	GF	GA	Pts
USA	10	7	1	2	16	6	22
Mexico	10	7	1	2	22	9	22
Costa Rica	10	5	1	4	15	14	16
Trinidad and Tob	10	4	1	5	10	15	13
Guatemala	10	3	2	5	16	18	11
Panama	10	0	2	8	4	21	2

					FIFA ranking			
1	18 Aug 04	Away	Jamaica	42	D	1 1	Ching 88
2	04 Sep 04	Home	El Salvador	114	W	2 0	Ching 5, Donovan 68
3	08 Sep 04	Away	Panama	88	D	1 1	Jones 90
4	09 Oct 04	Away	El Salvador	114	W	0 2	McBride 29, Johnson 75
5	13 Oct 04	Home	Panama	88	W	6 0	Donovan 21, 56, Johnson 69, 84, 86, A.Torres 89og
6	17 Nov 04	Home	Jamaica	42	D	1 1	Johnson 15
7	09 Feb 05	Away	Trinidad & Tobago	57	W	1 2	Johnson 23, Lewis 53
8	27 Mar 05	Away	Mexico	6	L	2 1	Lewis 58
9	30 Mar 05	Home	Guatemala	60	W	2 0	Johnson 11, Ralston 69
10	04 Jun 05	Home	Costa Rica	22	W	3 0	Donovan 10, 62, McBride 87
11	08 Jun 05	Away	Panama	88	W	0 3	Bocanegra 6, Donovan 19, McBride 39
12	17 Aug 05	Home	Trinidad & Tobago	57	W	1 0	McBride 2
13	03 Sep 05	Home	Mexico	6	W	2 0	Ralston 53, Beasley 57
14	07 Sep 05	Away	Guatemala	60	D	0 0	
15	08 Oct 05	Away	Costa Rica	22	L	3 0	
16	12 Oct 05	Home	Panama	88	W	2 0	Martino 51, Twellman 57
	Average FIFA ranking of opposition		50				

MAIN PLAYER PERFORMANCES IN QUALIFICATION

Match: 1 2 3 4 5 6 7 8 9 10 11 12 13 14 15 16
Venue: A H A A H H A A H H A H H A A H
Result: D W D W W W D W L W W W W D L W

	Appearances	Started	Subbed on	Subbed off	Mins played	% played	Goals	Yellow	Red
Goalkeepers									
Tim Howard	3	3	0	0	270	18.8	0	0	0
Kasey Keller	12	12	0	0	1080	75.0	0	0	0
Defenders									
Chris Albright	6	5	1	1	430	29.9	0	0	0
Greg Berhalter	7	5	2	0	460	31.9	0	2	0
Carlos Bocanegra	10	10	0	2	868	60.3	1	2	0
Steve Cherundolo	6	6	0	2	509	35.3	0	0	0
Corey Gibbs	5	5	0	0	450	31.3	0	1	0
Frankie Hejduk	7	6	1	0	557	38.7	0	2	0
Pablo Mastroeni	8	6	2	2	532	36.9	0	0	0
Oguchi Onyewu	7	6	1	0	528	36.7	0	2	1
Eddie George Pope	8	8	0	2	710	49.3	0	1	0
Midfielders									
DaMarcus Beasley	11	11	0	2	957	66.5	1	2	0
Bobby Convey	6	5	1	1	441	30.6	0	2	1
Clint Dempsey	7	2	5	1	259	18.0	0	1	0
Eddie Lewis	9	7	2	2	653	45.3	2	1	0
Santino Quaranta	5	2	3	1	216	15.0	0	0	0
Steve Ralston	9	6	3	3	562	39.0	2	0	0
Claudio Reyna	6	6	0	0	540	37.5	0	1	0
Kerry Zavagnin	5	5	0	2	423	29.4	0	0	0
Forwards									
Brian Ching	6	4	2	1	396	27.5	2	0	0
Landon Donovan	14	13	1	2	1177	81.7	6	0	0
Ed Johnson	7	4	3	2	433	30.1	7	0	0
Brian McBride	12	9	3	4	801	55.6	4	0	0
Taylor Twellman	5	3	2	1	265	18.4	1	0	0

FINAL PROSPECTS

The USA will be one of the best-prepared and fittest sides at the World Cup.

They are building a good World Cup track record and look stronger than they did going into 2002.

Their target man Brian McBride is having his best Premiership season ever and DaMarcus Beasley has rewarded PSV manager Guus Hiddink's faith in him. Beasley replaced Chelsea-bound Robben in 2004/5, and helped PSV win the Dutch title. He was their top-scorer in the Champions League, with four.

LA Galaxy's Landon Donovan and Leeds left winger Eddie Lewis both hit seven goals in qualifying.

Carlos Bocanegra has moved into the centre of Fulham's defence, the vastly experienced Kasey Keller (now at Monchengladback) adds authority and left back Jonathan Spector, 20, is now playing more regularly at Charlton.

THE MANAGER

Bruce Arena, 55, is on course to be the most successful US coach ever.

His efforts with the Olympic team, reputation for developing youngsters and success with DC United got him the job after the disappointing 1998 Finals. That meant he had four years to prepare for the 2002 Finals.

Arena's reputation is one of meticulous preparation associated with coaches in American sport.

It's that attention to detail Arena uses, together with teamwork, to overcome any disadvantage that the US has with a weaker domestic league.

Bruce Arena

GROUP FIXTURES

CZECH REPUBLIC	Mon 12 June 1700 BST
ITALY	Sat 17 June 2000 BST
GHANA	Thur 22 June 1500 BST

Washington D.C.

Zone	North, Central America & Caribbean
Population	296,860,019
Capital	Washington DC
Language	English
Top league	Major League Soccer
Major clubs	**Capacities**
Houston 1836 (San Jose)	33,000
Los Angeles Galaxy	27,000
New England Revs	68,700

Where likely squad players play:

In Premiership	5
In other major five European Leagues	6
Outside major European Leagues	12

Number of American players playing:

In Premiership	8
In other major five European Leagues	10

World Cup record

1930 -	Semi-finals	1974 -	Did not qualify
1934 -	Round 1	1978 -	Did not qualify
1938 -	Withdrew	1982 -	Did not qualify
1950 -	Group 4th	1986 -	Did not qualify
1954 -	Did not qualify	1990 -	Group 4th
1958 -	Did not qualify	1994 -	Last 16
1962 -	Did not qualify	1998 -	Group 4th
1966 -	Did not qualify	2002 -	Quarter-finals
1970 -	Did not qualify		

THE SQUAD

Goalkeepers	Club side	Age	QG
Marcus Hahnemann	Reading	33	1
Tim Howard	Man Utd	27	3
Kasey Keller	B M'gladbach	36	12
Defenders			
Chris Albright	LA Galaxy	27	6
Greg Berhalter	Energie Cottbus	32	7
Carlos Bocanegra	Fulham	27	10
Steve Cherundolo	Hannover 96	27	6
Corey Gibbs	Den Haag	26	5
Frankie Hejduk	Columbus Crew	31	7
Chad Marshall	Columbus Crew	21	2
Pablo Mastroeni	Colorado Rapids	29	8
John O'Brien	Den Haag	28	1
Oguchi Onyewu	Standard Liege	24	7
Eddie George Pope	Real Salt Lake City	32	8
Jonathan Spector	Charlton	20	2
Greg Vanney	Dallas	31	3
Midfielders			
Chris Armas	Chicago Fire	33	3
DaMarcus Beasley	PSV Eindhoven	24	11
Bobby Convey	Reading	23	6
Clint Dempsey	New England Rev	23	7
Eddie Lewis	Leeds	32	9
Santino Quaranta	Washington DC Utd	21	5
Steve Ralston	New England Rev.	31	9
Claudio Reyna	Man City	32	6
Kerry Zavagnin	Kansas City Wizards	31	5
Forwards			
Freddy Adu	DC United	17	-
Brian Ching	Houston 1836	28	6
Landon Donovan	LA Galaxy	24	14
Ed Johnson	Kansas City Wizards	22	7
Brian McBride	Fulham	33	12
Pat Noonan	New England Rev.	25	4
Taylor Twellman	New England Rev.	26	5

■ Probable   ■ Possible   **QG** Qualification Games

KEY PLAYER

BRIAN MCBRIDE FULHAM

Brian McBride provides the cutting edge to the USA's build-up play. The Fulham centre forward is their most experienced striker and bursts a lung to get on the end of crosses. His goals for Fulham this season make him one of the top Premiership strikers.

Usually used as the lone striker in a 4-5-1, formation with support coming through from midfield.

Playing record	12 mths lge	wcq
Appearances:	38	12
Minutes played:	2815	801
Percentage played:	74.5%	55.6%
Goals scored:	15	4
Percentage share:	25.86	13.79
Cards:	Y2, R0	Y0, R0
Strike rate:	188mins	200mins
Strike rate ranking:	39th	35th

AGE 33   **STRIKER**   **WORLD RANKING 226**

ROUTE TO THE FINALS

Two things stood between the Czech Republic and the top of Europe's Group 1: the young Dutch stars and a disgraced former Chelsea striker.

Romania's Adrian Mutu was playing his way back from his drug's ban when he hit two goals to hand the Czechs their second qualifying defeat.

The original group favourites had already lost their first game to an experimental Dutch side in Amsterdam.

The loss to Romania meant they had to beat Marco van Basten's team in Prague to have any chance of an automatic qualifying place. Without the free-scoring Jan Koller, or Bochum's forward Vratislav Lokvenc, Milan Baros led the attack and earned a penalty. Tomas Rosicky stepped up but Edwin van der Sar saved his spot kick brilliantly.

A minute later, Holland struck when the recalled Rafael van der Vaart drove home. Barry Opdam headed a second and the Czechs had to qualify through the play-offs against Norway.

FINAL QUALIFYING TABLE
EUROPE GROUP 1

	P	W	D	L	GF	GA	Pts
Netherlands	12	10	2	0	27	3	32
Czech Republic	12	9	0	3	35	12	27
Romania	12	8	1	3	20	10	25
Finland	12	5	1	6	21	19	16
Macedonia FYR	12	2	3	7	11	24	9
Armenia	12	2	1	9	9	25	7
Andorra	12	1	2	9	4	34	5

European Group Play-offs
Czech Republic beat Norway

					FIFA ranking			
1	08 Sep 04	Away	Holland	4	L	2 0		
2	09 Oct 04	Home	Romania	29	W	1 0	Koller 36	
3	13 Oct 04	Away	Armenia	116	W	0 3	Koller 3, 76, Rosicky 30	
4	17 Nov 04	Away	Macedonia	93	W	0 2	Lokvenc 88, Koller 90	
5	26 Mar 05	Home	Finland	41	W	4 3	Baros 7, Rosicky 34, Polak 58, Lokvenc 87	
6	30 Mar 05	Away	Andorra	113	W	0 4	Jankulovski 31pen, Baros 40, Lokvenc 53, Rosicky 90pen	
7	04 Jun 05	Home	Andorra	113	W	8 1	Lokvenc 13, 90, Koller 29, Smicer 38, Galasek 52pen, Baros 80, Rosicky 86pen, Polak 87	
8	08 Jun 05	Home	Macedonia	93	W	6 1	Koller 42, 45, 49, 53, Rosicky 74pen, Baros 86	
9	03 Sep 05	Away	Romania	29	L	2 0		
10	07 Sep 05	Home	Armenia	116	W	4 1	Heinz 47, Polak 52, 76, Baros 58	
11	08 Oct 05	Home	Holland	4	L	0 2		
12	12 Oct 05	Away	Finland	41	W	0 3	Jun 6, Rosicky 51, Heinz 58	
13	12 Nov 05	Away	Norway	36	W	0 1	Smicer 31	
14	16 Nov 05	Home	Norway	36	W	1 0	Rosicky 35	
	Average FIFA ranking of opposition	62						

MAIN PLAYER PERFORMANCES IN QUALIFICATION

Match	1 2 3 4 5 6 7 8 9 10 11 12 13 14	Appearances	Started	Subbed on	Subbed off	Mins played	% played	Goals	Yellow	Red
Venue	A H A A H A H H A H H A A H									
Result	L W W W W W W W L W L W W W									
Goalkeepers										
Jaromir Blazek		1	1	0	0	90	7.1	0	0	0
Petr Cech		13	13	0	0	1170	92.9	0	0	0
Defenders										
Rene Bolf		6	6	0	1	508	40.3	0	0	0
Zdenek Grygera		11	10	1	1	919	72.9	0	0	0
Tomas Hubschmann		2	2	0	1	150	11.9	0	0	0
Marek Jankulovski		9	9	0	1	736	58.4	1	1	0
Martin Jiranek		5	5	0	3	355	28.2	0	0	0
Roman Tyce		2	2	0	2	120	9.5	0	1	0
Tomas Ujfalusi		14	14	0	0	1260	100.0	0	1	0
Midfielders										
Tomas Galasek		8	8	0	1	684	54.3	1	1	0
Jiri Jarosik		4	0	4	0	48	3.8	0	0	0
Radoslav Kovac		4	0	4	0	78	6.2	0	0	0
Pavel Nedved		2	2	0	0	180	14.3	0	1	0
Jaroslav Plasil		5	0	5	0	130	10.3	0	0	0
Karel Poborsky		11	11	0	1	977	77.5	0	0	0
Jan Polak		10	5	5	2	605	48.0	4	0	0
Tomas Rosicky		12	12	0	3	1051	83.4	7	0	0
Libor Sionko		3	2	1	1	184	14.6	0	1	0
Vladimir Smicer		8	6	2	5	495	39.3	2	1	0
Forwards										
Milan Baros		12	12	0	7	886	70.3	5	3	0
Marek Heinz		9	6	3	2	621	49.3	2	1	0
Tomas Jun		7	1	6	1	201	16.0	1	0	0
Jan Koller		8	8	0	2	685	54.4	9	0	0
Vratislav Lokvenc		7	4	3	1	352	27.9	5	0	0
Stepan Vachousek		5	4	1	2	340	27.0	0	0	0

FINAL PROSPECTS

Czechoslovakia boast one of the great World Cup pedigrees without ever having won the competition.

They were losing finalists to Italy in the first European World Cup in 1934 and went down 3-1 to Brazil in Chile in the 1962 final. Following the break up of the Soviet Bloc, the Czech Republic split from Slovakia, becoming two football teams for the 1993/4 season.

This is the first World Cup final for the new Czechs but they are one of the powers of world football with a record, which FIFA currently rates, as the second best in world football - behind Brazil (we give the FIFA average for the year above).

The team is sprinkled around some of the top club sides in Europe with the influential Karel Poborsky as the only one of the likely first XI to play domestic football – with Dynamo Ceske – and even he seems to have half Europe's top clubs on his C.V.

Pavel Nedved is one huge bonus for the Czechs; the Juventus midfielder returned from international retirement for the two play-off games against Norway and is still a key player for the runaway Italian

> **"When the Czech Republic have everybody fit, they are a country to be reckoned with."**
> Martin Jol

league leaders.

They have the best goalkeeper in the world in Chelsea's Petr Cech and their strike force revolves around the 2.02m tower that is Dortmund's Jan Koller. Milan Baros may not yet have set the Premiership alight for either Liverpool or Aston Villa, but his pace makes him an effective foil for the lofty presence of Koller. Baros finished Euro 2004 as the tournament's top scorer. Koller has to be fit. He hit nine goals in the qualification games, where the Czechs were outscored only by Mexico.

The midfield, anchored by captain Tomas Galasek of Ajax is one of the best units in international football. Galasek suffered an injury during qualification but he is now back and performing better than ever for Ajax, who are about to extend his contract.

If they avoid injuries to their strongest XI, Karel Bruckner's guile could take the Czechs into the semi-finals; any slip-up in the group stage means a last 16 game against Brazil.

GROUP FIXTURES

USA	Mon 12 June 1700 BST
GHANA	Sat 17 June 1700 BST
ITALY	Thur 22 June 1500 BST

● Prague

Zone	Europe
Population	10,228,003
Capital	Prague
Language	Czech
Top league	Gambrinus Liga
Major clubs	**Capacities**
Sparta Prague	10,000
FK Teplice	18,200
Slavia Prague	19,000

Where likely squad players play:

In Premiership	3	In Spain	-
In Holland	2	In France	4
In Italy	3	In Germany	3

Number of Czech players playing:

In Premiership	10	In Spain	0
In Holland	3	In France	4
In Italy	4	In Germany	14

World Cup record (1984 - 2002 as the Czech Rep)

1930 -	Did not enter	1974 -	Did not qualfiy
1934 -	Runners-up	1978 -	Did not qualfiy
1938 -	Quarter-finals	1982 -	Group 3rd
1950 -	Did not enter	1986 -	Did not qualfiy
1954 -	Group 3rd	1990 -	Quarter-finals
1958 -	Group 3rd	1994 -	Did not qualify
1962 -	Runners-up	1998 -	Did not qualify
1966 -	Did not qualfiy	2002 -	Did not qualify
1970 -	Group 4th		

KEY PLAYER

JAN KOLLER B DORTMUND

A cruciate ligament injury in the left knee of Jan Koller has dented Czech hopes. The highest scorer in Czech history, who reached 40 international goals in August 2005, had his operation in October but expects to be fit for the World Cup. The tall Dortmund forward is deceptively nimble and dangerous in the air.

Top Czech players are Nedved and Cech.

Playing record	12 mths lge	wcq
Appearances:	18	8
Minutes played:	1462	685
Percentage played:	42.7%	54.4%
Goals scored:	9	9
Percentage share:	16.36	24.32
Cards:	Y1, R0	Y0, R0
Strike rate:	162mins	76mins
Strike rate ranking:	24th	2nd

AGE 33   **STRIKER**   **WORLD RANKING 167**

THE SQUAD

	Club side	Age	QG
Goalkeepers			
Jaromir Blazek	Sparta Prague	33	1
Petr Cech	Chelsea	24	13
Defenders			
Rene Bolf	Auxerre	32	6
Zdenek Grygera	Ajax	26	11
Tomas Hubschmann	Shakhtar Donetsk	24	2
Marek Jankulovski	AC Milan	29	9
Martin Jiranek	Spartak Moscow	27	5
Pavel Mares	Zenit St Petersburg	30	1
David Rozehnal	Paris SG	25	7
Roman Tyce	1860 Munich	29	2
Tomas Ujfalusi	Florentina	28	14
Midfielders			
Tomas Galasek	Ajax	33	8
David Jarolim	Hamburg	27	1
Jiri Jarosik	Birmingham	28	4
Radoslav Kovac	Sparta Prague	26	4
Pavel Nedved	Juventus	33	2
Jaroslav Plasil	AS Monaco	24	5
Karel Poborsky	Dynamo Ceske	34	11
Jan Polak	Nuremberg	25	10
Tomas Rosicky	B Dortmund	25	12
Libor Sionko	Austria Vienna	29	3
Tomas Sivok	Sparta Prague	22	2
Rudolf Skacel	Hearts	26	1
Vladimir Smicer	Bordeaux	33	8
Forwards			
Milan Baros	Aston Villa	24	12
Marek Heinz	Galatasaray	28	9
Tomas Jun	Besiktas	23	7
Jan Koller	B Dortmund	33	8
Vratislav Lokvenc	Salzburg	32	7
Jiri Stajner	Hannover 96	30	2
Stepan Vachousek	Austria Vienna	26	5

■ Probable ■ Possible **QG** Qualification Games

KEY GOALKEEPER

PETR CECH
CHELSEA

Chelsea's success is built on a record-busting defence. As Arjen Robben pointed out, it's a lot easier to win games when you don't concede any goals.

Petr Cech rewrote the record book in his first season in the Premiership for clean sheets and lowest number of goals conceded. Yes, he had a good defence in front of him, but the most astonishing statistic was that he saved 9.9 shots on target for every goal conceded. The Premiership keepers between them averaged 5.5 shots on target per goal conceded. In three previous seasons, no one had ever bettered 6.6 before!

Cech was at Sparta Prague and making his mark in the Champions League when he was signed by Rennes. His performances for the Czechs in Euro 2004 tempted Chelsea to make a bid of £10.3m. That put him in competition with the impressive Italian Carlo Cudicini at the start of the 2004/5 season but Cech won Jose Mourinho's vote and has been first choice ever since.

He is one of our Top Four Keepers.

AGE 24	WORLD RANKING 7

KEY DEFENDERS

TOMAS UJFALUSI
FIORENTINA

Tomas Ujfalusi was rumoured to be a 'Real deal' last summer on the back of defiant performances in defence for Fiorentina.

Madrid had spotted that he had the best defensive stats in a poor season for the 'Viola' as they narrowly escaped relegation. He stayed put and is still a key player for Fiorentina.

Playing record	12 mths lge	wcq
Appearances:	37	14
Minutes played:	3330	1260
Percentage played:	82.2%	100.0%
Goals conceded:	43	12
Clean sheets:	10	7
Cards:	Y4, R0	Y1, R0
Defensive rating:	77mins	105mins
Defensive ranking:	75th	62nd

AGE 28	WORLD RANKING 493

DAVID ROZEHNAL
PARIS SG

Playing record	12 mths lge	wcq
Appearances:	25	7
Minutes played:	2230	564
Percentage played:	59.0%	44.8%
Goals conceded:	22	3
Clean sheets:	11	5
Cards:	Y4, R0	Y1, R0
Defensive rating:	101mins	188mins
Defensive ranking:	38th	30th

AGE 25	WORLD RANKING 913

ZDENEK GRYGERA
AJAX

Zdenek Grygera can play anywhere across the back line and is in good form at Ajax.

He suffered from a torn hamstring last season but recovered to finish the season strongly.

Playing record	12 mths lge	wcq
Appearances:	26	11
Minutes played:	2250	919
Percentage played:	59.5%	72.9%
Goals conceded:	24	8
Clean sheets:	11	5
Cards:	Y6, R1	Y0, R0
Defensive rating:	94mins	115mins
Defensive ranking:	47th	58th

AGE 26	WORLD RANKING 913

MAREK JANKULOVSKI
AC MILAN

Marek Jankulovski is a wing back who plays in the defence for the Czech Republic but flies forward to devastating effect.

Like Milan Baros he began his career at Banik Ostrava and made his debut for the Czechs in 2000. After Euro 2000 he moved to Napoli in Serie A but as they were relegated, he moved to Udinese.

Playing on the left flank, he helped Udinese to a Champions League spot for the first time in the club's history in 2004/5 and was signed by AC Milan. Jankulovski works hard for the Republic and has impressive stamina.

Playing record	12 mths lge	wcq
Appearances:	29	9
Minutes played:	1579	736
Percentage played:	39.0%	58.4%
Goals scored:	1	1
Goals conceded:	19	5
Cards:	Y5, R0	Y1, R0
Power rating:	53mins	46mins
Power ranking:	58th	53rd

AGE 29	WORLD RANKING 1113

TOMAS ROSICKY B DORTMUND

Tomas Rosicky is the heir to Pavel Nedved's crown as midfield hub of the Czech Republic team. Both players are pacy, hard-working midfielders with plenty of guile and an eye for goal.

A revelation in the Bundesliga when he provided the spark to take Dortmund to the title in 2002, Rosicky is likely to move on after the World Cup.

Playing record	12 mths lge	wcq
Appearances:	33	12
Minutes played:	2784	1051
Percentage played:	81.4%	83.4%
Goals scored:	4	7
Goals conceded:	36	9
Cards:	Y5, R1	Y0, R0
Power rating:	63mins	32mins
Power ranking:	96th	14th

AGE 25   **MIDFIELDER**   **WORLD RANKING 157**

KEY MIDFIELDERS

PAVEL NEDVED
JUVENTUS

Pavel Nedved was one of many prominent players who retired from international football after Euro 2004 and was persuaded back for one last hurrah. The Juventus midfielder is at the top of his game.

He is one of our Top 12 Midfielders.

AGE 33	WORLD RANKING 26

KAREL POBORSKY
DYNAMO BUDEJOVICE

Karel Poborsky is another highly experienced member of the Czech squad who is still playing and still hugely influential.

Ther former Manchester United winger, first showed his paces in Euro 96 as one of the Czech stars who reached the final. He was the first Czech player to reach 100 appearances.

AGE 34	WORLD RANKING –

TOMAS GALASEK
AJAX

The tough tackling Tomas Galasek is the Czech Republic's midfield minder.

He was first capped in 1995 and represented the Czechs in every game in the ultimately unsuccessful 2002 World Cup qualifying crusade. In 2000, he switched from Dutch side Willem II to giants Ajax.

He has been a regular at the club, winning Dutch league titles and is a pivotal player in the team. Although they are having a poor season by their standards, Galasek is apparently having a blinder and his performances have persuaded coach Danny Blind to extend his contract.

Playing record	12 mths lge	wcq
Appearances:	24	8
Minutes played:	1985	684
Percentage played:	52.5%	54.3%
Goals scored:	5	1
Goals conceded:	28	5
Cards:	Y2, R0	Y1, R0
Power rating:	47mins	28mins
Power ranking:	34th	7th

AGE 33	WORLD RANKING 522

VLADIMIR SMICER
BORDEAUX

Vladimir Smicer is a veteran of the Czech Republic's Euro 1996 run to the final.

Along with Nedved, Poborsky and Galasek he gives the Czechs one of the most experienced midfields in World Football.

The wide midfield player joined Liverpool in 1999 and had many years in or around the fringes of the team, without ever winning the fans over to his side. He had the last laugh though, coming on to score a vital goal in Liverpool's Champions League triumph last summer.

He played only 330 minutes for Rafael Benitez in the league last season and moved on to French side Bordeaux for 2005/6.

Playing record	12 mths lge	wcq
Appearances:	35	8
Minutes played:	1772	495
Percentage played:	46.9%	39.3%
Goals scored:	3	2
Goals conceded:	15	5
Cards:	Y2, R0	Y1, R0
Power rating:	84mins	31mins
Power ranking:	137th	12th

AGE 33	WORLD RANKING 987

KEY STRIKERS

VRATISLAV LOKVENC
RED BULL SALZBURG

Vratislav Lokvenc is the player Karel Bruckner will turn to if Jan Koller struggles for fitness.

The striker has experience with Bundesliga clubs Kaiserslautern and Bochum, for whom he top-scored last season with ten goals. This season he is playing for Red Bull Salzburg in Austria and will have to step up a class if called on by the Czechs.

AGE 33	WORLD RANKING –

THE MANAGER

The seeds of the success of the current Czech Republic team were sown in 1997 when coach Karel Bruckner was put in charge of the Czech Under-21 team.

He led them to second spot in the 2000 European Under-21 Championship with Milan Baros scoring the goals and Petr Cech keeping them out.

His craggy features and sweep of white hair have earned him the nickname Kleki Petra because of his resemblance to a Red Indian character on a popular Czech TV show.

Bruckner was promoted to the full international side in 2001, and many of the Under-21 team moved up with him. He is a keen tactical thinker, plays chess and is regarded as a master of set pieces. He out-thought Dick Advocaat with his substitutions in the most thrilling game of Euro 2004.

In one of his teams in the 1980s, two players went to take the same free kick, collided and fell over. While opponents laughed, a third player took the kick to an unmarked forward, who duly scored. You'll have seen Manchester United use the same ploy.

KEY STRIKER

MILAN BAROS ASTON VILLA

Milan Baros forms half of an unusual striking partnership for the Czech Republic. He teams up with the lanky presence of Jan Koller and it works!

Baros claimed the Golden Boot in Euro 2004 with five goals and helped the Czechs to 35 goals in their qualification games. He brings genuine pace, movement and unsettles defenders with his direct running.

Playing record	12 mths lge	wcq
Appearances:	30	12
Minutes played:	2245	886
Percentage played:	60.8%	70.3%
Goals scored:	6	5
Percentage share:	12.00	13.51
Cards:	Y7, R1	Y3, R0
Strike rate:	374mins	177mins
Strike rate ranking:	77th	30th

| AGE 24 | STRIKER | WORLD RANKING 888 |

F

Position	1st	**2nd**	3rd	4th	5th	6th	7th	8th
Group	E	**F**	C	A	D	H	B	G
Total FIFA ranking	89	**93**	95	96	101	109	117	138

AUSTRALIA V JAPAN
Kaiserslautern, Monday 12th June 1400 BST

This match will feature the neat passing of Japan's midfielders against the Premiership wing play of Australia.
Harry Kewell and Brett Emerton will be aiming to take the ball wide and fire in crosses to feed strikers John Aloisi and Mark Viduka and hit midfielder Tim Cahill's late runs into the box.

Both sides had good defensive records in qualifying but Australia's attack contains a variety of different threats and more menace than the Japanese faced in qualifying.
The Socceroos' rugged and experienced defence will also ask a lot of Japan but it will be a fascinating clash of football cultures.

BRAZIL V CROATIA
Berlin, Tuesday 13th June 2000 BST

Brazil will be keen to get their World Cup campaign off to a winning start and although Croatia are not the attacking force they used to be, they can certainly be a difficult side to break down.
The Croatian defence, superbly marshalled by Robert Kovac of Juventus, proved just how mean it can be with six clean sheets in ten

qualifying matches and Brazil may have to show a little patience in their opening game.
Nico Kovac will be important to Croatia, protecting the defence, breaking up attacks and growling at colleagues - just like a Balkan Roy Keane. At 35, it's asking a lot but he's still a major force for Hertha Berlin in the German Bundesliga.

JAPAN V CROATIA
Nuremberg, Sunday 18th June 1400 BST

This clash between Japan and Croatia is likely to be a game of cat and mouse. The Japanese should dominate the middle of the park, while Croatia's tactics will be based around a solid defence and waiting to hit their opponents on the break. Ivan Klasnic's partnership with Miroslav Klose is raining goals for Werder Bremen (32 between them). If he clicks with Dado Prso, Croatia will win.

BRAZIL V AUSTRALIA
Munich, Sunday 18th June 1700 BST

Australia had a good Confederations Cup result against Brazil in 2001 but this Brazil team are a class apart and Australia lost to everyone in the 2005 Confederations Cup.
Man of the match could be Mark Schwarzer in the Australian goal or perm any Brazilian from around 15.

Croatia's Niko Kranjcar

JAPAN V BRAZIL
Dortmund, Thursday 22nd June 2000 BST

These teams played out a 2-2 draw in last summer's Confederations Cup with a strong Brazilian line-up scoring through Robinho and Ronaldinho while Japan answered with goals from Celtic-bound Shansuke Nakamura and Masashi Oguro in the 88th minute. However, Brazil hit a hefty 28 shots in the game and may

have done better if 19 of them hadn't flown wide.
Japan's Hidetoshi Nakata is becoming more influential for Bolton. Here's an opportunity to use everything he's learnt from Sam Allardyce about getting under the skin of top-rated teams.

CROATIA V AUSTRALIA
Stuttgart, Sunday 18th June 2000 BST

Probably the game which settles who joins Brazil in the last 16. Australia will be looking to keep it tight and Croatia may need more than a draw. The Croatians have had some poor results in recent friendlies but their wins against Sweden are a better guide to their resolve. It will come down to a test of character and sporting determination with

two strong defences dictating the result. Croatia's defence is better and their national pride is awesome.
The rising young star of Croatian football, Niko Kranjcar, was a controversial choice when father Zlatko put him into the side but the youngster provides the flair in midfield and dad needs it now.

MARTIN JOL'S VIEW

Group F is one of the most difficult groups to predict. Brazil will finish top, but who will be runners-up? It is hard to decide because there is not much daylight between Croatia, Japan and Australia.

There is no doubt that Brazil are everyone's favourites. They have the world's best player in their side in the shape of Ronaldinho. But by picking out the Barcelona star, we forget a lot of other top performers.

Brazil come to the tournament with good defenders such as Cafu, Edmilson, Lucio, Luisao (one of the tallest defenders in the tournament and Player of the Year in Portugal) and that wily old fox Roberto Carlos.

In midfield there are an absurd number of quality players to choose from. For example, if Emerson and Gilberto Silva play in central midfield, other stars like Kaka, Ze Roberto and Renato - not to mention Lyon's playmaker Juninho - will all have cause to complain to coach Carlos Alberto Parreira.

Adriano (the best target striker in the world) will be playing up front with Ronaldo, leaving Julio Baptista and Lyon's Fred out of the team. And then there is also Robinho who, if given the chance, could also be one of the best young players of the tournament.

"They have the world's best player in their side in the shape of Ronaldinho"

Croatia are, on paper, the best of the other three sides in the group, and remember, they finished third at the 1998 World Cup. They have shown they have the mental resolve to bounce back after a disappointing result and that could be an important asset in a long tournament. Their best players are the Kovac brothers, Robert and Nico, and Josip Simunic, the 1.95m tall defender of Hertha Berlin. Others to watch out for are Ivan Klasnic of Werder Bremen, who is a very good striker and will link up well with the pony-tailed Dado Prso of Glasgow Rangers.

Australia are an example of a country where the coach is the star. My fellow Dutchman Guus Hiddink has proved – after reaching the last four at the last two World Cup finals with Holland and Korea – that he knows what it takes to be successful at a big tournament. They don't have any real stars in the field, although Tim Cahill of Everton, Brett Emerton (ex Feyenoord and now

KEY MATCH

Blackburn), Harry Kewell (Liverpool), Mark Viduka (Middlesbrough) and Lucas Neill (Blackburn) are all well known names in England. Their most important player in my opinion will be John Aloisi, because of his knack of finding the back of the net – he's a real goal machine. He is often overlooked because he plays for little known Alaves in Spain. The former Coventry striker hit four goals in last year's Confederation Cup. The top-flight experience of many of their players and the sports mentality of the Australians makes me think they might finish second in this group.

In Japan football is becoming more and more important and that really does mean something as the country has a population of almost 130 million. They have a team filled with good players, but lack the technical skills of the Croatians and the physical strength of the Australians. Players like Junichi Inamoto, Shunsuke Nakamura, Shinji Ono and Naohiro Takahara have all done well at the highest level, but the country's biggest star is Hidetoshi Nakata – a superb technician and a cult figure in Japan.

Japan's trio of Nakata, Ono and Nakamura combine to make up what is probably the best midfield in Asia. They are a team for the connoisseurs but likely to be too lightweight to make it through.

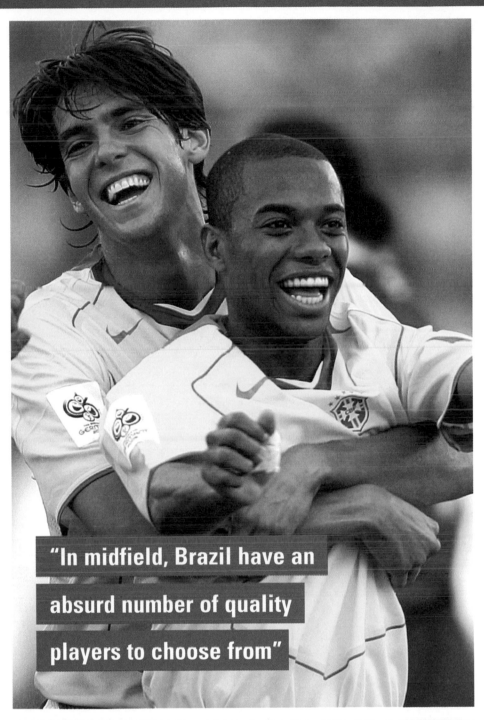

"In midfield, Brazil have an absurd number of quality players to choose from"

MARTIN JOL'S PREDICTIONS FOR THE TOP TWO TEAMS FROM THIS GROUP

Schedule of play is on page 80

GROUP STAGE	LAST SIXTEEN	QUARTER-FINALS
FIRST GROUP F	v SECOND GROUP E	v FIRST GROUP H or SECOND GROUP G
BRAZIL →	**BRAZIL v CZECH REPUBLIC** →	**BRAZIL v UKRAINE**
SECOND GROUP F	v FIRST GROUP E	v FIRST GROUP G or SECOND GROUP H
AUSTRALIA →	**AUSTRALIA v ITALY** →	**ITALY v FRANCE**

GROUP F
BRAZIL, CROATIA, AUSTRALIA, JAPAN

GROUP E
ITALY, GHANA, USA, CZECH REPUBLIC

GROUP G
FRANCE, SWITZERLAND, SOUTH KOREA, TOGO
GROUP H
SPAIN, UKRAINE, TUNISIA, SAUDI ARABIA

If England top their group and keep winning, they will meet Brazil in the semi-finals with the winner to take on either Argentina or Italy.

ROUTE TO THE FINALS

Brazil qualified by beating Argentina to first place on goal difference after both sides ended up with 24 points.

An impressive 3-0 home victory over Venezuela in their last qualifier in October, saw the world champions snatch top spot from Argentina, who lost 1-0 away to Uruguay in their last match.

Brazil won nine, drew seven and lost two of their qualifiers – 1-0 to Argentina in Buenos Aires and by the same score to Ecuador at high altitude in Quito.

Ronaldo was top scorer in the group with ten goals, three of them coming in a home win over Argentina when the Real Madrid striker won and converted a hat-trick of penalties. Adriano scored six goals from just six starts.

The main-stays of the team during qualification were Ronaldo, Cafu, Ze Roberto, Kaka, Roque Junior and Roberto Carlos who all made more than 14 appearances, while Dida played all but two of the games in goal.

For final qualification table see Paraguay.

	Date	Venue	Opposition	FIFA ranking	Result	Score	Scorers
1	07 Sep 03	Away	Colombia	25	W	1 2	Ronaldo 22, Kaka 61
2	10 Sep 03	Home	Ecuador	35	W	1 0	Ronaldinho 12
3	16 Nov 03	Away	Peru	68	D	1 1	Rivaldo 21pen
4	19 Nov 03	Home	Uruguay	18	D	3 3	Kaka 20, Ronaldo 28, 86
5	31 Mar 04	Away	Paraguay	30	D	0 0	
6	02 Jun 04	Home	Argentina	3	W	3 1	Ronaldo 16pen, 67pen, 90pen
7	06 Jun 04	Away	Chile	72	D	1 1	Fabiano 16
8	05 Sep 04	Home	Bolivia	96	W	3 1	Ronaldo 1, Ronaldinho 12pen, Adriano 44
9	09 Oct 04	Away	Venezuela	66	W	2 5	Kaka 5, 34, Ronaldo 48, 50, Adriano 75
10	13 Oct 04	Home	Colombia	25	D	0 0	
11	17 Nov 04	Away	Ecuador	35	L	1 0	
12	27 Mar 05	Home	Peru	68	W	1 0	Kaka 74
13	30 Mar 05	Away	Uruguay	18	D	1 1	Emerson 67
14	05 Jun 05	Home	Paraguay	30	W	4 1	Ronaldinho 32pen, 41pen, Ze Roberto 70, Robinho 82
15	08 Jun 05	Away	Argentina	3	L	3 1	Roberto Carlos 71
16	04 Sep 05	Home	Chile	72	W	5 0	Juan 11, Robinho 21, Adriano 27, 29, 90
17	09 Oct 05	Away	Bolivia	96	D	1 1	Pe.Juninho 25
18	12 Oct 05	Home	Venezuela	66	W	3 0	Adriano 28. Ronaldo 51. Roberto Carlos 61
	Average FIFA ranking of opposition			46			

MAIN PLAYER PERFORMANCES IN QUALIFICATION

	Appearances	Started	Subbed on	Subbed off	Mins played	% played	Goals	Yellow	Red
Goalkeepers									
Julio Cesar	2	2	0	0	180	11.1	0	0	0
Nelson Dida	16	16	0	0	1440	88.9	0	0	0
Defenders									
Alex	11	2	9	2	287	17.7	0	1	0
Juliano Belletti	2	2	0	0	180	11.1	0	2	0
Cafu	15	15	0	0	1350	83.3	0	3	0
Cicinho	1	1	0	0	90	5.6	0	0	0
Edmilson	3	3	0	1	259	16.0	0	0	0
Juan	10	9	1	0	819	50.6	1	2	0
Angelo De Sousa Junior	2	2	0	0	180	11.1	0	0	0
Lucio	10	10	0	0	888	54.8	0	1	1
Roberto Carlos	15	15	0	1	1325	81.8	2	1	0
Roque Junior	14	14	0	0	1260	77.8	0	3	0
Midfielders									
Emerson	9	9	0	5	673	41.5	1	1	0
Gilberto Silva	10	7	3	0	689	42.5	0	3	0
Pernambucano Juninho	11	7	4	7	554	34.2	1	0	0
Ricardo Kaka	15	13	2	7	1112	68.6	5	2	0
Anderson Luisao	2	2	0	0	180	11.1	0	0	0
Renato	13	6	7	3	654	40.4	0	0	0
Ricardo Rodrigues	2	0	2	0	72	4.4	0	0	0
Jose Ze Roberto	14	14	0	3	1207	74.5	1	2	0
Forwards									
Adriano	9	6	3	2	563	34.8	6	1	0
Luis Fabiano	4	2	2	1	233	14.4	1	0	0
Ricardo Oliveira	2	1	1	1	78	4.8	0	0	0
Robinho	8	4	4	2	439	27.1	2	0	0
Ronaldinho	11	11	0	3	909	56.1	4	3	0
Ronaldo	15	15	0	2	1285	79.3	10	1	0

Match: 1 2 3 4 5 6 7 8 9 10 11 12 13 14 15 16 17 18
Venue: A H A H A H A H A H A H A H A H A H
Result: W W D D D W D W W W D L W D W L W D W

FINAL PROSPECTS

Brazil are favourites to win the World Cup for a sixth time when the tournament gets going in Germany.

Head coach Carlos Alberto Parreira will have a star-studded squad of players to work with and his biggest headache will probably be choosing which of his galaxy of superstars should be in the starting line-up and who should be left on the bench.

Brazil's attacking options are endless, with Ronaldinho, Ronaldo, Oliveira, Adriano and Robinho all capable of winning a match single-handedly.

AC Milan's Dida has matured into one of the best goalkeepers in the world and has become Brazil's first-choice shot-stopper, although he has not been at his very best for his club this season.

Parreira has already confirmed that 35-year-old right-back Cafu will captain the side, if fit. His full back partner will be the indefatigable Roberto Carlos.

Bayern Munich central defender Lucio was outstanding at the last World Cup and is the linchpin at the back. Fellow central defender Roque Junior of Bayer Leverkusen has his critics, but has rarely let his country down.

Juventus midfielder Emerson and Arsenal's Gilberto Silva can play a holding role, if necessary in the middle of the park, while the playmakers ahead of them include Kaka, Juninho, Ze Roberto and Julio Baptista.

Brazil have quality players in every position and the vast majority of the squad currently play for top-flight European clubs. An astonishing 161 Brazilians are registered with clubs in

> **"Adriano (the best target striker in the world) will be playing up front with Ronaldo."**
> Martin Jol

Europe's top six leagues. They will be used to the pitch and climatic conditions.

The five-times world champions will expect to stroll through Group F but could face Italy in the last 16 and Spain in the quarter-finals.

Brazil's soccer-mad supporters will expect a convincing and stylish victory in Germany.

It's hard to think of any previous tournament where the quality and depth of their squad has looked so formidable.

GROUP FIXTURES

CROATIA	Tues 13 June 2000 BST
AUSTRALIA	Sun 18 June 1700 BST
JAPAN	Thurs 22 June 2000 BST

Brasilia

Zone	South America
Population	187,412,164
Capital	Brasilia
Language	Portuguese
Top league	Campeonato
Major clubs	**Capacities**
Sao Paulo	80,000
Corinthians	38,800
Cruzeiro	82,000

Where likely squad players play:

In Premiership	1	In Spain	7
In Holland	2	In France	1
In Italy	6	In Germany	3

Number of Brazilian players playing:

In Premiership	5	In Spain	43
In Holland	13	In France	32
In Italy	36	In Germany	32

World Cup record

1930 -	Group 2nd	1974 -	Fourth place
1934 -	Round 1	1978 -	Third place
1938 -	Third place	1982 -	Round 2
1950 -	Runners-up	1986 -	Quarter-finals
1954 -	Quarter-finals	1990 -	Last 16
1958 -	Champions	1994 -	Champions
1962 -	Champions	1998 -	Runners-up
1966 -	Group 3rd	2002 -	Champions
1970 -	Champions		

KEY PLAYER

RONALDINHO BARCELONA

Real Madrid were being humiliated by their old rivals Barcelona – a 3-0 defeat in front of their home fans.
Yet the proud Real fans weren't booing! They were applauding, first grudgingly then enthusiastically, the skills of one man – Ronaldinho. He had twice cut through their defence to score superb individual goals and had run the game throughout.

Consistently voted the world's best player by his peers, Ronaldinho joined Barca in 2003 and helped transform them into arguably the best club side in the world. His only weakness used to be not scoring enough goals and he's put that right!
Ronaldinho is a Top 12 Striker
Other Brazilian Top Players are Lucio, Juninho, Kaka and Ronaldo

AGE 26	STRIKER	WORLD RANKING 5

THE SQUAD

Goalkeepers	Club side	Age	QG
Julio Cesar	Inter Milan	26	2
Nelson Dida	AC Milan	32	16
Heurelho Gomes	PSV Eindhoven	24	1
Defenders			
Alex	PSV Eindhoven	23	11
Juliano Belletti	Barcelona	29	2
Cafu	AC Milan	35	15
Cicinho	Real Madrid	25	1
Edmilson	Barcelona	29	3
Gilberto	Hertha Berlin	29	1
Juan	B Leverkusen	27	10
Junior	Sao Paulo	32	2
Lucio	Bayern Munich	28	10
Anderson Luisao	Benfica	25	2
Gustavo Nery	W Bremen	28	1
Roberto Carlos	Real Madrid	33	15
Roque Junior	B Leverkusen	29	14
Midfielders			
Julio Cesar Baptista	Real Madrid	24	3
Diego	Porto	21	1
Edu	Valencia	28	5
Elano	Shakhtar Donetsk	24	1
Emerson	Juventus	30	9
Gilberto Silva	Arsenal	29	10
Pernambucano Juninho	Lyon	31	11
Ricardo Kaka	AC Milan	24	15
Renato	Seville	27	13
Jose Ze Roberto	Bayern Munich	31	14
Forwards			
Adriano	Inter Milan	24	9
Luis Fabiano	Seville	25	4
Ricardo Oliveira	Real Betis	26	2
Robinho	Real Madrid	22	8
Ronaldinho	Barcelona	26	11
Ronaldo	Real Madrid	29	15

■ Probable ■ Possible **QG** Qualification Games

KEY GOALKEEPER

NELSON DIDA
AC MILAN

Nelson Dida currently holds the goalkeeping jersey for Brazil but the competition is mounting.

The 1.96m tall keeper played for two of Brazil's most famous clubs Cruzeiro and Corinthians, before joining FC Lugano in Switzerland. A move to AC Milan saw him establish himself as one of the top keepers in Italy's Serie A. He gets down quickly for a big man and has a reputation as a penalty saver.

Dida has not been at his best for Milan this season and coach Carlos Algerto Parreira has warned him about his form but he is a class act, who has rarely let his country down.

Playing record	12 mths lge	wcq
Appearances:	42	16
Minutes played:	3780	1440
Percentage played:	95.5%	88.9%
Goals conceded:	35	15
Clean sheets:	17	6
Cards:	Y0, R0	Y0, R0
Defensive rating:	108mins	96mins
Defensive ranking:	9th	14th

AGE 32 | **WORLD RANKING 62**

KEY DEFENDERS

LUCIO
BAYERN MUNICH

Lucio came to the fore in the 2001/2 season as the central defender keeping Bayer Leverkusen's triple trophy assault on track.

He was out-playing top Bundesliga forwards in the German league and cup games and Manchester United's strikers in the semi-finals of the Champions League.

And, when he had a spare moment, he was racing forward to join the attack.

Lucio and Leverkusen's German stars ended up three times losers, beaten in two finals and runners-up in the league.

However, most of them met up again two months later in the 2002 World Cup final and this time Lucio did get his hands on a trophy when Brazil beat Germany.

He is still one of the best Bundesliga defenders, only now he's playing with Bayern Munich - and he's also won the German league and cup double that eluded him in 2002.

He is a Top 12 Defender.

AGE 28 | **WORLD RANKING 28**

ROQUE JUNIOR
B LEVERKUSEN

Playing record	12 mths lge	wcq
Appearances:	18	14
Minutes played:	1522	1260
Percentage played:	45.7%	77.8%
Goals conceded:	31	16
Clean sheets:	0	3
Cards:	Y2, R2	Y3, R0
Defensive rating:	49mins	79mins
Defensive ranking:	109th	77th

AGE 29 | **WORLD RANKING 881**

ROBERTO CARLOS
REAL MADRID

Roberto Carlos remains one of the best attacking left-backs around. He is world renowned for his forays up the flank and ferocious free-kick, and despite his age, is still an effective threat for Brazil.

Playing record	12 mths lge	wcq
Appearances:	40	15
Minutes played:	3576	1325
Percentage played:	96.9%	81.8%
Goals conceded:	36	12
Clean sheets:	17	6
Cards:	Y6, R0	Y1, R0
Defensive rating:	99mins	110mins
Defensive ranking:	36th	61st

AGE 33 | **WORLD RANKING 134**

CAFU
AC MILAN

Cafu is Brazil's most capped player with over 140 caps and has been first-choice right back for over a decade. In 2002 he became the first player to appear in three World Cup finals and has already been named Brazil's captain for the 2006 tournament.

Playing record	12 mths lge	wcq
Appearances:	26	15
Minutes played:	1792	1350
Percentage played:	45.3%	83.3%
Goals conceded:	15	14
Clean sheets:	14	6
Cards:	Y3, R0	Y3, R0
Defensive rating:	119mins	96mins
Defensive ranking:	17th	69th

AGE 35 | **WORLD RANKING 259**

THE MANAGER

Carlos Alberto Parreira guided Brazil to World Cup glory in 1994 and is now in his third spell as head coach of the South American giants.

Parreira's current stint in charge of the Selecao began when he took over from Luiz Felipe Scolari after Brazil's 2002 World Cup-winning campaign. His previous periods were 1983-84 and 1991-94.

His first involvement with the Brazilian national set-up came in 1970 when he acted as fitness trainer for the squad that won the World Cup against Italy in Mexico in such brilliant style.

Parreira's globetrotting coaching career has also seen him lead three other countries – Kuwait (1982), United Arab Emirates (1990) and Saudi Arabia (1998) – to the World Cup finals.

At club level, he has been involved with a huge range of clubs including Vasco da Gama, New York Metro Stars, Valencia, and Fenerbahce.

Parreira never played professional football.

ONE TO WATCH

ROBINHO REAL MADRID

Robinho is known as the Pearl of Brazilian football. A free-scoring striker capable of some outrageous pieces of skill, he moved to Spain in summer 2005 when Real Madrid signed him for £12m from FC Santos. He was one of Brazil's stars when they when they won the 2005 Confederations Cup. He can find space with jinking runs and calmly puts away his chances.

Playing record	12 mths lge	wcq
Appearances:	24	8
Minutes played:	1730	439
Percentage played:	46.9%	27.1%
Goals scored:	7	2
Percentage share:	8.64	5.71
Cards:	Y3, R0	Y0, R0
Strike rate:	247mins	219mins
Power ranking:	58th	40th

AGE 22   **STRIKER**   **WORLD RANKING –**

KEY MIDFIELDERS

EMERSON
JUVENTUS

The skipper of Brazil going into the 2002 World Cup, Emerson Ferreira da Rosa saw his chances of lifting the trophy end when he dislocated his shoulder.

Cafu took over and led the Brazilians to a resounding victory.

Emerson is a midfield all-rounder who, alongside Patrick Vieira, makes up the heart of the Juventus engine room.

He has played in Europe since 1997, first for Bayer Leverkusen and then for Roma, who he helped to a Serie A title in his first season, 2000/1.

He moved to Italian league champions Juventus when the Turin club signed him for the start of the 2004/5 season.

Playing record	12 mths lge	wcq
Appearances:	37	9
Minutes played:	3203	673
Percentage played:	80.9%	41.5%
Goals scored:	1	1
Goals conceded:	24	7
Cards:	Y4, R0	Y1, R0
Power rating:	50mins	42mins
Power ranking:	45th	36th

AGE 30	WORLD RANKING 50

GILBERTO
HERTHA BERLIN

Playing record	12 mths lge	wcq
Appearances:	26	1
Minutes played:	2105	57
Percentage played:	63.2%	3.5%
Goals scored:	3	0
Goals conceded:	25	1
Cards:	Y2, R2	Y0, R0
Power rating:	54mins	1000mins
Power ranking:	59th	136th

AGE 29	WORLD RANKING 251

KAKA
AC MILAN

Ricardo Kaka is the man charged with making all Brazil's attacking talent click.

The AC Milan youngster is the playmaker behind the front two for the world champions. He is a Top 12 Midfielder.

AGE 24	WORLD RANKING 24

GILBERTO SILVA
ARSENAL

Playing record	12 mths lge	wcq
Appearances:	31	10
Minutes played:	2686	689
Percentage played:	72.8%	42.5%
Goals scored:	2	0
Goals conceded:	21	8
Cards:	Y4, R1	Y3, R0
Power rating:	55mins	53mins
Power ranking:	64th	81st

AGE 29	WORLD RANKING 197

ZE ROBERTO
BAYERN MUNICH

Bayern Munich midfielder Ze Roberto can operate equally as well on the the left wing or as a holding player in front of the back four. His versatility will be a great asset in Germany.

Playing record	12 mths lge	wcq
Appearances:	27	14
Minutes played:	1927	1207
Percentage played:	57.9%	74.5%
Goals scored:	1	1
Percentage share:	1.23	2.86
Cards:	Y3, R0	Y2, R0
Strike rate:	927mins	207mins
Power ranking:	90th	37th

AGE 31	WORLD RANKING 499

KEY STRIKERS

ADRIANO
INTER MILAN

Adriano is a quick, powerful striker who is dangerous in the air. He struck 16 league goals for Inter Milan last season as the team finished third in the Italian league.

A shoulder injury limited his effectiveness at the start of the 2005-06 campaign but he has regained his fitness and goalscoring form.

He signed for Parma at the start of the 2002/3 season and lined up with Romanian striker Adrian Mutu.

The two seemed to bring out the best in each other and goals flowed. Inter re-signed him from their financially troubled rivals in 2004 and the Brazilian's career has flourished since returning to the San Siro.

He was the Player of the Tournament for Brazil when they won the 2005 Confederations Cup and is likely to beat off the challenge from Robinho for a place in the Brazilian starting line-up alongside Ronaldo.

Playing record	12 mths lge	wcq
Appearances:	36	9
Minutes played:	2567	563
Percentage played:	64.8%	34.8%
Goals scored:	14	6
Percentage share:	19.44	17.14
Cards:	Y1, R0	Y1, R0
Strike rate:	183mins	94mins
Power ranking:	32nd	8th

AGE 24	WORLD RANKING 122

KEY STRIKER

RONALDO REAL MADRID

Ronaldo will go down in history as the player who won and lost a World Cup for Brazil.
In 1998 he suffered a mysterious illness just before the final against France, played when clearly not fit and was widely thought to have cost Brazil their chance.
However, he won the cup in 2002 when he scored twice as Brazil beat Germany.

He has still not won over the Real Madrid fans but he did lead Brazil through their qualifying campaign, scoring ten times.
He also scored 21 goals for Real last season while Raul was struggling.
He remains Brazil's number one striker despite the continued good form of Adriano and the emergence of Robinho, who is now his club colleague at Real.

AGE 29   STRIKER   WORLD RANKING 9

ROUTE TO THE FINALS

Croatia reached their third successive World Cup finals after finishing top of European Group 8, ahead of fellow qualifiers Sweden.

The tough group also included Hungary and Bulgaria, but the Croatians were unbeaten, winning seven and drawing three of their ten matches. They ending up with 24 points, the same number as Sweden, but claimed top spot after recording home and away victories over their Scandinavian rivals.

A 3-0 home win against Hungary in their first match set the tone for Croatia's excellent campaign. This was followed by a 1-0 win over Sweden in Gothenburg, with Darijo Srna scoring with a 63rd-minute free-kick.

Srna was Croatia's match-winner again when they beat the Swedes 1-0 in Zagreb last October. This time the Shakhtar Donestsk midfielder hit the winner from the penalty spot on 56 minutes. A goalless draw with Hungary four days later secured first place.

Manager Zlatko Kranjcar turned his shortage of top-class resources to advantage in qualifying by operating from a tight-knit group of top club players.

He used his experienced defenders and ball-winning midfielders to make the team incredibly hard to break down. The side only conceded five goals in the ten qualifiers.

Dado Prso burdened the responsibility of netting the goals and top-scored with five but Niko Kranjcar, who plays as a deep-lying striker notched two and Srna five from midfield.

FINAL QUALIFYING TABLE
EUROPE GROUP 8

	P	W	D	L	GF	GA	Pts
Croatia	10	7	3	0	21	5	24
Sweden	10	8	0	2	30	4	24
Bulgaria	10	4	3	3	17	17	15
Hungary	10	4	2	4	13	14	14
Iceland	10	1	1	8	14	27	4
Malta	10	0	3	7	4	32	3

					FIFA ranking				
1	04 Sep 04	Home	Hungary	67	W	**3 0**	Prso 31, 54, Gyepes 80og
2	08 Sep 04	Away	Sweden	13	W	**0 1**	Srna 63
3	09 Oct 04	Home	Bulgaria	42	D	**2 2**	Srna 16, 32pen
4	26 Mar 05	Home	Iceland	93	W	**4 0**	N.Kovac 39, 76, Simunic 71, Prso 90
5	30 Mar 05	Home	Malta	132	W	**3 0**	Prso 24, 35, Tudor 80
6	04 Jun 05	Away	Bulgaria	42	W	**1 3**	Babic 18, Tudor 58, Kranjcar 80
7	03 Sep 05	Away	Iceland	93	W	**1 3**	Balaban 56, 61, Srna 82pen
8	07 Sep 05	Away	Malta	132	D	**1 1**	Kranjcar 19
9	08 Oct 05	Home	Sweden	13	W	**1 0**	Srna 56pen
10	12 Oct 05	Away	Hungary	67	D	**0 0**	
	Average FIFA ranking of opposition			**69**			

MAIN PLAYER PERFORMANCES IN QUALIFICATION

Match	1 2 3 4 5 6 7 8 9 10	Appearances	Started	Subbed on	Subbed off	Mins played	% played	Goals	Yellow	Red
Venue	H A H H H A A A A H									
Result	W W D W W W W D W D									
Goalkeepers										
Tomislav Butina		8	8	0	0	720	80.0	0	0	0
Stipe Pletikosa		2	2	0	0	180	20.0	0	0	0
Defenders										
Robert Kovac		8	8	0	2	692	76.9	0	4	0
Anthony Seric		2	2	0	2	150	16.7	0	1	0
Dario Simic		4	2	2	1	261	29.0	0	0	0
Josip Simunic		8	8	0	0	720	80.0	1	3	0
Mario Tokic		5	3	2	0	294	32.7	0	1	0
Stjepan Tomas		5	5	0	0	450	50.0	0	1	0
Igor Tudor		8	8	0	0	720	80.0	2	2	0
Midfielders										
Marko Babic		9	9	0	1	801	89.0	1	3	0
Ivica Banovic		1	0	1	0	14	1.6	0	0	0
Nico Kovac		9	9	0	1	765	85.0	2	2	0
Ivan Leko		3	3	0	2	230	25.6	0	0	0
Jerko Leko		7	1	6	1	208	23.1	0	0	0
Darijo Srna		9	8	1	0	727	80.8	5	3	0
Jurica Vranjes		5	4	1	0	374	41.6	0	1	0
Forwards										
Bosko Balaban		5	3	2	1	272	30.2	2	0	0
Ivan Bosnjak		6	1	5	2	153	17.0	0	0	0
Ivan Klasnic		8	7	1	5	487	54.1	0	0	0
Niko Kranjcar		9	8	1	3	678	75.3	2	2	0
Ivica Mornar		1	1	0	1	83	9.2	0	0	0
Ivica Olic		5	2	3	2	276	30.7	0	1	0
Dado Prso		9	8	1	2	735	81.7	5	1	0

FINAL PROSPECTS

Croatia will go to Germany expecting to make it through to at least the second round, even though they are drawn in the same group as world champions Brazil.

Croatia will be confident of getting the better of a Japanese side that may struggle at the back and also the Australians, despite the large number of Premiership players in the Socceroos squad.

The Croatians may no longer have that magnificent group of attacking players - Zvonimir Boban, Robert Prosinecki and Davor Suker – in their squad and the current side lacks creativity, but 21 goals in their ten qualifiers shows they can put the ball into the back of the net.

Head coach Zlatko Kranchar likes his team to play to a set pattern and build their attacks from the back. Croatia will be a difficult team to score goals against – they conceded just five in their ten qualifiers – and could emerge as one of the dark horses of the tournament.

A number of Croatian stars play their club football in Germany and will feel at home there. Australian-born central defender Josip Simunic and midfielder Nico Kovac (Robert's brother) are at Hertha Berlin, midfielder Marko Babic plays for Bayer Leverkusen, while pacy striker Ivan Klasnic has been playing Champions League football with Werder Bremen.

Klasnic was actually born in Hamburg and turned down an invitation to play for Germany in favour of Croatia, the birthplace of his parents.

> **"Croatia are, on paper, the best of the other three sides in the group, and remember, they finished third at the 1998 World Cup."**
> Martin Jol

Dado Prso has returned from a long lay-off with Rangers and their results without him show how important the pony-tailed striker is to the side.

Darijo Srna has a good scoring record from the flank and hit five in qualifying. Finally there's Serie A class at the back with Juventus' recent acquisition Robert Kovac and Igor Tudor from Siena.

They also have a possible young star of the tournament in the manager's son, Niko Kranjcar.

GROUP FIXTURES

BRAZIL	Tue 13 June 2000 BST
JAPAN	Sun 18 June 1400 BST
AUSTRALIA	Thu 22 June 2000 BST

KEY PLAYER

DADO PRSO RANGERS

Dado Prso leads the Croatian attack. He hit a record-equalling four goals for Monaco in a Champions League game against Deportivo in 2003/4. Monaco reached the final that year and Prso subsequently transferred to Rangers. He has a powerful build, good touch and is strong in the air.

Robert Kovac is a Top 12 Defender.

Playing record	12 mths lge	wcq
Appearances:	34	9
Minutes played:	2735	735
Percentage played:	74.1%	81.7%
Goals scored:	14	5
Percentage share:	19.18	23.81
Cards:	Y5, R1	Y1, R0
Strike rate:	195mins	147mins
Strike rate ranking:	44th	23rd

AGE 31 | **STRIKER** | **WORLD RANKING 761**

Zagreb

Zone	Europe
Population	4,493,147
Capital	Zagreb
Language	Croatian
Top league	Croatian 1 HNL
Major clubs	**Capacities**
Dinamo Zagreb	40,000
Hajduk Split	35,000
Rijeka	11,000

Where likely squad players play:

In Premiership	0	In Spain	0
In Holland	0	In France	0
In Italy	3	In Germany	6

Number of Croatian players playing:

In Premiership	1	In Spain	0
In Holland	1	In France	1
In Italy	4	In Germany	14

World Cup record

1930 -	Did not enter	1974 -	Did not enter
1934 -	Did not enter	1978 -	Did not enter
1938 -	Did not enter	1982 -	Did not enter
1950 -	Did not enter	1986 -	Did not enter
1954 -	Did not enter	1990 -	Did not enter
1958 -	Did not enter	1994 -	Did not enter
1962 -	Did not enter	1998 -	Third place
1966 -	Did not enter	2002 -	Group 3rd
1970 -	Did not enter		

THE SQUAD

Goalkeepers	Club side	Age	QG
Tomislav Butina	Club Brugge	31	8
Joey Didulica	Austria Vienna	28	0
Stipe Pletikosa	Hajduk Split	27	2
Vedran Runje	Standard Liege	29	0
Defenders			
Ivan Bosnjak	Dinamo Zagreb	27	0
Robert Kovac	Juventus	32	8
Ibica Karznac	Zenit	27	0
Anthony Seric	Panathinaikos	27	2
Dario Simic	AC Milan	30	4
Josip Simunic	Hertha Berlin	28	8
Mario Tokic	Austria Vienna	30	5
Stjepan Tomas	Galatasaray	30	5
Igor Tudor	Siena	28	8
Midfielders			
Marko Babic	B Leverkusen	25	9
Ivica Banovic	Nuremberg	25	1
Nico Kovac	Hertha Berlin	34	9
Ivan Leko	Club Brugge	28	3
Jerko Leko	Dinamo Kiev	26	7
Darijo Srna	Shakhtar Donetsk	24	9
Jurica Vranjes	W Bremen	26	5
Davor Vujrinuc	Rijeko	29	0
Forwards			
Bosko Balaban	Club Brugge	27	5
Ivan Bosnjak	Dinamo Zagreb	26	6
Ivan Klasnic	W Bremen	26	8
Niko Kranjcar	Dinamo Zagreb	21	9
Ivica Mornar	Portsmouth	32	1
Ivica Olic	CSKA Moscow	26	5
Dado Prso	Rangers	31	9

■ Probable ■ Possible **QG** Qualification Games

KEY GOALKEEPER

TOMISLAV BUTINA
CLUB BRUGGE

Tomislav Butina plays his club football in Belgium for Brugge, having joined them from Dinamo Zagreb in 2002.

He lines up behind one of the most formidable and experienced back-lines in the 2006 competition. He played in eight of the qualifying games – only missing out on the disappointing 1-1 draw with Malta and a 3-1 win over Iceland – with Shakhtar Donetsk's Stipe Pletikosa taking over for these two qualifiers.

If fit, Butina is likely to be first choice in Germany though, as his younger rival Pletikosa has let in some soft goals in previous tournaments.

AGE 31 | **WORLD RANKING -**

THE MANAGER

Zlatko 'Cico' Kranjcar took over as Croatia coach from Otto Baric after the team failed to progress beyond the group stage at Euro 2004.

As a player, Kranjcar made his name as a centre forward with his hometown club

KEY DEFENDERS

ROBERT KOVAC
JUVENTUS

Robert Kovac's reputation as one of the game's top man-markers has taken him to some of the best side's in Europe.

He was born in Berlin but retained Croatian nationality despite playing all his early club football in Germany.

He left Nuremberg for Bayer Leverkusen and after five years of rave notices at the BayArena, Bayern Munich coach Ottmar Hitzfeld took Kovac to join his brother Nico at the champions.

Robert Kovac won the Bundesliga in 2003 and again in 2005 before being enticed away to join Italian champions Juventus last summer. He's been a fixture at the back for Croatia through three tournaments.

He is a Top 12 Defender.

AGE 32 | **WORLD RANKING 104**

JOSIP SIMUNIC
HERTHA BERLIN

Playing record	12 mths lge	wcq
Appearances:	27	8
Minutes played:	2346	720
Percentage played:	70.5%	80.0%
Goals conceded:	32	5
Clean sheets:	10	4
Cards:	Y10, R0	Y3, R0
Defensive rating:	73mins	144mins
Defensive ranking:	84th	47th

AGE 28 | **WORLD RANKING 483**

Dinamo Zagreb and won 11 full international caps for Yugoslavia between 1977 and 1983.

He also won two caps for Croatia in the early 1990's after the country gained its independence from Yugoslavia.

Kranjcar ended his playing career in Austria with Rapid Vienna and then took up coaching. He moved back to Croatia and guided Dinamo Zagreb (twice) and then NK Zagreb to Croatian league title wins before taking charge of the national squad.

He has been an instant success, having brought in a number of promising young players, including his own son Niko, the Hajduk Split striker.

The 49-year-old Kranjcar has a softly-softly approach with the players but strongly denies he lacks authority.

KEY MIDFIELDERS

NICO KOVAC
HERTHA BERLIN

The experience of Nico Kovac is crucial to the Croatian team.

He plays in arguably the most effective midfield in the Bundesliga with Brazilian Gilberto and the inventive Yildiray Basturk, at Hertha Berlin. Kovac adds steel and purpose and he won the German title with Bayern Munich in 2003.

His Croatia debut came in 1996 and he was part of Davor Suker's team that finished third in the 1998 World Cup finals. His younger brother Robert plays in the Croatian defence.

Playing record	12 mths lge	wcq
Appearances:	33	9
Minutes played:	2669	765
Percentage played:	80.2%	85.0%
Goals scored:	3	2
Goals conceded:	32	5
Cards:	Y7, R0	Y2, R0
Power rating:	58mins	38mins
Power ranking:	74th	25th

AGE 34 | **WORLD RANKING 149**

MARKO BABIC
B LEVERKUSEN

Playing record	12 mths lge	wcq
Appearances:	24	9
Minutes played:	1279	801
Percentage played:	37.4%	89.0%
Goals scored:	2	1
Goals conceded:	25	5
Cards:	Y6, R0	Y3, R0
Power rating:	47mins	50mins
Power ranking:	35th	72nd

AGE 24 | **WORLD RANKING 867**

JURICA VRANJES
W BREMEN

Playing record	12 mths lge	wcq
Appearances:	25	5
Minutes played:	1055	374
Percentage played:	30.8%	41.6%
Goals scored:	1	0
Goals conceded:	9	2
Cards:	Y1, R0	Y1, R0
Power rating:	48mins	53mins
Power ranking:	39th	82nd

AGE 26 | **WORLD RANKING 935**

KEY STRIKERS

NIKO KRANJAR
Dinamo Zagreb

No one was too surprised when coach Zlatko Kranjcar put his son into the team.

Niko Kranjcar had long been seen as the next great Croatian footballer and had played in all the nation's youth teams. He can play as a striker or in midfield.

AGE 22 | **WORLD RANKING -**

IVAN KLASNIC
W BREMEN

Playing record	12 mths lge	wcq
Appearances:	28	8
Minutes played:	2094	487
Percentage played:	62.9%	54.1%
Goals scored:	14	0
Percentage share:	17.50	0.00
Cards:	Y1, R0	Y0, R0
Strike rate:	150mins	-
Power ranking:	20th	-

AGE 26 | **WORLD RANKING 240**

ONE TO WATCH

IGOR TUDOR SIENA

Croatia has important experience and power in 1.92m Igor Tudor. He played three seasons at Hadjuk Split before joining Juventus in 1998 where he was honed into a far more tactically aware player.

Three Scudetto titles later, he moved on to Siena in March 2005 helping them avoid relegation last season. He can play a holding role in midfield or at centre half.

Playing record	12 mths lge	wcq
Appearances:	32	8
Minutes played:	2795	720
Percentage played:	70.6%	80.0%
Goals conceded:	50	2
Clean sheets:	8	6
Cards:	Y12, R1	Y2, R0
Defensive rating:	56mins	360mins
Defensive ranking:	107th	15th

AGE 28 | **DEFENDER** | **WORLD RANKING 984**

ROUTE TO THE FINALS

Australia have reached the World Cup finals for the first time in 32 years.

They qualified by the skin of their teeth, beating Uruguay 4-2 on penalties at the end of a dramatic Oceania-South America play-off at Sydney's Telstra Stadium in November.

Uruguay, who finished fifth in the South American Group, won the first leg 1-0 in Montevideo, but Marco Bresciano's 34th minute goal gave Australia a 1-0 victory in the second match to set up a nail-biting penalty shoot-out in front of their own fans.

Substitute John Aloisi converted the decisive spot-kick to send Australia through after Middlesbrough goalkeeper Mark Schwarzer had produced brilliant saves to deny Dario Rodriguez and Marcelo Zalayeta.

Australia had earlier cruised through their Oceania qualifiers. The Socceroos won four of their five group matches, scoring 21 goals and conceding three. Tim Cahill top-scored for the Aussies, hitting seven from midfield.

FINAL QUALIFYING TABLE
OCEANIA STAGE 2

	P	W	D	L	GF	GA	Pts
Australia	5	4	1	0	21	3	13
Solomon Islands	5	3	1	1	9	6	10
New Zealand	5	3	0	2	17	5	9
Fiji	5	1	1	3	3	10	4
Tahiti	5	1	1	3	2	24	4
Vanuatu	5	1	0	4	5	9	3

Group Play-off
Australia beat The Solomon Islands
S America and Oceania Play-off
Australia beat Uruguay

#	Date		Venue	FIFA ranking	Result			Scorers
1	29 May 04	Home	New Zealand	106	W	1	0	Bresciano 40
2	31 May 04	Home	Tahiti	132	W	9	0	Cahill 14, 47, Skoko 43, Simon 44og, Sterjovski 51, 61, 74, Zdrilic 85, Chipperfield 89
3	02 Jun 04	Home	Fiji	137	W	6	1	Madaschi 6, 50, Cahill 39, 66, 75, Elrich 89
4	04 Jun 04	Away	Vanuatu	146	W	0	3	Aloisi 25, 85, Emerton 81
5	06 Jun 04	Away	Solomon Islands	134	D	2	2	Cahill 50, Emerton 52
6	03 Sep 05	Home	Solomon Islands	134	W	7	0	Culina 20, Viduka 36, 43, Cahill 57, Chipperfield 64, Thompson 68, Emerton 89
7	06 Sep 05	Away	Solomon Islands	134	W	1	2	Thompson 19, Emerton 58
8	12 Nov 05	Away	Uruguay	18	L	1	0	
9	16 Nov 05	Home	Uruguay	18	W	1	0	Bresciano 35
	Average FIFA ranking of opposition	107						

MAIN PLAYER PERFORMANCES IN QUALIFICATION

Match	1 2 3 4 5 6 7 8 9	Appearances	Started	Subbed on	Subbed off	Mins played	% played	Goals	Yellow	Red
Venue	H H H A A H A A H									
Result	W W W W D W W L W									
Goalkeepers										
Zeljko Kalac		6	6	0	0	540	64.3	0	1	0
Mark Schwarzer		3	3	0	0	300	35.7	0	0	0
Defenders										
Patrick Kisnorbo		3	2	1	0	186	22.1	0	2	1
Adrian Madaschi		4	3	1	0	289	34.4	2	0	0
Lucas Neill		4	4	0	0	390	46.4	0	1	0
David Tarka		2	2	0	1	135	16.1	0	0	0
Tony Vidmar		7	7	0	0	660	78.6	0	2	0
Midfielders										
Mark Bresciano		5	3	2	1	347	41.3	2	1	0
Tim Cahill		6	6	0	1	525	62.5	7	0	0
Scott Chipperfield		6	6	0	1	546	65.0	2	1	0
Jason Culina		4	4	0	0	390	46.4	1	1	0
Ahmad Elrich		4	0	4	0	162	19.3	0	0	0
Brett Emerton		8	8	0	2	694	82.6	4	1	0
Vincenzo Grella		8	7	1	0	680	81.0	0	1	0
Harry Kewell		2	1	1	0	179	21.3	0	1	0
Stan Lazaridis		4	3	1	1	249	29.6	0	1	0
Jade North		5	4	1	0	398	47.4	0	0	0
Josip Skoko		6	5	1	2	396	47.1	1	0	0
Forwards										
John Aloisi		7	5	2	2	414	49.3	2	1	0
Alex Brosque		3	2	1	2	153	18.2	0	0	0
Archie Thompson		3	1	2	1	170	20.2	2	0	0
Mark Viduka		4	4	0	2	333	39.6	2	0	0
Massimiliano Vieri		3	3	0	3	169	20.1	0	0	0
David Zdrilic		3	2	1	1	185	22.0	1	0	0

FINAL PROSPECTS

When the Socceroos last qualified for the World Cup finals in was held in Germany – in 1974.

They lost their first two group matches, managed a meaningless goalless draw against Chile and returned home without having scored a goal.

However, this Australia are a much stronger side and have a world-class head coach in Guus Hiddink. Their squad is packed with full-time professionals who play for top-flight European clubs.

Goalkeeper Mark Schwarzer is back in favour at Middlesbrough, having being dropped in January. Striker Mark Viduka also plays for Boro but is having a bits and pieces season. Defender Lucas Neill and midfielder Brett Emerton team up on the right flank at Blackburn, while midfielder Tim Cahill and winger Harry Kewell are both having good runs of form on Merseyside.

Cahill is a real find, taking his Everton form into the qualifiers he top-scored in

> **"The top-flight experience of many of their players and the sports mentality of the Australians makes me think they might finish second in this group."**
> Martin Jol

the Oceania Group with seven goals.

Don't underestimate John Aloisi, who's having a top-scoring season in Spain with relegation battling Alaves. He also has an astonishing scoring record at international level.

The Socceroos have had some good results in recent years, against France and Brazil in the 2001 Confederations Cup, and they beat England 3-1 in a friendly in 2003.

The match will be remembered for the quality of the Australian victory but it also saw striker Wayne Rooney make his debut for England.

They will be well-prepared by Hiddink and expect to reach the second round. The match against Croatia will probably decide which of the two sides join Brazil in the last 16.

There is a strange rivalry here as Australia has a large Balkans population and some of the Croatian players come from Australia.

GROUP FIXTURES

JAPAN	Mon 12 June 1400 BST
BRAZIL	Sun 18 June 1700 BST
CROATIA	Thu 22 June 2000 BST

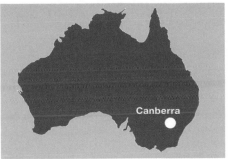

Canberra

Zone	Oceania
Population	20,153,745
Capital	Canberra
Language	English
Top league	Hyundai A-League
Major clubs	**Capacities**
Queensland Roar	52,000
Sydney FC	41,000
Melbourne Victory	18,500

Where likely squad players play:

In Premiership	8
In other major five European Leagues	3
Outside major European Leagues	12

Number of Australian players playing:

In Premiership	10
In other major five European Leagues	10

World Cup record

1930 -	Did not enter	1974 -	Group 4th
1934 -	Did not enter	1978 -	Did not qualify
1938 -	Did not enter	1982 -	Did not qualify
1950 -	Did not enter	1986 -	Did not qualify
1954 -	Did not enter	1990 -	Did not qualify
1958 -	Did not enter	1994 -	Did not qualify
1962 -	Did not enter	1998 -	Did not qualify
1966 -	Did not qualify	2002 -	Did not qualify
1970 -	Did not qualify		

KEY PLAYER

KEY PLAYER TIM CAHILL EVERTON

Tim Cahill has perfected the run into the opponent's box. It's a mix of pace, timing and anticipation but it leads to goals. He hit 11 league goals in his first season in the Premiership, taking Everton to a Champions League place. Another seven followed as he top-scored for the Socceroos in their successful World Cup qualifying ties.

Appearances:	35	5
Minutes played:	2961	405
Percentage played:	80.2%	64.3%
Goals scored:	9	7
Goals conceded:	33	3
Cards:	Y10, R0	Y0, R0
Power rating:	96mins	16mins
Power ranking:	140th	2nd

AGE 26   **MIDFIELDER**   **WORLD RANKING** 189

THE SQUAD

Goalkeepers	Club side	Age	QG
Ante Covic	Hammarby	30	0
Zeljko Kalac	AC Milan	33	6
Mark Schwarzer	Middlesbrough	33	3
Defenders			
Simon Colosimo	Perth Glory	27	2
Patrick Kisnorbo	Leicester	25	3
Stephen Laybutt	Gent	28	1
Adrian Madaschi	Dundee	23	4
Lucas Neill	Blackburn	28	4
Tony Popovic	Crystal Palace	32	3
David Tarka	Perth Glory	23	2
Tony Vidmar	NAC Breda	35	7
Midfielders			
Mark Bresciano	Parma	26	5
Tim Cahill	Everton	26	6
Scott Chipperfield	Basel	30	6
Jason Culina	PSV Eindhoven	25	4
Ahmad Elrich	Fulham	25	4
Brett Emerton	Blackburn	27	8
Vincenzo Grella	Parma	26	8
Harry Kewell	Liverpool	27	2
Stan Lazaridis	Birmingham	33	4
John McKain	Politehnica Timisoara	23	1
Jade North	Newcastle Jets	24	5
Josip Skoko	Stoke	30	6
Luke Wilkshire	Bristol City	24	1
Forwards			
John Aloisi	Alaves	30	7
Alex Brosque	Westerlo	22	3
Mile Sterjovski	Basel	27	5
Archie Thompson	PSV Eindhoven	27	3
Mark Viduka	Middlesbrough	30	4
Massimiliano Vieri	Triestina	27	3
David Zdrilic	Sydney	32	3

■ Probable ■ Possible **QG** Qualification Games

KEY GOALKEEPER

MARK SCHWARZER
MIDDLESBROUGH

Middlesbrough's brave goalkeeper Mark Schwarzer is one of the longest-serving keepers currently playing in the Premiership.

Last December he passed 250 games for his club – only the fifth foreign player to reach that milestone in the Premiership.

A tall keeper at 1.96m, Schwarzer is a solid performer but prone to the odd mistake, which keeps him out of the world-class bracket. Socceroos fans can buy signed photographs of one of Schwarzer's two penalty saves against Uruguay that took Australia to the World Cup finals. The cost – just $660 Australian.

Playing record	12 mths lge	wcq
Appearances:	27	3
Minutes played:	2430	300
Percentage played:	67.5%	35.7%
Goals conceded:	34	1
Clean sheets:	9	2
Cards:	Y0, R0	Y0, R0
Defensive rating:	71mins	300
Defensive ranking:	20th	-

AGE 33 **WORLD RANKING 1032**

KEY DEFENDERS

LUCAS NEILL
BLACKBURN

Lucas Neill has all the competitive spirit you expect from a sporting Australian.

He patrols the right flank at Blackburn, and had 36 league appearances last season.

Neill's uncompromising style can cause flashpoints on the pitch but it suits both club and country.

Playing record	12 mths lge	wcq
Appearances:	37	4
Minutes played:	3270	390
Percentage played:	88.6%	46.4%
Goals conceded:	39	2
Clean sheets:	16	2
Cards:	Y12, R1	Y1, R0
Defensive rating:	84mins	98mins
Defensive ranking:	59th	-

AGE 28 **WORLD RANKING 605**

ANTHONY VIDMAR
NAC BREDA

Playing record	12 mths lge	wcq
Appearances:	19	7
Minutes played:	1599	660
Percentage played:	42.3%	78.6%
Goals conceded:	35	2
Clean sheets:	4	5
Cards:	Y2, R0	Y2, R0
Defensive rating:	46mins	330mins
Defensive ranking:	112nd	-

AGE 35 **WORLD RANKING 1403**

KEY MIDFIELDERS

BRETT EMERTON
BLACKBURN

Brett Emerton will link up with Blackburn team-mate Lucas Neill on the Australian right flank.

The tall deceptive winger, who's faster than he looks, should score more but has 11 in 45 games for Australia. He can be an inconsistent player who moves in and out of a game.

Playing record	12 mths lge	wcq
Appearances:	36	8
Minutes played:	2190	694
Percentage played:	59.3%	82.6%
Goals scored:	2	4
Goals conceded:	26	5
Cards:	Y2, R0	Y1, R0
Power rating:	78mins	29mins
Power ranking:	120th	11th

AGE 27 **WORLD RANKING 317**

MARK BRESCIANO
PARMA

Playing record	12 mths lge	wcq
Appearances:	37	5
Minutes played:	2736	347
Percentage played:	67.6%	41.3%
Goals scored:	4	2
Goals conceded:	55	2
Cards:	Y1, R1	Y1, R0
Power rating:	67mins	31mins
Power ranking:	105th	9th

AGE 26 **WORLD RANKING 975**

THE MANAGER

Guus Hiddink became Australia's national coach in July 2005.

He succeeded Frank Farina, who stepped down by 'mutual consent' after the Socceroos failed to win a game in last summer's Confederations Cup.

Hiddink now combines his roles as manager of Dutch side PSV Eindhoven with that of Australia, and will remain in charge of the Socceroos until the end of the World Cup finals in Germany.

After a moderate playing career, which included spells with Dutch clubs PSV and NEC, Hiddink moved into coaching and has been in demand ever since.

The 49-year-old Dutchman has built up an impressive CV and is now rated one of the best in world football. At club level, he has been successful at PSV, Fenerbahce, Valencia and Real Madrid, while on the international stage, he guided Holland to the 1998 World Cup semi-finals and four years later led hosts South Korea on a remarkable run into the last four.

KEY STRIKERS

MARK VIDUKA
MIDDLESBROUGH

The World Cup may have come a couple of seasons too late for Mark Viduka.

The former Leeds striker has suffered injuries and is struggling for form and time on the pitch at Middlesbrough this season. However, for Australia he will be re-united with Harry Kewell who helped Viduka become a 22-goals-a-season man at Leeds. He has skippered the Aussies since September.

Playing record	12 mths lge	wcq
Appearances:	21	4
Minutes played:	1252	333
Percentage played:	34.8%	39.6%
Goals scored:	3	2
Percentage share:	0.38	6.67
Cards:	Y0, R0	Y0, R0
Strike rate:	417mins	-
Strike rate ranking:	78th	-

AGE 30   **WORLD RANKING 1776**

JOHN ALOISI
ALAVES

Playing record	12 mths lge	wcq
Appearances:	35	7
Minutes played:	1977	414
Percentage played:	91.5%	49.3%
Goals scored:	10	2
Percentage share:	41.67	6.67
Cards:	Y3, R0	Y1, R0
Strike rate:	198mins	188mins
Strike rate ranking:	41st	33rd

AGE 30   **WORLD RANKING 483**

ONE TO WATCH

HARRY KEWELL LIVERPOOL

Harry Kewell is enjoying a revival at Liverpool and is back to his darting, twisting best ahead of the World Cup.

The 16-year-old, who left New South Wales for Leeds youth team in 1996, was rated one of the best wingers in the Premiership when he joined Liverpool from Leeds in 2003. This season's return to form has made him a regular in the starting line-up.

Playing record	12 mths lge	wcq
Appearances:	21	2
Minutes played:	1510	179
Percentage played:	39.0%	21.3%
Goals scored:	2	0
Goals conceded:	12	1
Cards:	Y1, R0	Y1, R0
Power rating:	63mins	-
Power ranking:	94th	-

AGE 27   **MIDFIELDER**   **WORLD RANKING 1471**

ROUTE TO THE FINALS

Japan finished top of the final Asian Zone B group table, two points ahead of Iran, who also qualified for the finals in Germany.

They conceded just five goals in 12 qualifiers, but failed to score more than two goals in a game themselves, other than against a weak India side, who were hammered 7-0 at home in Saitama and 4-0 away in Calcutta.

Japan became the first country other than hosts Germany to be certain of their place at the 2006 finals after beating Korea DPR (not to be confused with the finalists South Korea) 2-0 in June 2005.

Celebrations in Japan, however, were muted as expectations for the national side are now so high, that inconsistent performances throughout qualifying had left doubts about their chances

of making an impact at the finals in Germany.

Head coach Zico, the former Brazilian star, faced a lot of criticism for not getting the team to play to its full potential after Japan's triumph at the 2004 Asian Cup.

He is still experimenting with his formations following qualification and played six across midfield - to widespread scorn - in a recent friendly against the USA, which ended in a 3-2 defeat.

**FINAL QUALIFYING TABLE
ASIA STAGE 3 – GROUP B**

	P	W	D	L	F	A	Pts
Japan	6	5	0	1	9	4	15
Iran	6	4	1	1	7	3	13
Bahrain	6	1	1	4	4	7	4
Korea DPR	6	1	0	5	5	11	3

				FIFA ranking			
1	18 Feb 04	Home	Oman	67	W	**1 0**	Kubo 90
2	31 Mar 04	Away	Singapore	99	W	**1 2**	Takahara 33, Fujita 81
3	09 Jun 04	Home	India	133	W	**7 0**	Kubo 12, Fukunishi 25, Nakamura 29, Suzuki 54, Nakazawa 65, 76, Ogasawara 68
4	08 Sep 04	Away	India	133	W	**0 4**	Suzuki 45, Ono 60, Fukunishi 71, Miyamato 87
5	13 Oct 04	Away	Oman	67	W	**0 1**	Suzuki 52
6	17 Nov 04	Home	Singapore	99	W	**1 0**	Tamada 13
7	09 Feb 05	Home	North Korea	89	W	**2 1**	Ogasawara 4, Oguro 90
8	25 Mar 05	Away	Iran	18	L	**2 1**	Fukunishi 33
9	30 Mar 05	Home	Bahrain	51	W	**1 0**	Salmeen 71og
10	03 Jun 05	Away	Bahrain	51	W	**0 1**	Ogasawara 34
11	08 Jun 05	Away	North Korea	89	W	**0 2**	Yanagisawa 67, Oguro 89
12	17 Aug 05	Home	Iran	18	W	**2 1**	Kaji 28, Oguro 76
	Average FIFA ranking of opposition			67			

MAIN PLAYER PERFORMANCES IN QUALIFICATION

Match	1 2 3 4 5 6 7 8 9 10 11 12	Appearances	Started	Subbed on	Subbed off	Mins played	% played	Goals	Yellow	Red
Venue	H A H A A H H A H A A H									
Result	W W W W W W W L W W W W									
Goalkeepers										
Yoshikatsu Kawaguchi		7	7	0	0	630	58.3	0	0	0
Seigo Narazaki		4	4	0	0	360	33.3	0	0	0
Defenders										
Alessandro Santos		10	9	1	0	821	76.0	0	4	0
Akira Kaji		11	11	0	0	990	91.7	1	2	0
Atsuhiro Miura		2	2	0	0	180	16.7	0	1	0
Tsuneyasu Miyamoto		12	12	0	1	1051	97.3	1	0	0
Yuji Nakazawa		9	9	0	0	810	75.0	2	1	0
Makoto Tanaka		7	7	0	2	587	54.4	0	2	0
Keisuke Tsuboi		3	3	0	0	270	25.0	0	0	0
Midfielders										
Yasuhito Endo		5	4	1	2	332	30.7	0	0	0
Takashi Fukunishi		9	9	0	0	810	75.0	3	1	0
Junichi Inamoto		5	3	2	0	275	25.5	0	2	0
Shunsuke Nakamura		8	7	1	3	614	56.9	1	2	0
Hidetoshi Nakata		5	5	0	0	450	41.7	0	2	0
Koji Nakata		3	2	1	0	195	18.1	0	0	0
Mitsuo Ogasawara		9	5	4	2	511	47.3	3	0	0
Shinji Ono		5	5	0	2	417	38.6	1	2	0
Forwards										
Mashasi Oguro		4	1	3	0	156	14.4	3	0	0
Takayuki Suzuki		9	5	4	4	451	41.8	3	1	0
Naohiro Takahara		7	6	1	4	509	47.1	1	0	0
Keiji Tamada		9	5	4	4	427	39.5	1	0	0
Atsushi Yanagisawa		5	4	1	4	314	29.1	1	0	0

FINAL PROSPECTS

Japan will find it difficult to reach the knockout stage in Germany after being drawn in a tough looking Group F, along with world champions Brazil, Croatia and Australia. All four teams will be optimistic of making the last 16.

With players of the calibre of midfielders Hidetoshi Nakata, Shunsuke Nakamura and Shinji Ono, all of whom have played top-flight European football, Japan are able to compete with the very best international sides, but a lack of a world-class striker could find them struggling to score sufficient goals against well-organised defences.

A good showing at the 2005 Confederations Cup, where they beat Euro 2004 champions Greece and drew with Brazil, would have boosted the confidence of coach Zico and his players going into the tournament.

THE MANAGER

Former Brazilian star Zico became Japan coach when he took over from Frenchman Philippe Troussier after the 2002 World Cup finals.

The 52-year-old, who shone on the field in a Brazilian shirt at the 1982 and 1986 World Cup finals, has extensive knowledge of Japanese football, having been a player and then general manager at J-League giants Kashima Antlers throughout the 1990s.

He is still tinkering with the squad and was widely criticised for the 3-6-1 formation tried in a February friendly defeat against the US.

Zico has declared himself available to continue after the World Cup but is unlikely to get the opportunity.

Zico

GROUP FIXTURES

AUSTRALIA	Mon 12 June 1400 BST
CROATIA	Sun 18 June 1400 BST
BRAZIL	Thu 22 June 2000 BST

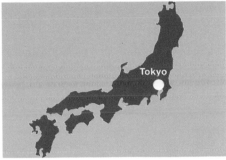

Tokyo

Zone	Asia
Population	127,417,000
Capital	Tokyo
Language	Japanese
Top league	J League
Major clubs	**Capacities**
Yokohama F. Marinos	72,300
Urawa Red Diamonds	21,500 & 63,700
Kashima Antlers	41,800

Where likely squad players play:

In Premiership	2
In other major five European Leagues	1
Outside major European Leagues	20

Number of Japanese players playing:

In Premiership	2
In other major five European Leagues	4

World Cup record

1930 -	Did not enter	1974 -	Did not qualify
1934 -	Did not enter	1978 -	Did not qualify
1938 -	Withdrew	1982 -	Did not qualify
1950 -	Did not enter	1986 -	Did not qualify
1954 -	Did not qualify	1990 -	Did not qualify
1958 -	Did not enter	1994 -	Did not qualify
1962 -	Did not enter	1998 -	Group 4th
1966 -	Did not enter	2002 -	Last 16
1970 -	Did not qualify		

THE SQUAD

Goalkeepers	Club side	Age	QG
Yoichi Doi	FC Tokyo	32	1
Yoshikatsu Kawaguchi	Jubilo Iwata	30	7
Seigo Narazaki	Grampus Eight	30	4
Defenders			
Alessandro Santos	Urawa Reds	28	10
Akira Kaji	Gamba Osaka	26	11
Yasuyuki Konno	FC Tokyo	23	1
Naoki Matsuda	Yokohama	29	1
Atsuhiro Miura	Vissel Kobe	31	2
Tsuneyasu Miyamoto	Gamba Osaka	29	12
Yuji Nakazawa	Yokohama	28	9
Makoto Tanaka	Jubilo Iwata	31	7
Keisuke Tsuboi	Urawa Reds	26	3
Nobuhisa Yamada	Urawa Reds	30	1
Midfielders			
Yuki Abe	Ichihara Chiba	24	1
Yasuhito Endo	Gamba Osaka	26	5
Toshiya Fujita	Grampus Eight	34	4
Takashi Fukunishi	Jubilo Iwata	29	9
Junichi Inamoto	West Brom	26	5
Masashi Motoyama	Kashima Antlers	26	2
Shunsuke Nakamura	Celtic	27	8
Hidetoshi Nakata	Bolton	29	5
Koji Nakata	Basel	26	3
Mitsuo Ogasawara	Kashima Antlers	27	9
Shinji Ono	Urawa Reds	26	5
Forwards			
Tatsuhiko Kubo	Yokohama	29	3
Mashasi Oguro	FC Grenoble	26	4
Yoshito Okubo	Mallorca	24	1
Takayuki Suzuki	Crvena Zvezda	30	9
Naohiro Takahara	Hamburg	27	7
Keiji Tamada	Grampus Eight	26	9
Atsushi Yanagisawa	Messina	29	5

■ Probable ■ Possible **QG** Qualification Games

KEY PLAYER

SHINJI ONO URAWA REDS

While Hidetoshi Nakata is the biggest star to emerge from Japan's J league, the best player is Shinji Ono. He won the UEFA Cup with Feyenoord in 2001/2 at his peak but has been hampered by a series of injuries in the last two seasons. He has just returned to Japan and his first club Urawa Red Diamonds and is back in the national squad. Nakata, Ono and Nakamura are vital.

Playing record	12 mths lge	wcq
Appearances:	15	5
Minutes played:	1021	417
Percentage played:	27.7%	38.6%
Goals scored:	4	1
Goals conceded:	22	3
Cards:	3, 0	2, 0
Power rating:	-	-
Power ranking:	-	-

AGE 26 **MIDFIELDER** **WORLD RANKING** -

12th ANDERSON DECO
BARCELONA

With Champions League and Uefa Cup medals already in the bag with FC Porto and a Spanish league title from his first season at Barcelona, Deco will be aiming for international success.

Although born in Brazil, Deco has qualified to play for Portugal and did so to great effect on his debut, scoring the goal that beat Brazil! His time on the ball helps Portugal keep possession and he is a constant danger around the edge of the box with his sharp dribbling and sure passing.

Playing record	12 mths lge	wcq
Appearances:	34	11
Minutes played:	2778	927
Percentage played:	73.5%	85.8%
Goals scored:	6	1
Goals conceded:	28	4
Cards:	Y12, R1	Y2, R0
Power rating:	41mins	31mins
Power ranking:	12th	12th

AGE 28 | **WORLD RANKING 27**

11th PAVEL NEDVED
JUVENTUS

Pavel Nedved adds quality to the Czech midfield. He is the only outfield player currently at a world class club and his record in Serie A shows why.

He helped Lazio to their first title for 26 years in 2001. He was bought by Juventus for £25m and immediately won the title twice with them.

Voted European Footballer of the Year in 2003, Nedved is a pacy left-sided midfielder with good touch and he can cut in from the wing and strike a fierce shot.

Playing record	12 mths lge	wcq
Appearances:	32	2
Minutes played:	2662	180
Percentage played:	65.7%	14.3%
Goals scored:	6	0
Goals conceded:	24	0
Cards:	Y6, R0	Y1, R0
Power rating:	41mins	-
Power ranking:	9th	-

AGE 33 | **WORLD RANKING 26**

10th ESTEBAN CAMBIASSO
INTER MILAN

Esteban Cambiasso was sitting on the bench at the Bernabeu not playing for Real Madrid or Argentina and watching his career drift away.

He impressed as a youngster and moved from Argentinos Juniors to Real Madrid at the age of just 16.

His spell in Real's reserves finally ended when Inter Milan signed him in 2004/5 to partner countryman Juan Sebastian Veron in their midfield. He was arguably their best player and revived his international career.

Playing record	12 mths lge	wcq
Appearances:	38	8
Minutes played:	3167	617
Percentage played:	78.2%	38.1%
Goals scored:	6	0
Goals conceded:	25	7
Cards:	Y5, R0	Y1, R1
Power rating:	49mins	62mins
Power ranking:	46th	94th

AGE 25 | **WORLD RANKING 25**

9th RICARDO KAKA
AC MILAN

Kaka deservedly won the Uefa Midfield Player of the Year Award in 2005 after a series of dazzling performances for club and country.

He made an instant impression when he joined AC Milan from Sao Paulo for £8.5m as a 21-year-old in summer 2003, scoring ten times in his first season as the Italian giants stormed to the Serie A title. A player with confidence and flair Kaka shines out – even in Brazil's star-studded line-up. As a playmaker he is second only to Riquelme.

Playing record	12 mths lge	wcq
Appearances:	41	15
Minutes played:	3083	1112
Percentage played:	76.1%	68.6%
Goals scored:	11	5
Goals conceded:	27	8
Cards:	Y4, R0	Y2, R0
Power rating:	45mins	43mins
Power ranking:	25th	41st

AGE 24 | **WORLD RANKING 24**

8th JUNINHO PERNAMBUCANO
LYON

A graceful right-sided midfielder and dead-ball specialist, Juninho is one of the major reasons why Lyon have dominated French domestic football in recent seasons.

Famed for his spectacular goals from unstoppable free kicks, he has also added flair and imagination to the Lyon line-up since moving to France from Vasco da Gama in 2001. His excellent club form has won him a regular place in the Brazilian squad but not yet the first XI.

Playing record	12 mths lge	wcq
Appearances:	36	11
Minutes played:	3083	554
Percentage played:	79.7%	34.2%
Goals scored:	11	1
Goals conceded:	27	2
Cards:	Y4, R0	Y0, R0
Power rating:	57mins	43mins
Power ranking:	72nd	40th

AGE 31 **WORLD RANKING 23**

7th MICHAEL ESSIEN
CHELSEA

The most expensive player in African history, the 'new Vieira', a reckless tackler; Michael Essien leaves his mark. Most notably in the power and athleticism he brings to the midfield, but also on Didi Hamann's knee.

The Ghanaian twice won the French League title with Lyon before Chelsea spent a club record £24.4m for him. He is an all-round talent, breaking up attacks; surging forward from midfield at pace and hitting crisp defence-splitting passes.

Playing record	12 mths lge	wcq
Appearances:	22	8
Minutes played:	1782	658
Percentage played:	47.1%	73.1%
Goals scored:	0	3
Goals conceded:	10	2
Cards:	Y5, R0	Y3, R0
Power rating:	41mins	51mins
Power ranking:	11th	76th

AGE 23 **WORLD RANKING 22**

6th PHILLIP COCU
PSV EINDHOVEN

A technically gifted and versatile midfielder, Cocu is a superb passer of the ball, who scores goals and controls games from deep.

He is influential for both Holland and PSV Eindhoven. The experienced Cocu enjoyed a successful six-year spell at Barcelona before re-joining PSV at the beginning of last season. He proved an inspiration, helping PSV to a Dutch League and Cup double and on a memorable run to the semi-finals of the Champions League.

Playing record	12 mths lge	wcq
Appearances:	38	8
Minutes played:	3352	629
Percentage played:	88.7%	58.2%
Goals scored:	10	3
Goals conceded:	19	2
Cards:	Y4, R1	Y0, R1
Power rating:	43mins	35mins
Power ranking:	16th	18th

AGE 35 **WORLD RANKING 16**

5th MICHAEL BALLACK
BAYERN MUNICH

One of the most coveted midfielders in world football, Germany captain Michael Ballack is a dynamo on the pitch with great vision, drive and attacking intent.

He suffered disappointment at the 2002 World Cup where he scored the semi-final goal against South Korea that took Germany to the final, but a booking just a few minutes earlier in the game, meant he was suspended from the game against Brazil. He's in phenomenal scoring form for Bayern Munich in the Champions League this year.

Playing record	12 mths lge	int
Appearances:	29	13
Minutes played:	2505	1182
Percentage played:	73.2%	71.6%
Goals scored:	20	9
Goals conceded:	25	21
Cards:	Y9, R0	Y1, R0
Power rating:	38mins	41mins
Power ranking:	5th	33rd

AGE 29 **WORLD RANKING 15**

4th
CLAUDE MAKELELE
CHELSEA

A fierce midfield ball-winner, Claude Makelele's diminutive size belies his tough-tackling approach.

His ability to read the game and protect his defence makes him an important player at international level for France. Makelele won a Champions League and Spanish league winner's medal with Real Madrid before joining Chelsea in 2003 for £16m. He missed only two games last season as Chelsea strolled to the Premiership title. He also missed a penalty - but scored the rebound!

Playing record	12 mths lge	wcq
Appearances:	35	4
Minutes played:	2902	360
Percentage played:	76.8%	40.0%
Goals scored:	1	0
Goals conceded:	19	1
Cards:	Y8, R0	Y2, R0
Power rating:	44mins	72mins
Power ranking:	22nd	104th

AGE 33	WORLD RANKING 14

3rd
STEVEN GERRARD
LIVERPOOL

A multi-talented midfielder, Steve Gerrard is capable of changing the course of a game single-handedly.

The inspirational Liverpool captain has the ability to beat players and score important (not to mention stunning) goals at both club and international level.

Gerrard can play in any position across the middle of the park. He will be one of the key players for England in Germany where his combination of skill and tenacity will be vital to the team's progress.

Playing record	12 mths lge	wcq
Appearances:	37	7
Minutes played:	3195	588
Percentage played:	84.5%	65.3%
Goals scored:	10	2
Goals conceded:	26	4
Cards:	Y5, R0	Y0, R0
Power rating:	73mins	49mins
Power ranking:	111th	70th

AGE 26	WORLD RANKING 13

2nd
JUAN RIQUELME
VILLARREAL

Juan Riquelme is the creative hub for both Villarreal and Argentina.

He failed to settle at Barcelona when he moved to Spain, and it was only after he joined Villarreal 12 months later that he rediscovered the prodigious form he showed in South America. After a slow start to qualifying, Argentina manager Jose Pekerman, plumped for Riquelme – ahead of Pablo Aimar or Juan Sebastian Veron – as the playmaker for his team. He sets the tempo and direction of the side's attacks.

Playing record	12 mths lge	wcq
Appearances:	32	9
Minutes played:	2797	723
Percentage played:	72.3%	44.6%
Goals scored:	16	3
Goals conceded:	32	7
Cards:	Y3, R0	Y0, R0
Power rating:	56mins	60mins
Power ranking:	68th	92nd

AGE 27	WORLD RANKING 12

THE TOP MIDFIELDER

ENGLAND FRANK LAMPARD

Frank Lampard is widely considered the most complete midfielder currently playing in the Premiership and perhaps the world.

He is quick, creative, and intelligent, has a superb range of passing, can tackle and scores plenty of goals. He was voted runner-up to Ronaldinho as FIFA's 2005 Player of the Year.

Playing record	12 mths lge	wcq
Appearances:	40	10
Minutes played:	3600	889
Percentage played:	95.2%	98.8%
Goals scored:	20	5
Goals conceded:	23	5
Cards:	Y5, R0	Y0, R0
Power rating:	47mins	52mins
Power ranking:	31st	80th

1st

AGE 27 CHELSEA WORLD RANKING 1

G

Position	1st	2nd	3rd	4th	5th	6th	7th	8th
Group	E	F	C	A	D	H	B	G
Total FIFA ranking	89	93	95	96	101	109	117	138

SOUTH KOREA V TOGO
Frankfurt, Tuesday 13 JUNE 1400 BST

South Korea's organisation should be too much for an unsettled Togo who are coming off a poor African Cup of Nations campaign, with an disgruntled star and a new coach at the helm. The Koreans will want to notch up a few goals and usually play three up front with Ji-Sung Park adding extra penetration from either flank.

This game could also give Chu-Young Park – the new Korean find – a chance to shine. He only played in the final three games of qualifying but the 19-year-old scored twice and came closest in the final Saudi game that the Koreans dominated from start to finish and should have won comfortably.

FRANCE V SWITZERLAND
Stuttgart, Tuesday 13 JUNE 1700 BST

These close European neighbours know each other well and played out two draws in qualifying. They will both expect to go through and see a draw as a good start before going on to tackle two sides they would both expect to beat. The French started slowly at the last

World Cup and will show Rennes' top scorer, Alexander Frei, plenty of respect up front. This game is made for the deep-lying midfield skills of Johann Vogel. He may be short of match practice at AC Milan but he'll be making sure Zidane can't settle on the ball.

FRANCE V SOUTH KOREA
Leipzig, Sunday 18 June 2000 BST

France to win with Trezeguet's power and Henry's finesse too much for the Korean defence to cope with. Even if the Koreans can rediscover the organisation of the last World Cup, they would still need a huge slice of luck to scrape a draw if France hit their form.

This could be a good chance for Zidane to parade the skills, which thrill the Bernabeu, but Vieira is the key to dominating the midfield and giving Zidane his platform.
Dick Advocaat will have the Koreans prepared to close down the flair play of the French.

TOGO V SWITZERLAND
Dortmund, Monday 19 June 1400 BST

The Swiss players survived the furore in Turkey; they are tight unit and the best side ever to represent their country. This is the game for them to prove why they are there.
Raphael Wicky may miss the French game and be saved to unlock both Togo and South Korea from midfield.

TOGO V FRANCE
Cologne, Friday 23 June 2000 BST

Togo qualified ahead of Senegal and the Senegalese must still haunt French dreams from the group phase of the last World Cup. And, Togo is another small French-speaking outpost of France's colonial past; could lightning strike twice? No. Togo's attack got them to Germany but they shipped goals to poor sides in qualifying and again in the African Cup of Nations.
France's front pair should do the damage. Henry has class but Trezeguet has form and more to prove.

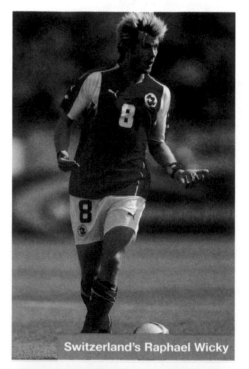

Switzerland's Raphael Wicky

SWITZERLAND V SOUTH KOREA
Hanover, Friday 23 June 2000 BST

If everything else has gone to our predictions this is the game to decide second place. South Korea's self-belief may have been stripped away against France and that should leave the Swiss in a better frame of mind to win this game. They have the added incentive of wanting to

enthuse their supporters before Euro 2008 which they will be co-hosting with Austria. Young-Pyo Lee will have to live up to his former tag as 'the best left back in Holland' in this game. Another key man will be Korea's coach Dick Advocaat, using all his knowledge to try to beat the Swiss.

MARTIN JOL'S VIEW

France must be the favourites in a group that doesn't look too difficult. They will be desperate not to repeat the mistakes of the last World Cup tournament when they crashed out in the first phase, without even scoring a goal.

That had a lot to do with the system they played - an uncompromising 4-4-2 - in which even international stars like Thierry Henry (in my opinion the best player in the Premier League in the last decade) and Zinedine Zidane looked very ordinary.

I expect that this time France will get the freedom to express themselves, which means that – especially in this group – they will be too strong for the other teams.

Defensively they are second-to-none. In Lilian Thuram, William Gallas, Jean-Alain Boumsong, Willy Sagnol and Sebastien Squillaci they have a very strong group.

Their midfield too - with Claude Makelele, Ludovic Giuly, Zidane and Patrick Vieira – is world class. Players like Robert Pires and Vikash Dhorasoo will not even be making the team.

With players like Henry and David Trezeguet leading the attack (leaving Nicolas Anelka, Djibril Cisse and Sylvain Wiltord hungry on the bench), France must be one of the World Cup favourites.

"Thierry Henry – in my opinion the best player in the Premier League in the last decade."

Coach Raymond Domenech has more than enough superstars and he will win this group without any sweat.

Switzerland have a stronger team this time. Their young players will all be gaining experience for the European Championships that will be held in their country (with Austria as co-hosts) in two years time. This is important for young players such as my Reto Ziegler (now at Wigan), Arsenal's Philippe Senderos, Christoph Spycher of Eitracht Frankfurt, Tranquillo Barnetta, Valon Behrami, and Johan Vonlanthen.

More experienced team-mates such as Stephane Henchoz, Rafael Wicky, Alexander Frei and Johann Vogel, will add enough quality to enable them to surprise everybody. Turkey found out just how determined the Swiss were during the play-offs.

KEY MATCH

Four years ago, South Korea were the surprise team of the tournament, reaching the semi-finals. They had a lot of opposition mistakes in almost every game to thank for their progress but let us call it the luck that goes with playing at home. However, they were good enough to take advantage and sometimes they made their own luck and Guus Hiddink played an important role in this.

The best-known players are Young-Pyo Lee and Ji-Sung Park, who both played at PSV for Hiddink, and are currently playing for my Tottenham and for Manchester United.

South Korea's rookey is Chu-Young Park. I expect a fascinating tournament and I will follow them with a lot of interest. One reason is that once again, they have a Dutch coach, the 'Little General' Dick Advocaat, but I don't expect them to perform as well as they did four years ago, especially without the home advantage.

Togo is another African unknown. Surprisingly enough they managed to eliminate Senegal, one of the better countries. Their best player is without doubt Emmanuel Adebayor, who moved to Arsenal in the January transfer window.

However, most of the players of Togo play in the lower leagues of Europe and that will cost them dear when they have to perform on football's highest platform.

"With players like Henry and Trezeguet leading the attack, France must be one of the favourites"

MARTIN JOL'S PREDICTIONS FOR THE TOP TWO TEAMS FROM THIS GROUP   For the full draw please see page 80

GROUP STAGE	LAST SIXTEEN	QUARTER-FINALS
FIRST GROUP G	v SECOND GROUP H	v FIRST GROUP E or SECOND GROUP F
FRANCE →	**FRANCE v SPAIN** →	**FRANCE v ITALY**
SECOND GROUP G	v FIRST GROUP H	v FIRST GROUP F or SECOND GROUP E
SWITZERLAND →	**SWITZERLAND v UKRAINE** →	**UKRAINE v BRAZIL**

GROUP G	GROUP H	GROUP E
FRANCE, SWITZERLAND, SOUTH KOREA, TOGO	SPAIN, UKRAINE, TUNISIA, SAUDI ARABIA	ITALY, GHANA, USA, CZECH REPUBLIC
		GROUP F
		BRAZIL, CROATIA, AUSTRALIA, JAPAN

Even as runners-up, France would still be favourites in the last 16 but Brazil would then be waiting in the quarter-final.

FRANCE

ROUTE TO THE FINALS

The return of Zinedine Zidane from international retirement was the highlight of France's struggle to qualify for the World Cup.

Les Bleus had enough talent to have made light of the admittedly competitive European Group 4, but couldn't pull clear of a pack of Israel, Switzerland and the Republic of Ireland.

These four countries played out draw after draw with each other. France picked off Cyprus and the Faroes but played out goalless draws against Israel, Ireland and the Swiss. David Trezeguet finally scored in Israel but a late equaliser shared the points. Then Zidane announced his return followed by a breakthrough in Dublin. The defence stood firm against early Irish pressure and Henry netted his 30th French goal to record a vital win.

Not there yet - they only managed a tight 1-1 draw with Switzerland in the next game and , although they thrashed Cyprus in the final match, they could still have finished in the play-offs. To put them there the Swiss needed to beat Ireland in Dublin but they ran into Given.

FINAL QUALIFYING TABLE
EUROPE GROUP 4

	P	W	D	L	F	A	Pts
France	10	5	5	0	14	2	20
Switzerland	**10**	**4**	**6**	**0**	**18**	**7**	**18**
Israel	10	4	6	0	15	10	18
Rep of Ireland	10	4	5	1	12	5	17
Cyprus	10	1	1	8	8	20	4
Faroe Islands	10	0	1	9	4	27	1

European Group play-off
Switzerland beat Turkey

					FIFA ranking			
1	04 Sep 04	Home	Israel	47	D	**0 0**		
2	08 Sep 04	Away	Faroe Islands	131	W	**0 2**	Giuly 31, Cisse 72	
3	09 Oct 04	Home	Rep of Ireland	16	D	**0 0**		
4	13 Oct 04	Away	Cyprus	105	W	**0 2**	Wiltord 38, 38, Henry 72, 72	
5	26 Mar 05	Home	Switzerland	42	D	**0 0**		
6	30 Mar 05	Away	Israel	47	D	**1 1**	Trezeguet 50	
7	03 Sep 05	Home	Faroe Islands	131	W	**3 0**	Cisse 13, 76, Olsen 19og	
8	07 Sep 05	Away	Rep of Ireland	16	W	**0 1**	Henry 67	
9	08 Oct 05	Away	Switzerland	42	D	**1 1**	Cisse 52	
10	12 Oct 05	Home	Cyprus	105	W	**4 0**	Zidane 29, Wiltord 31, Dhorasoo 43, Giuly 84	

Average FIFA ranking of opposition	58

MAIN PLAYER PERFORMANCES IN QUALIFICATION

Match	1 2 3 4 5 6 7 8 9 10	Appearances	Started	Subbed on	Subbed off	Mins played	% played	Goals	Yellow	Red
Venue	H A H A H A H A A H									
Result	D W D W D D W W D W									
Goalkeepers										
Fabien Barthez		4	4	0	0	360	40.0	0	0	0
Gregory Coupet		6	6	0	0	540	60.0	0	0	0
Defenders										
Jean-Alain Boumsong		6	6	0	0	540	60.0	0	0	0
Alou Diarra		4	1	3	0	185	20.6	0	0	0
William Gallas		10	10	0	0	900	100.0	0	0	0
Gael Givet		7	6	1	0	542	60.2	0	0	0
Anthony Reveillere		1	1	0	0	90	10.0	0	0	0
Willy Sagnol		5	5	0	1	448	49.8	0	2	0
Mikael Silvestre		2	2	0	0	180	20.0	0	0	0
Sebastien Squillaci		5	4	1	0	375	41.7	0	0	0
Lilian Thuram		4	4	0	1	345	38.3	0	0	0
Midfielders										
Olivier Dacourt		2	2	0	2	152	16.9	0	0	0
Vikash Dhorasoo		4	3	1	1	258	28.7	1	0	0
Patrice Evra		3	2	1	0	205	22.8	0	0	0
Ludovic Giuly		4	2	2	0	245	27.2	2	0	0
Claude Makelele		4	4	0	0	360	40.0	0	2	0
Benoit Pedretti		3	3	0	0	270	30.0	0	0	0
Robert Pires		4	3	1	1	250	27.8	0	0	0
Patrick Vieira		9	9	0	1	708	78.7	0	2	1
Zinedine Zidane		4	4	0	2	305	33.9	1	1	0
Forwards										
Djibril Cisse		6	3	3	1	403	44.8	4	0	0
Thierry Henry		6	6	0	3	472	52.4	3	0	0
Florent Malouda		4	3	1	1	291	32.3	0	0	0
Louis Saha		2	2	0	1	98	10.9	0	0	0
David Trezeguet		2	2	0	0	180	20.0	1	1	0
Sylvain Wiltord		8	7	1	3	612	68.0	3	0	0

FINAL PROSPECTS

A few countries have strength in depth, France have brilliance in depth. If they click and the selection and tactics work, they can recapture the dominance of 1998.

The A list of stars: Henry, Zidane, Makelele, Thuram, Giuly, Trezeguet, Vieira, Sagnol, Gallas, Coupet; easily bears comparison with Brazil. And the generation coming through includes top centre back Sebastien Squillaci, Vikash Dhorasoo and Florent Malouda in midfield and Anthony Reveillere at full-back.

Everyone one of them is an in-form star with a top European club.

None of which quite explains the stuttering against dogged but hardly world class teams in qualification. If it wasn't for the brilliance of Ireland's Shay Given against the Swiss, France would have been in the play-offs.

Coach Raymond Domenech has been tinkering with the team and the formation, trying a 5-3-2 in November's friendly against Germany, playing Reveillere and

> **"They will be desperate not to repeat the mistakes of the last World Cup tournament"**
> Martin Jol

Sagnol as wing-backs to try and find some width.

It ended 0-0 and was their 17th game undefeated under Domenech but there have been nine draws and five blank sheets, and Germany are the only top-20 side they have faced since Euro 2004.

Henry is in good form despite Arsenal's midfield problems and Trezeguet is scoring impressively for Inter Milan this season, although neither seems to be doing so for France.

There are many players that Domenech could look to if he wanted to freshen up the squad but the French squad has become a hard group to break into.

Are we worried? Not really; a dogged defence is often a good route to the finals and even if Domenech doesn't get the tactics right, there is enough talent on the pitch to prevent them getting beaten.

They should win a weak-looking Group G even if they start slowly against the Swiss. If the other results pan out, and they keep winning, they don't meet Brazil until the final.

GROUP FIXTURES

SWITZERLAND	Tue 13 June 1700 BST
SOUTH KOREA	Sun 18 June 2000 BST
TOGO	Fri 23 June 2000 BST

Paris

Zone	Europe
Population	60,771,476
Capital	Paris
Language	French
Top league	Ligue 1
Major clubs	**Capacities**
Lyon	44,000
Marseille	60,000
Paris QQ	49,000

Where likely squad players play:

In France			11
In Premiership			6
In Italy	3	In Holland	0
In Spain	2	In Germany	1

Number of French players playing:

In France			410
In Premiership			40
In Italy	12	In Holland	5
In Spain	14	In Germany	10

World Cup record

1930 -	Group 3rd	1974 -	Did not qualify
1934 -	Round 1	1978 -	Group 3rd
1938 -	Quarter-finals	1982 -	Fourth place
1950 -	Did not qualify	1986 -	Third place
1954 -	Group 3rd	1990 -	Did not qualify
1958 -	Third place	1994 -	Did not qualify
1962 -	Did not qualify	1998 -	Champions
1966 -	Group 4th	2002 -	Group 4th
1970 -	Did not qualify		

KEY PLAYER

THIERRY HENRY ARSENAL

Thierry Henry didn't always have Va-Va-Voom. Juventus spent £14m on the 21-year-old World Cup winner in 1999 but his stay in Italy was short and frustrating.
He was played out of position on the wing, and he wasn't given time to adapt to the defensive nature of Serie A.
After 16 games, his former manager at Monaco, Arsene Wenger, stepped in and took him to Arsenal for £10.5m. He converted him back into a centre forward. The Premiership is still reeling! Henry is not only the most prolific striker the league has seen in recent years, he also does a lot of damage around the box and regularly features at the top of our 'Assists' chart.
Henry is one of our Top 12 Players: as are Coupet, Gallas, Makelele and Trezeguet.

AGE 28 | **STRIKER** | **WORLD RANKING 19**

THE SQUAD

Goalkeepers	Club side	Age	QG
Fabien Barthez	Marseille	34	4
Gregory Coupet	Lyon	33	6
Defenders			
Jean-Alain Boumsong	Newcastle	26	6
Patrice Evra	Man Utd	25	3
William Gallas	Chelsea	28	10
Gael Givet	AS Monaco	24	7
Bernard Mendy	Paris SG	24	1
Anthony Reveillere	Lyon	26	1
Willy Sagnol	Bayern Munich	29	5
Mikael Silvestre	Man Utd	28	2
Sebastien Squillaci	AS Monaco	25	5
Lilian Thuram	Juventus	34	4
Midfielders			
Olivier Dacourt	Roma	31	2
Vikash Dhorasoo	Paris SG	32	4
Alou Diarra	Lens	24	4
Ludovic Giuly	Barcelona	29	4
Claude Makelele	Chelsea	33	4
Florent Malouda	Lyon	25	4
Rio Mavuba	Bordeaux	22	1
Camel Meriem	AS Monaco	26	1
Benoit Pedretti	Lyon	25	3
Robert Pires	Arsenal	32	4
Jerome Rothen	Paris SG	28	1
Patrick Vieira	Juventus	29	9
Zinedine Zidane	Real Madrid	33	4
Forwards			
Djibril Cisse	Liverpool	24	6
Sydney Govou	Lyon	26	4
Thierry Henry	Arsenal	28	6
Louis Saha	Man Utd	27	2
David Trezeguet	Juventus	28	2
Sylvain Wiltord	Lyon	32	8

■ Probable ■ Possible **QG** Qualification Games

KEY GOALKEEPER

GREGORY COUPET
LYON

Gregory Coupet learned a lot about the game from his father, a professional goalkeeper who played for Hazebrouck in France's second division.

Having started his career with Saint-Etienne, Coupet moved to local rivals Lyon in 1997. He has been a regular in their championship winning side ever since.

Coupet is one of our Top Four Keepers.

AGE 33	WORLD RANKING 18

FABIEN BARTHEZ
MARSEILLE

At international level, **Fabien Barthez** has been selected ahead of Coupet but with the Marseille and former Manchester United star retiring this year, Coupet is likely to collect a lot more caps for his bulging trophy cabinet.

AGE 34	WORLD RANKING 454

KEY DEFENDERS

SEBASTIEN SQUILLACI
AS MONACO

Sebastien Squillaci is expected to be one of the mainstays of the French national team for at least the next five years or so.

He is a tall goal-scoring central defender who is fast on his feet. Squillaci started his professional career with his hometown club Toulon before joining Monaco in 1998. His French debut came in 2004.

Playing record	12 mths lge	wcq
Appearances:	23	5
Minutes played:	1893	375
Percentage played:	50.1%	41.7%
Goals conceded:	20	0
Clean sheets:	10	5
Cards:	Y2, R1	Y0, R0
Defensive rating:	95mins	-
Defensive ranking:	42nd	-

AGE 25	WORLD RANKING 398

WILLY SAGNOL
BAYERN MUNICH

Playing record	12 mths lge	wcq
Appearances:	35	5
Minutes played:	3047	448
Percentage played:	91.5%	49.8%
Goals conceded:	24	1
Clean sheets:	16	4
Cards:	Y5, R0	Y2, R0
Defensive rating:	127mins	448mins
Defensive ranking:	13th	11th

AGE 28	WORLD RANKING 86

LILIAN THURAM
JUVENTUS

This summer Lilian Thuram stands on the threshold of greatness.

A top European defender for ten years he earned his 110th French cap in the international against Germany in November. The French record is 116 and belongs to Thuram's former team-mate Marcel Desailly.

He was a World Cup winner in France's famous back-four in 1998. He played out of position at full back and rampaged forward to score twice in the semi-finals against Croatia. He is the only surviving member of a backline which included Desailly, Laurent Blanc and Bixente Lizarazu.

Like Zidane, Thuram retired after Euro 2004 but was tempted back to help 'Les Bleus' qualify from a tough group.

At club level, Thuram made 37 appearances for Juventus as they won the Scudetto last season, recording 19 clean sheets - the top defence in Serie A.

This season they are top of the league and Thuram is playing as solidly and regularly as ever, suggesting he's still at the top of his game and will soon become the most capped player in French football.

Playing record	12 mths lge	wcq
Appearances:	36	4
Minutes played:	3119	345
Percentage played:	78.8%	38.3%
Goals conceded:	27	1
Clean sheets:	16	3
Cards:	Y4, R1	Y0, R0
Defensive rating:	116mins	345mins
Defensive ranking:	22nd	17th

AGE 34	WORLD RANKING 113

THE MANAGER

Coach Raymond Domenech succeeded Jacques Santini (who left for Tottenham) after the disappointment of Euro 2004.

The former Under 21 coach won the role from among 41 applicants but France is a side not living up to the undoubted brilliance of its players. Domenech is accused of losing control, amid bust-ups with a number of perceived troublemakers. France were second in the FIFA Rankings when he took over, at the end of a lacklustre qualification they had slipped to ninth.

The out-of-favour group include Robert Pires who complained about the coach. Johan Micoud is in top form at Werder Bremen and could add creativity to the midfield but is seen as too awkward a customer. Another is Nicolas Anelka, recently called up for a friendly.

The press hailed the returning trio of Zidane, Makelele and Thuram, forcing Domenech's hand to select them, so one of Patrick Vieira, Vikash Dhorasoo and Florent Malouda has to be left out.

KEY DEFENDER

WILLIAM GALLAS CHELSEA

John Terry wins the headlines, Ricardo Carvalho cost nearly £14m more to bring to Stamford Bridge, but William Gallas is very much the unsung hero of the Chelsea defence.

He's good in the air, formidably strong and a terrific tackler. Gallas is a central defender but has the pace to play at full back and is versatile enough to do it on either side.

In his 28 appearances last season, Chelsea only conceded ten league goals while he was on the pitch and enjoyed 19 clean sheets.

He won his 37th cap for France last November and may have edged ahead of Lilian Thuram in France's defensive pecking order.

Gallas is a Top 12 defender.

AGE 28   **DEFENDER**   **WORLD RANKING 3**

KEY MIDFIELDERS

PATRICK VIEIRA
JUVENTUS

Patrick Vieira has been one of the most influential midfielders in European football for nearly ten years.

He was the heart and soul of the Arsenal side that won league and cup doubles in both 1997/98 and 2001/2. Following a £13.7m transfer to Juventus in July 2005, he is building on that success in Italian football.

In 2002, Vieira became the Arsenal club captain and lifted the 2003 FA Cup before leading them in their 'Untouchables' 2003/4 season in which they didn't lose a single game. He combines athleticism, power, fine technique and a commanding presence.

Playing record	12 mths lge	wcq
Appearances:	21	9
Minutes played:	1890	708
Percentage played:	47.7%	78.7%
Goals scored:	4	0
Goals conceded:	16	2
Cards:	Y8, R0	Y2, R1
Power rating:	44mins	64mins
Power ranking:	21st	98th

AGE 29	WORLD RANKING 48

CLAUDE MAKELELE
CHELSEA

Claude Makelele does the same job for France as he does for Chelsea.

He protects the defence, knits play together, and keeps possession. No one does it better, and Zidane gets the platform he needs to destroy teams.

He's one of our Top 12 Midfielders.

AGE 33	WORLD RANKING 14

LUDOVIC GIULY
BARCELONA

France's rich selection of attacking talent has restricted the exciting Ludovic Giuly to 17 caps - mostly from the bench - and three goals.

However, don't be surprised to see him make a breakthrough in the summer. He was in irrepressible form leading a moderate Monaco side to the 2004 Champions League final. In his debut season for Barcelona, he out-scored Ronaldinho, with 11 league goals.

Playing record	12 mths lge	wcq
Appearances:	33	4
Minutes played:	2256	245
Percentage played:	61.1%	27.2%
Goals scored:	13	2
Goals conceded:	25	0
Cards:	Y2, R0	Y0, R0
Power rating:	43mins	82mins
Power ranking:	19th	111th

AGE 29	WORLD RANKING 74

FLORENT MALOUDA
LYON

Lyon's Florent Malouda is the best left-midfield playing in France and has nine caps for Les Bleus.

Playing record	12 mths lge	wcq
Appearances:	34	5
Minutes played:	2476	381
Percentage played:	65.5%	42.3%
Goals scored:	5	0
Goals conceded:	19	5
Cards:	Y2, R0	Y0, R0
Power rating:	59mins	76mins
Power ranking:	79th	108th

AGE 25	WORLD RANKING 80

KEY STRIKERS

ZINEDINE ZIDANE
REAL MADRID

Zinedine Zidane is the most expensive player in football history.

He was France's starring midfielder when they won the World Cup in 1998 and scored two goals in the final against Brazil. He moved from Juventus to become the most costly of Real Madrid's 'Galacticos' and made a return in the 2002 Champions League final by striking a glorious goal as Real beat Bayer Leverkusen.

One of the greatest midfielders ever to have played the game, his decision to come out of international retirement and help France qualify for the 2006 World Cup was a lift for the country as much as the team and took affect immediately with a crucial win in Dublin.

He combines pace, control, vision and breathtaking skill to make him the most creative of modern midfielders.

Playing record	12 mths lge	wcq
Appearances:	29	4
Minutes played:	2199	305
Percentage played:	59.6%	33.9%
Goals scored:	9	1
Goals conceded:	27	1
Cards:	Y4, R1	Y1, R0
Power rating:	45mins	38mins
Power ranking:	26th	24th

AGE 33	WORLD RANKING 127

KEY STRIKER

DAVID TREZEGUET Juventus

Injuries have limited David Trezeguet's club appearances in recent seasons and consequently France dropped him. Manager Raymond Domenech lost faith in the forward after his sending off against Israel and he only featured in two qualifiers. However, he forced his way back into selection with scintillating form for Juventus is Serie A. Trezeguet scored 23 goals in 27 games for Juventus, leaving club colleagues Zlatan Ibrahimovic and Alessandro Del Piero trailing in his wake.

Originally, a club colleague of Thierry Henry at Monaco, Trezeguet looks in even more devastating form than the Arsenal man. France aren't scoring enough – expect Trezeguet to add to his 60 caps.

Trezeguet is one of our Top 12 Strikers.

| AGE 28 | STRIKER | WORLD RANKING 17 |

ROUTE TO THE FINALS

Switzerland had to battle all the way to get to the World Cup Finals and they will be stronger for the experience.

First came the Group 4 struggle with France, Israel, the Republic of Ireland and Switzerland all playing draws against each other. Everyone beat the Faroe Islands and Cyprus but no one could record a victory against any other of the top four sides.

The Swiss top-scored, thanks to a six-goal hammering of the Faroes in their first game. Then came the draws with their main rivals, all waiting to see who would blink first. Switzerland had at least to finish even in Dublin in their final game to earn a runners-up spot on goal difference. It was a 0-0 draw.

However, the battle wasn't over. They beat Turkey in their home play-off with goals by

Philippe Senderos and Valon Behrami in Berne. Turkey threw everything at the Swiss in Istanbul, winning 4-2 to level on goal difference but going out on the away goals rule. A fight between players immediately after the game led to FIFA placing a ban on the Turkish side.

FINAL QUALIFYING TABLE
EUROPE GROUP 4

	P	W	D	L	F	A	Pts
France	10	5	5	0	14	2	20
Switzerland	10	4	6	0	18	7	18
Israel	10	4	6	0	15	10	18
Rep of Ireland	10	4	5	1	12	5	17
Cyprus	10	1	1	8	8	20	4
Faroe Islands	10	0	1	9	4	27	1

European Group Play-offs

Switzerland beat Turkey

					FIFA ranking			
1	04 Sep 04	Home	Faroe Islands	131	W	**6 0**	Vonlanthen 10, 14, 57, Rey 29, 44, 55
2	08 Sep 04	Home	Rep of Ireland	16	D	**1 1**	H.Yakin 17
3	09 Oct 04	Away	Israel	47	D	**2 2**	Frei 26, Vonlanthen 34
4	26 Mar 05	Away	France	4	D	**0 0**	
5	30 Mar 05	Home	Cyprus	105	W	**1 0**	Frei 88, 88
6	04 Jun 05	Away	Faroe Islands	131	W	**1 3**	Wicky 25, Frei 73, 86
7	03 Sep 05	Home	Israel	47	D	**1 1**	Frei 5
8	07 Sep 05	Away	Cyprus	105	W	**1 3**	Frei 15, Senderos 70, Gygax 84
9	08 Oct 05	Home	France	4	D	**1 1**	Magnin 79
10	12 Oct 05	Away	Rep of Ireland	16	D	**0 0**	
11	12 Nov 05	Home	Turkey	12	W	**2 0**	Senderos 24, Behrami 86
12	16 Nov 05	Away	Turkey	12	L	**4 2**	Frei 2pen, Streller 84
	Average FIFA ranking of opposition			58			

MAIN PLAYER PERFORMANCES IN QUALIFICATION

Match	1 2 3 4 5 6 7 8 9 10 11 12	Appearances	Started	Subbed on	Subbed off	Mins played	% played	Goals	Yellow	Red
Venue	H H A A H A H A H A H A									
Result	W D D D W W D W D D W L									
Goalkeepers										
Pascal Zuberbuhler		12	12	0	0	1080	100.0	0	1	0
Defenders										
Stephane Grichting		1	0	1	0	8	0.7	0	0	0
Bernt Haas		3	3	0	0	270	25.0	0	0	0
Stephane Henchoz		2	0	2	0	31	2.9	0	1	0
Johan Lonfat		4	2	2	2	102	9.4	0	2	0
Ludovic Magnin		10	7	3	1	704	65.2	1	2	0
Patrick Muller		12	12	0	0	1080	100.0	0	0	0
Philippe Senderos		8	8	0	0	720	66.7	2	0	0
Murat Yakin		3	3	0	1	240	22.2	0	0	0
Midfielders										
Tranquillo Barnetta		9	9	0	5	717	66.4	0	1	0
Ricardo Cabanas		10	9	1	1	808	74.8	0	1	0
Philipp Degen		9	9	0	1	765	70.8	0	1	0
Daniel Gygax		10	7	3	2	660	61.1	1	0	0
Benjamin Huggel		4	0	4	0	180	16.7	0	1	0
Christoph Spycher		6	5	1	2	398	36.9	0	0	0
Johann Vogel		12	12	0	0	1080	100.0	0	1	0
Johan Vonlanthen		10	8	2	5	683	63.2	4	0	0
Raphael Wicky		6	6	0	2	531	49.2	1	4	0
Reto Ziegler		3	2	1	2	123	11.4	0	0	0
Forwards										
Alex Frei		10	10	0	1	882	81.7	8	1	0
Mauro Lustrinelli		2	0	2	0	17	1.6	0	0	0
Alexandre Rey		2	2	0	1	165	15.3	3	0	0
Marco Streller		3	1	2	2	170	15.7	1	1	0
Hakan Yakin		6	4	2	2	369	34.2	1	0	0

FINAL PROSPECTS

The battling Swiss captain Johann Vogel sums up the dogged spirit of his side. He makes life extremely difficult for opponents, raises his game against superior sides but almost never scores (81 caps – two goals).

The Swiss qualified for Euro 2004, drew against Croatia but lost out to Wayne Rooney and Thierry Henry. They have since managed two draws against France in qualifying though and will feel confident in the Group G game against their neighbours.

The French league's top scorer Rennes' Alexander Frei has hit 23 goals in his 42 caps. He is their best chance of reaching the latter stages. Johan Vonlanthen, 20, eclipsed Rooney to become the youngest-ever European Championships scorer in Euro 2004. The South Korea game will be crucial and should decide the runners-up spot.

THE MANAGER

The Switzerland coach Jakob 'Kobi' Kuhn took charge in 2001 and has led them through the most successful period in the team's history. Kuhn won six Swiss championship winners' medals in midfield for FC Zurich and 63 international caps.

The Swiss went a full year and 14 games without defeat, before losing to Turkey in the final play-off game.

He has helped turn Hamburg midfielder Raphael Wicky, Arsenal stopper Philippe Senderos and Bayer Leverkusen's Tranquillo Barnetta into capable internationals.

Jakob Kuhn

GROUP FIXTURES

FRANCE	Tue 13 June 1700 BST
TOGO	Mon 19 June 1400 BST
SOUTH KOREA	Fri 23 June 2000 BST

● Bern

Zone	Europe
Population	7,498,505
Capital	Berne
Language	German, Fre nch, Italian
Top league	FL Super League
Major clubs	**Capacities**
FC Basel	42,000
FC Zurich	19,500
Grasshoppers	17,800

Where likely squad players play:

In Premiership	3	In Spain	0
In Holland	0	In France	6
In Italy	3	In Germany	9

Number of Swiss players playing:

In Premiership	4	In Spain	2
In Holland	3	In France	9
In Italy	1	In Germany	13

World Cup record

1930 -	Did not enter	1974 -	Did not qualify
1934 -	Quarter-finals	1978 -	Did not qualify
1938 -	Quarter-finals	1982	Did not qualify
1950 -	Group 3rd	1986	Did not qualify
1954 -	Quarter-finals	1990 -	Did not qualify
1958 -	Did not qualify	1994 -	Last 16
1962 -	Group 4th	1998 -	Did not qualify
1966 -	Group 4th	2002 -	Did not qualify
1970 -	Did not qualify		

THE SQUAD

Goalkeepers	Club side	Age	QG
Pascal Zuberbuhler	Basel	35	12
Fabio Coltorti	Grasshoppers	25	0
Defenders			
Philipp Degen	B Dortmund	23	9
Stephane Grichting	Auxerre	27	1
Bernt Haas	Bastia	28	3
Stephane Henchoz	Wigan	31	2
Johan Lonfat	Sochaux	32	4
Ludovic Magnin	Stuttgart	27	10
Patrick Muller	Lyon	29	12
Alain Rochat	Rennes	23	1
Philippe Senderos	Arsenal	21	8
Murat Yakin	Basel	31	3
Midfielders			
Tranquillo Barnetta	B Leverkusen	21	9
Valon Behrami	Lazio	21	2
Ricardo Cabanas	Cologne	27	10
Daniel Gygax	Lille	24	10
Benjamin Huggel	Eintr Frankfurt	28	4
Xavier Margairaz	Zurich	22	1
Christoph Spycher	Eintr Frankfurt	28	6
Johann Vogel	AC Milan	29	12
Johan Vonlanthen	Brescia	20	10
Raphael Wicky	Hamburg	29	6
Reto Ziegler	Wigan	20	3
Forwards			
Alexander Frei	Rennes	26	10
Thomas Haberli	Young Boys Bern	32	1
Mauro Lustrinelli	Sparta Prague	30	2
Alexandre Rey	Neuchatel	33	2
Marco Streller	Cologne	24	3
Hakan Yakin	Stuttgart	29	6

■ Probable ■ Possible **QG** Qualification Games

KEY PLAYER

ALEXANDER FREI RENNES

Alexander Frei was a journeyman striker flitting between Swiss clubs before he moved to struggling French side Rennes. He started hitting the net; topping the French league charts with 20 in 2003/4.
Last season he repeated the feat, his 20 goals lifting Rennes up to fourth place. The Swiss are a hard-working team but he gives them potency up front.

Playing record	12 mths lge	wcq
Appearances:	36	10
Minutes played:	2980	882
Percentage played:	80.8%	81.7%
Goals scored:	16	8
Percentage share:	30.19	34.78
Cards:	Y5, R0	Y1, R0
Strike rate:	186mins	110mins
Strike rate ranking:	35th	14th

AGE 26   **STRIKER**   **WORLD RANKING** 105

SOUTH KOREA

ROUTE TO THE FINALS

After the unimagined success of a semi-final spot under Guus Hiddink in 2002, the expectation level for the Taeguk Warriors was sky-high.

However, Hiddink was a hard man to replace and the Koreans were held to a disastrous goalless draw by the lowly Maldives in the first stage of qualifying. Out went Portuguese coach Humberto Coelho, replaced by Dutchman Jo Bonfrere.

He took them into Asia's last eight but an early defeat by Saudi Arabia (ranked level with the Koreans by FIFA) knocked confidence. The final qualifying game was between the two Asian Group 1 finalists. Saudi were solid defensively so despite dominating possession and the best

efforts of teen striker Chu-Young Park, Korea went down 1-0. The Warriors had already qualified but not in the style expected of semi-finalists, Bonfrere was despatched and Dick Advocaat put in charge for the final preparation. Dong-Gook Lee hit five goals in qualifying but lost his place to Chu-Young Park towards the end of the campaign.

FINAL QUALIFYING TABLE
ASIA STAGE 3 – GROUP A

	P	W	D	L	F	A	Pts
Saudi Arabia	6	4	2	0	10	1	14
South Korea	6	3	1	2	9	5	10
Uzbekistan	6	1	2	3	7	11	5
Kuwait	6	1	1	4	4	13	4

#	Date	Venue	Opponent	FIFA ranking	Result		Scorers
1	18 Feb 04	Home	Lebanon	114	W	**2 0**	Cha 32, BK Cho 51
2	31 Mar 04	Away	Maldives	141	D	**0 0**	
3	09 Jun 04	Home	Vietnam SR	108	W	**2 0**	Ahn 29, Do-Heon Kim 61
4	08 Sep 04	Away	Vietnam SR	108	W	**1 2**	DG Lee 63, CS Lee 76
5	13 Oct 04	Away	Lebanon	114	D	**1 1**	JC Choi 8
6	17 Nov 04	Home	Maldives	141	W	**2 0**	Do-Heon Kim 66, DG Lee 80
7	09 Feb 05	Home	Kuwait	59	W	**2 0**	DG Lee 24, Y-P Lee 81
8	25 Mar 05	Away	Saudi Arabia	30	L	**2 0**	
9	30 Mar 05	Home	Uzbekistan	54	W	**2 1**	Y-P Lee 54, DG Lee 61
10	03 Jun 05	Away	Uzbekistan	54	D	**1 1**	CY.Park 90
11	08 Jun 05	Away	Kuwait	59	W	**0 4**	CY.Park 19, DG.Lee 29, Chung 55, Ji-Sung Park 61
12	17 Aug 05	Home	Saudi Arabia	30	L	**0 1**	
	Average FIFA ranking of opposition			84			

MAIN PLAYER PERFORMANCES IN QUALIFICATION

Match	1 2 3 4 5 6 7 8 9 10 11 12	Appearances	Started	Subbed on	Subbed off	Mins played	% played	Goals	Yellow	Red
Venue	H A H A A H H A H A A H									
Result	W D W W D W W L W D W L									
Goalkeepers										
Woon-Jae Lee		12	12	0	0	1080	100.0	0	0	0
Defenders										
Byung-Kuk Cho		3	3	0	0	270	25.0	1	0	0
Jin-Chul Choi		6	6	0	0	540	50.0	1	0	0
Dong-Jin Kim		7	7	0	2	586	54.3	0	1	1
Han Yoon Kim		2	2	0	0	180	16.7	0	1	0
Jin Kyu Kim		3	3	0	0	270	25.0	0	0	0
Young Chul Kim		1	1	0	0	90	8.3	0	0	0
Min-Sung Lee		2	2	0	1	155	14.4	0	1	0
Young-Pyo Lee		11	11	0	0	990	91.7	2	1	0
Dong-Hyuk Park		4	4	0	0	360	33.3	0	1	0
Jae Hong Park		5	5	0	0	450	41.7	0	2	0
Sang-Chul Yoo		6	6	0	2	516	47.8	0	0	0
Kyoung-Youl You		5	5	0	0	450	41.7	0	1	0
Midfielders										
Kyung-ho Chung		6	1	5	0	222	20.6	1	1	0
Do-Heon Kim		7	3	4	2	268	24.8	2	1	0
Jung-Woo Kim		5	1	4	0	191	17.7	0	2	0
Nam-Il Kim		5	5	0	1	405	37.5	0	2	0
Ji-Sung Park		8	8	0	0	720	66.7	1	0	0
Ki-Hyeon Seol		9	6	3	3	559	51.8	0	1	0
Chong-Gug Song		5	5	0	1	383	35.5	0	1	1
Forwards										
Jung-Hwan Ahn		9	8	1	4	613	56.8	1	1	0
Doo-Ri Cha		6	6	0	2	467	43.2	1	1	0
Chung-Soo Lee		6	5	1	2	464	43.0	1	0	0
Dong-Gook Lee		8	7	1	4	573	53.1	5	0	0
Chu Young Park		3	3	0	0	270	25.0	2	0	0

FINAL PROSPECTS

One big difference over the 2002 World Cup team is that South Korea now have some big club stars.

Ji-Sung Park and Young-Pyo Lee played key roles in PSV Eindhoven's 2004/5 Dutch league title win and Champions League campaign.

Now at Manchester United and Spurs respectively, they can bring European experience to the Korean enthusiasm for soccer. Doo-Ri Cha plays up front in the Bundesliga for Eintracht Frankfurt while Eul-Yong Lee is a pacy winger and free-kick expert at Turkish Premier side, Trabzonspor. Another Park, Chu-Young, is only 20 but the striker was Young Asia Player of the Year in 2004 and scored twice in the qualifiers.

Another big difference is no home crowd, no Hiddink and far less preparation. Qualification from Group G may still come on the back of a first game win against Togo.

THE MANAGER

Dick Advocaat arrived in South Korea with the task of raising morale after a below par qualification.

"We still have eight months to go and we can do well," said the Dutchman, promising to rebuild confidence.

Advocaat has plenty of international experience, having coached Holland twice. The first time he took them to the quarter-finals of the 1994 World Cup. He had a good spell at PSV before taking himself and a host of Dutch stars off to Glasgow for Rangers in 1998. Put back in charge of the Dutch, he led them to the semi-finals of Euro 2004.

Dick Advocaat

GROUP FIXTURES

TOGO	Tue 13 June 1400 BST
FRANCE	Sun 18 June 2000 BST
SWITZERLAND	Fri 23 June 2000 BST

Seoul

Zone	Asia
Population	48,764,470
Capital	Seoul
Language	Korean
Top league	K League
Major clubs	**Capacities**
FC Seoul	64,600
Suwon Bluewings	44,000
FC Incheon	52,100

Where likely squad players play:

In South Korea	18
In Premiership	2
In other major five European Leagues	1
Outside major European Leagues	2

Number of South Korean players playing:

In Premiership	2
In other major five European Leagues	3

World Cup record

1930 -	Did not enter	1974 -	Did not qualify
1934 -	Did not enter	1978 -	Did not qualify
1938 -	Did not enter	1982 -	Did not qualify
1950 -	Did not enter	1986 -	Group 4th
1954 -	Group 4th	1990 -	Group 4th
1958 -	Did not enter	1994 -	Group 3rd
1962 -	Did not qualify	1998 -	Group 4th
1966 -	Withdrew	2002 -	Fourth place
1970 -	Did not qualify		

THE SQUAD

Goalkeepers	Club side	Age	QG
Woon-jae Lee	Samsung Bluewings	33	12
Jun-ho Cho	Bucheon SK	33	0
Young-kwang Kim	Chunnam Dragons	22	0
Defenders			
Byung-Kuk Cho	Chunnam Dragons	24	3
Jin-Chul Choi	Jeoniu	35	6
Dong-Jin Kim	FC Seoul	24	7
Han Yoon Kim	FC Seoul	31	2
Jin Kyu Kim	Jubilo Iwata	21	3
Tae-Young Kim	Chunman Dragons	35	2
Min-Sung Lee	Pusan Daewoo	32	2
Young-Pyo Lee	Tottenham	29	11
Dong-Hyuk Park	Ulsan Tigers	27	4
Jae Hong Park	Chunman Dragons	27	5
Sang-Chul Yoo	Ulsan Tigers	34	6
Kyoung-Youl You	Ulsan Tigers	27	5
Midfielders			
Ji-Hoon Baek	FC Seoul	21	1
Kyung-ho Chung	Ulsan Tigers	26	6
Do-Heon Kim	Seongnam Chunma	23	7
Jung-Woo Kim	Grampus Eight	24	5
Nam-Il Kim	Samsung Bluewings	32	5
Eul-Yong Lee	Trabzonspor	30	2
Ji Sung Park	Man Utd	25	8
Ki-Hyeon Seol	Wolverhampton	27	9
Chong-Gug Song	Samsung Bluewings	27	5
Forwards			
Jung-Hwan Ahn	Duisburg	30	9
Doo-Ri Cha	Eintr Frankfurt	25	6
Jae-Jin Cho	Shimizu S-Pulse	24	2
Sung-Kuk Choi	Ulsan Tigers	23	1
Chung-Soo Lee	Ulsan Tigers	24	6
Dong-Gook Lee	Pohang Steelers	27	8
Do Namkung	Gwangju Phoenix	24	2
Chu Young Park	FC Seoul	20	3

■ Probable ■ Possible **QG** Qualification Games

KEY PLAYER

JI-SUNG PARK MAN UTD

Ji-Sung Park began his international career as a defensive midfield player.
He was moved to the wing by Guus Hiddink. Park's simple direct running unnerves defences and he started scoring, most notably in the World Cup against Portugal. A Dutch league title at PSV led to his £4m move to United.

Top 12 defender: Young-Pyo Lee

Playing record	12 mths lge	wcq
Appearances:	23	8
Minutes played:	1275	720
Percentage played:	34.6%	66.7%
Goals scored:	1	1
Goals conceded:	14	4
Cards:	Y0, R0	Y0, R0
Power rating:	44mins	48mins
Power ranking:	22nd	64th

AGE 25   **MIDFIELDER**   **WORLD RANKING 147**

TOGO

ROUTE TO THE FINALS

Senegal, the conquerors of France in 2002, had stars playing in top teams across Europe. The Hawks of Togo had a lanky striker playing for Metz in the French second division.

Senegal were ranked in the top 30 teams in FIFA's international charts, Togo were barely in the top 100. At the time of the World Cup qualification draw, it seemed easy to predict the winners of African Group 1.

Togo scraped past Equatorial Guinea in the preliminaries and promptly lost away to Zambia in their first group game. The next match was at home to Senegal and Emmanuel Adebayor put the Hawks ahead after 29 minutes. Junior Senaya, who then played for Swiss minnows Concordia BS, struck twice in the second half.

Adebayor continued to pile on the goals as they beat Zambia, completed a double over disappointing Mali, drew with Senegal away and won through to Germany with a win in the Congo.

Adebayor's total of 11 goals included one in the pre-qualifying games against Equatorial Guinea. The league table and the results below does not include pre-qualifying.

FINAL QUALIFYING TABLE
AFRICA GROUP 1

	P	W	D	L	F	A	Pts
Togo	10	7	2	1	20	8	23
Senegal	10	6	3	1	21	8	21
Zambia	10	6	1	3	16	10	19
Congo	10	3	1	6	10	14	10
Mali	10	2	2	6	11	14	8
Liberia	10	1	1	8	3	27	4

#	Date		Opponent	FIFA ranking	Result			Scorers
1	05 Jun 04	Away	Zambia	65	L	1	0	
2	20 Jun 04	Home	Senegal	33	W	3	1	Adebayor 30, J.Senaya 76, 85
3	04 Jul 04	Away	Liberia	128	D	0	0	
4	05 Sep 04	Home	Congo	113	W	2	0	Adebayor 37, 80
5	10 Oct 04	Home	Mali	57	W	1	0	Adebayor 23
6	27 Mar 05	Away	Mali	57	W	1	2	M.Salifou 78, Toure 90
7	05 Jun 05	Home	Zambia	65	W	4	1	Adebayor 14, 90, Toure 45, Coubadja 61
8	18 Jun 05	Away	Senegal	33	D	2	2	Olufade 11, Adebayor 71
9	04 Sep 05	Home	Liberia	128	W	3	0	Adebayor 52, 90, Toure 69
10	08 Oct 05	Away	Congo	113	W	2	3	Adebayor 40, Coubadja 60, 70
	Average FIFA ranking of opposition			**79**				

Not including pre-qualifying games.

MAIN PLAYER PERFORMANCES IN QUALIFICATION

Match	1 2 3 4 5 6 7 8 9 10	Appearances	Started	Subbed on	Subbed off	Mins played	% played	Goals	Yellow	Red
Venue	A H A H H H A H A H									
Result	L W D W W W W D W W									
Goalkeepers										
Kossi Agassa		9	9	0	0	810	90.0	0	1	0
Ouro Tchagnirou		1	1	0	0	90	10.0	0	0	0
Defenders										
Jean-Paul Yaovi Abalo		9	9	0	0	810	90.0	0	1	0
Eric Akoto		7	6	1	2	515	57.2	0	0	1
Mohama Atte-Oudeyi		8	8	0	0	720	80.0	0	0	0
Abdoul Gafar Mamah		6	6	0	0	540	60.0	0	1	0
Dare Nibombe		8	7	1	0	668	74.2	0	1	0
Lantame Ouadja		3	0	3	0	46	5.1	0	0	0
Massamasso Tchangai		1	1	0	0	90	10.0	0	1	0
Midfielders										
Ismalia Atte-Oudeyi		1	1	0	0	90	10.0	0	0	0
Yao Aziawonou		9	7	2	0	728	80.9	0	0	0
Abdel Coubadja		6	6	0	2	517	57.4	3	3	0
Komlan Eninful		1	0	1	0	3	0.3	0	0	0
Alessandro Farias		1	0	1	0	15	1.7	0	0	0
Guyazou Kassim		3	2	1	0	194	21.6	0	1	0
Emmanuel Mathias		4	4	0	1	346	38.4	0	0	0
Jacques Romao		2	2	0	1	122	13.6	0	0	0
Moustapha Salifou		8	5	3	4	435	48.3	1	2	0
Tadjou Salou		1	1	0	1	52	5.8	0	0	0
Robert Souliemane		1	0	1	0	58	6.4	0	0	0
Sherif Toure		10	10	0	1	867	96.3	3	1	0
Forwards										
Emmanuel Sheyi Adebayor		10	9	1	2	812	90.2	10	0	0
Komlan Amewou		3	3	0	1	249	27.7	0	0	0
Adekamni Olufade		7	6	1	4	449	49.9	1	0	0

Key: ■ Played all 90 mins   ◄◄ Started but subbed off   ►► Subbed on   ■ On the bench   □ Not in the squad

FINAL PROSPECTS

Arsene Wenger may have his hands full with his new signing from Togo.

The tall striker Emmanuel Adebayor fell out with the French club Monaco for repeatedly missing training, claiming the Togo team was his priority. During the African Cup of Nations, Adebayor argued with Togo coach Stephen Keshi and refused to play in a 2-0 defeat against DR Congo. Ultimately, Keshi was sacked as a result.

The new Gunners striker is vital to Togo's slim chances. His 11 goals made him top-scorer in the African World Cup qualifiers and made-up 55% of his side's goals. He is the star, the only top-club regular and the side's talisman, while his height offers something unique in attack. Fellow striker Kader Toure barely played for Sochaux last season. Even with him, they will fall at the group stage.

THE MANAGER

The Togolese FA sacked manager Stephen Keshi following his row with star striker and new Arsenal signing, Emmanuel Adebayor, during the African Cup of Nations.

Keshi, a former Nigerian international, who captained his country in the 1994 World Cup in the USA, had worked wonders with the Togolese team. When the qualification tournament started, Togo were in the 90s in FIFA's World Rankings – the lowest ranking among any of the final qualifiers. They now stand at 56 (we show their average for the year above).

The new manager appointed is German Otto Pfister, 67, who managed Saudi in the 1994 World Cup, but player mutterings have cast this into doubt.

Stephen Keshi

GROUP FIXTURES

SOUTH KOREA	Tue 13 June 1400 BST
SWITZERLAND	Mon 19 June 1400 BST
FRANCE	Fri 23 June 2000 BST

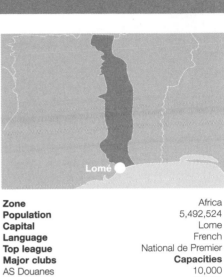

Lomé

Zone	Africa
Population	5,492,524
Capital	Lome
Language	French
Top league	National de Premier
Major clubs	**Capacities**
AS Douanes	10,000
Etolle Filante	10,000
Dynamio Togolals	10,000

Where likely squad players play:

In Togo	11
In Premiership	1
In other major five European Leagues	3
Outside major European Leagues	8

Number of Togolese players playing:

In Premiership	1
In other major five European Leagues	3

World Cup record

1930 -	Did not enter	1974 -	Did not qualify
1934 -	Did not enter	1978 -	Did not qualify
1938 -	Did not enter	1982 -	Did not qualify
1950 -	Did not enter	1986	Withdrew
1954 -	Did not enter	1990	Withdrew
1958 -	Did not enter	1994 -	Did not qualify
1962 -	Did not enter	1998 -	Did not qualify
1966 -	Did not enter	2002 -	Did not qualify
1970 -	Did not enter		

THE SQUAD

Goalkeepers	Club side	Age	QG
Kossi Agassa	Metz	27	9
Ouro Tchagnirou	Djollba	28	1
Defenders			
Jean-Paul Yaovi Abalo	Dunkerque	31	9
Eric Akoto	Admira Wacker	25	7
Mohama Atte-Oudeyi	Lokeren	25	8
Abdoul Gafar Mamah	105 Libreville	20	6
Dare Nibombe	Mons	29	8
Lantame Ouadja	-	28	3
Massamasso Tchangai	Benevento	27	1
Midfielders			
Ismalla Atte-Oudeyi	Douanes Lome	21	1
Yao Aziawonou	Young Boys Bern	26	9
Abdel Coubadja	Sochaux	27	6
Komlan Eninful	AS Douanes	21	1
Guyazou Kassim	Douanes Lome	24	3
Souleymane Mamam	Royal Antwerp	20	1
Emmanuel Mathias	Esperance Tunis	20	4
Jacques Romao	Louhans	22	2
Moustapha Salifou	Brest	23	8
Tadjou Salou	AS Douanes	31	1
Sherif Toure	Metz	25	10
Forwards			
Emmanuel Adebayor	Arsenal	22	10
Komlan Amewou	Hearts Kpando	22	3
Thomas Dossevi	Valenciennes	27	1
Adekamni Olufade	Al Siliya	26	7
Djima Oyawole	Shenzhen Jianlibao	29	1
Junior Senaya	YF Juve Zurich	22	9

■ Probable ■ Possible **QG** Qualification Games

KEY PLAYER

EMMANUEL ADEBAYOR ARSENAL

Togo's hopes rest on the tall slim shoulders of Emmanuel Adebayor, who gives them class and height up front.

Reminiscent of his Nigerian hero, Nwanko Kanu, Adebayor is a skilful forward whose 1.9m height is accompanied by pace and athleticism.

He played for FC Metz, then Monaco and scored on his debut for Arsenal.

Playing record	12 mths lge	wcq
Appearances:	3	10
Minutes played:	270	812
Percentage played:	7.5%	90.2%
Goals scored:	1	10
Percentage share:	1.37	50.00
Cards:	Y0, R0	Y0, R0
Strike rate:	-	81mins
Power ranking:	-	5th

AGE 22   **STRIKER**   **WORLD RANKING** 682

Position	1st	2nd	3rd	4th	5th	6th	7th	8th
Group	E	F	C	A	D	H	B	G
Total FIFA ranking	89	93	95	96	101	109	117	138

SPAIN V UKRAINE
UKRW DRAW Leipzig, Wednesday 14th June 1400 BST

Ukraine seem to be Andriy Shevchenko and a lot of players you've never heard of but there's an astonishing amount of European cup experience in their top teams. Chart successes in the Champions League and Uefa Cups in recent seasons and the Ukrainian league is in the top ten. Dinamo Kiev, Shakhtar Dontesk and Dnipro have all progressed in both cups. So of course have Barcelona, Real Madrid and Villarreal – the key difference is that the Ukrainian teams have more indigenous players.

While all eyes will inevitably be on Shevchenko, Ruslan Rotan could also prove influential; he is a dominant figure in midfield and scores vital goals. During qualifying Rotan was one of seven Dnipro players in Blokhin's squad. He has since moved to Kiev but is still the key player in the area of the pitch where Ukraine are weakest.

TUNISIA V SAUDI ARABIA
TUNW TUNW Munich, Wednesday 14th June 1700 BST

The 2004 African Cup of Nations winners, Tunisia had a disappointing tournament this year, going out in the quarter-finals. However, it took a penalty shoot out for a strong Nigerian side to put them out. Up front, Francileudo Dos Santos is often singled out but he only hit six of Tunisia's 25 goals in qualifying so there are other threats in the team. Tunisian skipper Hatem Trabelsi missed the first four qualifying games with injury and they got off to a stuttering start. The Ajax defender retuned and put the side back on track

SPAIN V TUNISIA
SPAW SPAW Hamburg, Monday 19th June 2000 BST

Spain's poor tournament form will mean anything less than a win against Ukraine will see the jitters set in. There's plenty of midfield talent in the Spanish squad but the one clear contender for a start, Barcelona's Xavi Hernandez has been out with a long-term injury. Joaquin was recently dropped, Vicente is in and out of the side, Reyes and Liverpool's Luis Garcia are demanding a place so Aragones has decisions to make.

When things get tough Carlos Puyol is Spain's rock in defence and the passion that he brings to his game should rub off on his forward colleagues.

SAUDI ARABIA V UKRAINE
UKRW UKRW Hamburg, Monday 19th June 1700 BST

Saudi Arabia may enjoy their best possession in this game but still look too lightweight to break through a solid Ukrainian defence, which only conceded three goals in its first seven qualifying games.

Saudi used 15 forwards in different permutations in 12 qualifying games. It either shows strength in depth or a lack of confidence.

SAUDI ARABIA V SPAIN
SPAW SPAW Kaiserslauten, Friday 23rd June 1500 BST

Spain to finish the group with a win but the Saudis will be determined to perform better than they did in the final group game of 2002 against Germany. Fernando Torres' beloved Atletico Madrid are having a tough mid-table season. The goals aren't flowing with eight from the first 23 games but this is his chance to show he's the Spanish Rooney.

UKRAINE V TUNISIA
UKRW DRAW Berlin, Friday 23rd June 1500 BST

Tunisia are strong in defence and only conceded three in the last six games following Trabelsi's return to the side. They will make Ukraine work for a final win and, by this stage, the Ukrainians may not need one. Shevchenko is the class act on the field and if Ukraine want to finish top of the group and avoid France, he's the man to earn them a win.

Tunisia's Francileudo Dos Santos

MARTIN JOL'S VIEW

I have always liked Spanish football and believe Spain's Primera Liga, together with the English Premiership are the two most attractive leagues in Europe.

Atletico Madrid centre forward Fernando Torres will be the star of the Spanish team this summer. He is only 22 but has everything a modern striker needs: speed, skill and a killer instinct in front of goal.

Spain will also have several other very good attacking players in their squad, such as Joaquin (Real Betis), Jose Antonio Reyes (Arsenal), Vicente (Valencia) and, of course, Real Madrid captain Raul. They will also have the experienced Carlos Puyol as the rock at the heart of their defence.

But with Spain you always have to wait and see if a group of 11 gifted individuals can play as a team. The Spaniards have seriously underperformed in the World Cup over the years with their best ever finish being fourth place… and that was achieved back in 1950!

In fact the Spanish rarely produce the goods at senior international football tournaments, while their youth teams strangely always seem to do well. However, the current Spanish side has played together for some time and can be expected to make it through to the knockout stages.

"Andriy Shevchenko's speed proves too much for almost every defence he plays against"

Ukraine were the first European country to qualify for the finals in Germany and they did it with three games in hand from a group that included Euro 2004 champions Greece and Turkey, who finished third at the 2002 World Cup. They are not the most attacking team in football, but will be very hard to beat.

They will rely heavily on AC Milan's Andriy Shevchenko. He is one of the best strikers in Europe and his speed has proved too much for almost every defence he played against.

Ukraine can be regarded as outsiders for the tournament and will surely survive this first round of group matches.

Tunisia left it late to book their place for this summer's tournament. It took a hard-fought 2-2 against North African rivals Morocco last October to secure qualification.

GROUP H

They were also not at their best at the 2006 Africa Cup of Nations. They have some good talents like defenders Karim Hagui (Strasbourg) and Karim Saidi (Feyenoord), while Hamed Namouchi has done well in midfield for Glasgow Rangers. Brazilian-born striker Francileudo Santos, who plays for Toulouse, will be their main threat up front. Tunisia coach Roger Lemerre guided France to glory at Euro 2000 but is likely to struggle this time to reach the second round.

Of all the countries, Saudi Arabia is the most unknown and I am sure they will not cause any upsets, as they hardly have any players performing regularly in European leagues.

Still, they have some good home-based players. One is goalkeeper Mbrouk Zaid, while their top-scorer and natural leader is still Sami Al Jaber, who has over 150 caps and will be appearing in his fourth World Cup finals.

He had a spell on loan at Wolverhampton back in 2000 but was beset by injuries at Molineux and returned home without making much of an impact. Saudi Arabia's head coach in qualifying was the 45-year old Argentinian Gabriel Calderon, who played in the 1990 World Cup final against Germany.

> "But with Spain you always have to see if a group of 11 individuals can play as a team"

MARTIN JOL'S PREDICTIONS FOR THE TOP TWO TEAMS FROM THIS GROUP
Schedule of play is on page 80

GROUP STAGE	LAST SIXTEEN	QUARTER-FINALS
FIRST GROUP H	v SECOND GROUP G	v FIRST GROUP F or SECOND GROUP E
UKRAINE	UKRAINE v SWITZERLAND	UKRAINE v BRAZIL
SECOND GROUP H	v FIRST GROUP G	v FIRST GROUP E or SECOND GROUP F
SPAIN	SPAIN v FRANCE	FRANCE v ITALY

GROUP H SPAIN, UKRAINE, TUNISIA, SAUDI ARABIA

GROUP G FRANCE, SWITZERLAND, SOUTH KOREA, TOGO

GROUP E ITALY, GHANA, USA, CZECH REPUBLIC
GROUP F BRAZIL, CROATIA, AUSTRALIA, JAPAN

The top two in this group can't meet a team from England's group until at least the semi-finals and even then France and Brazil stand in the way.

ROUTE TO THE FINALS

Spain have qualified for their eighth World Cup finals in a row but they made heavy weather of it.

They finished second in European Group 7, two points behind Serbia & Montenegro, which meant that Luis Aragones' side were in the play-offs. Spain won five of their ten qualifiers, but could only draw the remaining five.

The two games against Serbia were key to the oucome and after a goalless draw away, Raul and Kezman exchanged goals in Madrid.

Spain had to win a play-off over two legs against Slovakia to reach the 2006 finals. Slovakia finished second in European Group 3, ahead of Russia, and were rated as one of the most improved sides in Europe. However, they were without their Bundesliga star Marek Mintal and Spain finally found their form in the first leg in Madrid and trounced Slovakia 5-1.

Liverpool's supercharged Luis Garcia scored a hat-trick, with the other goals coming from his Anfield team-mate Fernando Morientes and Atletico Madrid's Fernando Torres. The second leg in Bratislava ended 1-1.

FINAL QUALIFYING TABLE
EUROPE GROUP 7

	P	W	D	L	F	A	Pts
Serbia and Mont	10	6	4	0	16	1	22
Spain	10	5	5	0	19	3	20
Bosnia-Herz	10	4	4	2	12	9	16
Belgium	10	3	3	4	16	11	12
Lithuania	10	2	4	4	8	9	10
San Marino	10	0	0	10	2	40	0

European Group Play-offs
Spain beat Slovakia

				FIFA ranking			
1	08 Sep 04	Away	Bosnia	74	D	1 1	Vicente 66
2	09 Oct 04	Home	Belgium	47	W	2 0	Luque 59, Raul 63
3	13 Oct 04	Away	Lithuania	97	D	0 0	
4	09 Feb 05	Home	San Marino	160	W	5 0	Joaquin 15, Torres 33, Raul 43,
							Guti 64, Del Horno 79
5	30 Mar 05	Away	Serbia & Montenegro	46	D	0 0	
6	04 Jun 05	Home	Lithuania	97	W	1 0	Luque 68
7	08 Jun 05	Home	Bosnia	74	D	1 1	Marchena 90
8	07 Sep 05	Home	Serbia & Montenegro	46	D	1 1	Raul 18
9	08 Oct 05	Away	Belgium	47	W	0 2	Torres 56, 59
10	12 Oct 05	Away	San Marino	160	W	0 6	Raul 1, Torres 10, 76pen, 88,
							Sergio 30, 49
11	12 Nov 05	Home	Slovakia	47	W	5 1	Garcia 10, 18, 74, Torres 65,
							Morientes 79
12	16 Nov 05	Away	Slovakia	47	D	1 1	Villa 70
	Average FIFA ranking of opposition			**78**			

MAIN PLAYER PERFORMANCES IN QUALIFICATION

Match	1 2 3 4 5 6 7 8 9 10 11 12	Appearances	Started	Subbed on	Subbed off	Mins played	% played	Goals	Yellow	Red
Venue	A H A H A H H H A A H A									
Result	D W D W D W D D W W W D									
Goalkeepers										
Iker Casillas		12	12	0	0	1080	100.0	0	0	0
Defenders										
Asier Del Horno		6	6	0	1	510	47.2	1	1	0
Juanito		3	1	2	0	218	20.2	0	0	0
Carlos Marchena		7	7	0	0	630	58.3	1	1	0
Pablo Ibanez		4	4	0	0	360	33.3	0	0	0
Carlos Puyol		11	11	0	2	862	79.8	0	1	0
Michel Salgado		10	10	0	0	900	83.3	0	0	0
Midfielders										
David Albelda		9	9	0	3	731	67.7	0	8	0
Guerrero Antonio Lopez		4	3	1	1	269	24.9	0	0	0
Ruben Baraja		6	3	3	2	285	26.4	0	0	0
Ivan De La Pena		3	3	0	1	225	20.8	0	0	0
Luis Garcia		3	1	2	1	130	12.0	3	0	0
Sanchez Joaquin		8	7	1	2	589	54.5	1	1	0
Gonzalez Sergio		4	2	2	0	209	19.4	2	1	0
Xabi Alonso		3	2	1	0	205	19.0	0	1	0
Xavi Hernandez		10	10	0	2	865	80.1	0	3	0
Forwards										
Alberto Luque		6	2	4	0	327	30.3	2	0	0
Fernando Morientes		3	0	3	0	82	7.6	1	1	0
Raul		12	11	1	3	978	90.4	4	0	0
Jose Antonio Reyes		7	5	2	3	430	39.8	0	1	0
Fernando Torres		10	10	0	6	679	62.9	7	1	0
Rodriguez Guillen Vicente		7	6	1	2	519	48.1	1	0	0
David Villa		3	1	2	1	126	11.7	1	1	0

FINAL PROSPECTS

Much has been said and written about Spain's failure to play to their full potential at World Cup finals.

They have not made it past the quarter-finals since 1950, when they finished in fourth place. Since then they have played at nine World Cup finals and every tournament has ended in disappointment.

They will start as one of the favourites in Germany this summer and again expectations will be high.

They have been drawn in what looks like being one of the easier groups, along with Ukraine, Tunisia and Saudi Arabia.

Coach Luis Aragones will expect his team to win all their group matches, but the question is can the Spaniards hold their collective form together for the duration of the tournament.

"Fernando Torres has everything a modern striker needs; speed, skill and a killer instinct"
Martin Jol

Atletico Madrid's Fernando Torres hit seven goals in the qualifiers and the 22-year-old striker could emerge as one of the stars of the finals.

Joaquin (Real Betis) and Vicente (Valencia) are quick skilful wingers who can open up any defence but Joaquin's form has been questioned.

Aragones will have options in the centre of midfield, with Barcelona's Xavi, Liverpool's Xabi Alonso and David Albelda of Valencia, all capable of winning ball and keeping possession. However, it is hardly a settled unit and its most trusted performer, Xavi, has been out with a long term injury.

The Spanish defence, which let in eight goals in 12 qualifiers, is marshalled by Barcelona skipper Carlos Puyol and will not be easily breached.

They have three stunning keepers but Real Madrid's Iker Casillas, who was always regarded as one of the best shot-stoppers in the world and has now improved his all-round game, will be preferred to Reina and Valdes.

Even if Aragones can get his team to play to their top form, they will meet France in the last 16 or Brazil in the quarter-finals.

This team is not one of Spain's strongest and either of those tests would prove too much for them. Another early exit.

GROUP FIXTURES

UKRAINE	Wed 14 June 1400 BST
TUNISIA	Mon 19 June 2000 BST
SAUDI ARABIA	Fri 23 June 1500 BST

Madrid

Zone		Europe
Population		40,341,013
Capital		Madrid
Language		Spanish
Top league		La Liga
Major clubs		**Capacities**
Barcelona		98,600
Real Madrid		80,300
Valencia		50,000

Where likely squad players play:

In Spain			18
In Premiership			5
In Italy	0	In France	0
In Holland	0	In Germany	0

Number of Spanish players playing:

In Spain			454
In Premiership			17
In Italy	3	In France	3
In Holland	3	In Germany	3

World Cup record

1930 -	Did not enter	1974 -	Did not qualify
1934 -	Quarter-finals	1978 -	Group 3rd
1938 -	Withdrew	1982 -	Round 2
1950 -	Fourth place	1986 -	Quarter-finals
1954 -	Did not qualify	1990 -	Last 16
1958 -	Did not qualify	1994 -	Quarter-finals
1962 -	Group 4th	1998 -	Group 3rd
1966 -	Group 3rd	2002 -	Quarter-finals
1970 -	Did not qualify		

THE SQUAD

Goalkeepers	Club side	Age	QG
Ikor Casillas	Real Madrid	25	12
Pepe Reina	Liverpool	23	0
Victor Valdes	Barcelona	24	0
Defenders			
Capdevila	Deportivo	28	1
Asier Del Horno	Chelsea	25	6
Ivan Helguera	Real Madrid	31	1
Juanito	Real Betis	29	3
Carlos Marchena	Valencia	26	7
Pablo Ibanez	Atl Madrid	24	4
Carlos Puyol	Barcelona	28	11
Enrique Romero	Deportivo	34	1
Michel Salgado	Real Madrid	30	10
Midfielders			
David Albelda	Valencia	28	9
Guerrero Lopez	Atl Madrid	24	5
Ruben Baraja	Valencia	30	6
Ivan De La Pena	Espanyol	30	3
Sanchez Joaquin	Real Betis	24	8
Javier Luis Garcia	Liverpool	27	3
Gonzalez Sergio	Deportivo	29	4
Juan Carlos Valeron	Deportivo	30	1
Rodriguez Vicente	Valencia	24	7
Sanchez Victor	Deportivo	30	2
Xabi Alonso	Liverpool	24	3
Xavi Hernandez	Barcelona	26	10
Forwards			
Alberto Luque	Newcastle	28	6
Fernando Morientes	Liverpool	30	3
Raul	Real Madrid	28	12
Jose Antonio Reyes	Arsenal	22	7
Raul Tamudo	Espanyol	28	2
Fernando Torres	Atl Madrid	22	10
David Villa	Valencia	24	3

■ Probable ■ Possible **QG** Qualification Games

KEY PLAYER

RAUL REAL MADRID

Raul is the golden boy of Spanish football and his record is outstanding. He became the youngest player to play for Real Madrid when he was just 17. Two years later, he won his first cap in 1996 against the Czech Republic and has gone on to become Spain's leading scorer of all time with over 40 goals.

Top 12 Players: Valdes, Puyol

Playing record	12 mths lge	wcq
Appearances:	27	12
Minutes played:	2017	978
Percentage played:	53.4%	90.6%
Goals scored:	10	4
Percentage share:	12.20	16.00
Cards:	Y0, R0	Y0, R0
Strike rate:	202mins	244mins
Strike rate ranking:	49th	44th

AGE 28 | **STRIKER** | **WORLD RANKING 93**

KEY GOALKEEPER

IKER CASILLAS
REAL MADRID

Iker Casillas is ahead in the pecking order of the trio of young, gifted Spanish keepers currently playing top-flight football.

He first won Spain's goalkeeping jersey from Santiago Canizares and Jose Molina in 2000 and is currently preferred to Barcelona's Victor Valdes and Liverpool's Jose Reina.

Casillas has spent his entire career at Real Madrid. An agile shot-stopper with lightning reflexes, he has been criticised for his ability with crosses but has worked hard to improve.

'Pepe' Reina is in excellent form for Liverpool whose manager, Rafael Benitez says he's the best keeper in Spain. Valdes is third choice but the Barcelona keeper's form makes him one of our Top Four Goalkeepers.

Playing record	12 mths lge	wcq
Appearances:	42	12
Minutes played:	3743	1080
Percentage played:	99.0%	100.0%
Goals conceded:	40	5
Clean sheets:	18	7
Cards:	Y1, R0	Y0, R0
Defensive rating:	94mins	216mins
Defensive ranking:	13th	6th

AGE 25 | **WORLD RANKING 101**

KEY DEFENDERS

MICHEL SALGADO
REAL MADRID

Michel Salgado is the right back for Real Madrid and Spain and he loves to attack.

Steve McManaman joked that Salgado only knew two words of English, 'cover me', which he shouted as he raced forward.

His position for Madrid is currently under threat from new Brazilian recruit Cicinho, whose attacking gallops are even more suicidal.

Playing record	12 mths lge	wcq
Appearances:	30	10
Minutes played:	2562	900
Percentage played:	67.8%	83.3%
Goals conceded:	23	5
Clean sheets:	15	5
Cards:	Y12, R0	Y3, R0
Defensive rating:	111mins	180mins
Defensive ranking:	29th	36th

AGE 30 | **WORLD RANKING 202**

PABLO IBANEZ
ATL MADRID

Playing record	12 mths lge	wcq
Appearances:	39	4
Minutes played:	3486	360
Percentage played:	92.2%	33.3%
Goals conceded:	31	2
Clean sheets:	20	2
Cards:	Y14, R1	Y0, R0
Defensive rating:	112mins	180mins
Defensive ranking:	27th	32nd

AGE 24 | **WORLD RANKING 333**

ASIER DEL HORNO
CHELSEA

Asier Del Horno is the Chelsea left back who uses his lightning pace to make marauding runs down the flank.

He joined last summer from Athletic Bilboa and is quick, strong in the tackle and a totally committed player, who is exceptionally good in the air. He poses a real threat in his opponent's penalty area – and not just at set pieces.

Playing record	12 mths lge	wcq
Appearances:	32	6
Minutes played:	2434	510
Percentage played:	64.4%	47.2%
Goals conceded:	22	2
Clean sheets:	18	4
Cards:	Y5, R0	Y1, R0
Defensive rating:	111mins	255mins
Defensive ranking:	31st	21st

AGE 25 | **WORLD RANKING 324**

CARLOS MARCHENA
VALENCIA

Playing record	12 mths lge	wcq
Appearances:	30	7
Minutes played:	2413	630
Percentage played:	63.8%	58.3%
Goals conceded:	30	2
Clean sheets:	11	5
Cards:	Y9, R2	Y1, R0
Defensive rating:	80mins	315mins
Defensive ranking:	69th	19th

AGE 27 | **WORLD RANKING 702**

THE MANAGER

Luis Aragones had previously turned down the job as manager of the Spanish national team before he was finally appointed in succession to Inaki Saez after Euro 2004.

The 68-year-old Aragones was born in Hortaleza, Madrid and made a name for himself as a centre forward with Atletico Madrid during the 1960s and early 1970s where his goal-scoring exploits and thunderous free-kicks earned him the nickname Zapatones (big boots). He also played for Real Betis, Oviedo and Recreativo.

When he retired as a player in 1974, he was made Atletico coach almost straightaway. He soon gained a reputation as a no-nonsense coach, with a very short temper. His outspoken comments have landed him in hot water with the authorities.

After guiding Atletico to the Spanish League and Cup double in 1996, Aragones moved on to manage seven of Spain's top clubs before eventually accepting the national team challenge.

KEY DEFENDER

CARLOS PUYOL BARCELONA

Carlos Puyol is the darling of the terraces at the Nou Camp. Barcelona's captain is defensively solid and hugely committed.

He played as a right back but a change in coach at Barcelona led to change in position. Raddy Antic – in a short spell in charge - moved Puyol to centre back, where he has thrived ever since.

He made 36 league appearances for Barcelona in their championship-winning 2004/5 season. He picked up 17 clean sheets and his Defensive rating of a goal conceded every 122 minutes was one of the top four in the Primera Liga.

He's been through the bad times with Barca so he's enjoying the good times now.

He is one of our Top 12 Defenders.

| AGE 28 | DEFENDER | WORLD RANKING 33 |

KEY MIDFIELDERS

HERNANDEZ XAVI
BARCELONA

Xavi Hernandez is the Barcelona midfield anchor who doubles as first choice in Spain's centre field.

His exceptional passing and ball control played a major role in helping Barcelona win the Spanish Primera Liga title for the first time in six years in 2005.

Playing record	12 mths lge	wcq
Appearances:	27	10
Minutes played:	2316	865
Percentage played:	61.3%	80.1%
Goals scored:	0	0
Goals conceded:	24	4
Cards:	Y2, R0	Y3, R0
Power rating:	42mins	48mins
Power ranking:	15th	64th

AGE 26 | **WORLD RANKING 68**

JOAQUIN
REAL BETIS

Joaquin is one of the most admired wingers in European football.

Chelsea felt the full force of his attacking play as he inspired Real Betis to become the first side to beat the Premier champions in 2005/6.

Playing record	12 mths lge	wcq
Appearances:	40	8
Minutes played:	3454	589
Percentage played:	91.4%	54.5%
Goals scored:	6	1
Goals conceded:	59	1
Cards:	Y3, R1	Y1, R0
Power rating:	65mins	49mins
Power ranking:	99th	70th

AGE 25 | **WORLD RANKING 187**

DAVID ALBELDA
VALENCIA

David Albelda is an uncompromising midfield player who came to prominence with a string of gutsy performances in 2001/2 when he helped Valencia win Spain's Primera Liga title.

He was even more influential in a second title triumph two seasons later.

Playing record	12 mths lge	wcq
Appearances:	38	9
Minutes played:	3381	731
Percentage played:	89.4%	67.7%
Goals scored:	2	0
Goals conceded:	35	2
Cards:	Y16, R1	Y8, R0
Power rating:	65mins	52mins
Power ranking:	98th	79th

AGE 28 | **WORLD RANKING 229**

XAVIER ALONSO
LIVERPOOL

Rafael Benitez was determined to pluck some jewels out of the Spanish Primera Liga when he joined as Liverpool manager. Top of his list was Xavier Alonso.

'Xabi', was signed for £10.7m from Real Sociedad to control games with a mix of short simple passes and raking through balls.

AGE 24 | **WORLD RANKING 270**

VICENTE
VALENCIA

Vicente Rodríguez Guillén is known simply as Vicente to the adoring fans of Valencia.

Since the young left winger arrived as an unknown from rivals Levante their team has emerged as a power in Spain's Primera Liga.

In 2001/2 Vicente took over the left midfield position from Argentinian Kily Gonzalez and the club won the league title. By the time they took their next title in 2003/4, Vicente was firing over crosses for Mista to turn into goals.

Playing record	12 mths lge	wcq
Appearances:	24	7
Minutes played:	1943	519
Percentage played:	51.4%	48.1%
Goals scored:	4	1
Percentage share:	6.67	4.00
Cards:	Y2, R0	Y0, R0
Strike rate:	486mins	519mins
Strike rate ranking:	87th	61st

AGE 24 | **WORLD RANKING 821**

KEY STRIKERS

JOSE ANTONIO REYES
ARSENAL

Jose Reyes made his debut for Spanish club Seville in the 1999/2000 season. He was soon an integral part of the first team, scoring eight goals in 34 games in 2002/3.

Seville signed him on a long-term contract but alerted a number of big clubs to his worth. Arsenal won Reyes' signature in January 2004 and he made a 13 appearances, scoring twice in the run in to the Premiership title.

He can play as a forward, or on either wing and has quick feet with a temper to match generating the odd red card. His recent performance for Arsenal in a 1-0 win at the Bernabeu will have done his World Cup chances no harm.

Playing record	12 mths lge	wcq
Appearances:	30	7
Minutes played:	2170	430
Percentage played:	58.8%	39.8%
Goals scored:	6	0
Percentage share:	8.22	0.00
Cards:	Y6, R0	Y1, R0
Strike rate:	362mins	-
Strike rate ranking:	76th	-

AGE 22 | **WORLD RANKING 298**

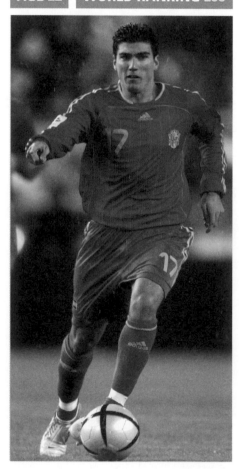

KEY STRIKER

FERNANDO TORRES ATL MADRID

As Raul's form stutters, Spain increasingly looks to Fernando Torres as their most natural finisher. He top-scored with seven goals in their qualifying games.
A Spanish Wayne Rooney, Torres was the youngest player ever to play for Atletico Madrid, he was also their youngest scorer and the youngest player ever to play for Spain on his debut in 2003.

Playing record	12 mths lge	wcq
Appearances:	41	10
Minutes played:	3613	679
Percentage played:	95.6%	62.9%
Goals scored:	18	7
Percentage share:	33.96	28.00
Cards:	Y7, R0	Y1, R0
Strike rate:	201mins	97mins
Strike rate ranking:	48th	9th

AGE 22   **STRIKER**   **WORLD RANKING 257**

ROUTE TO THE FINALS

Ukraine were the first European country to book a place in Germany with two games to spare when they drew with Georgia in September.

Yet, Europe Group 2 was one of the two toughest qualifying groups. It included runners-up Turkey, Denmark and Euro 2004 champions Greece.

Dynamo Kiev's Olekander Shovkovskyi showed why he is one of the most reliable goalkeepers in Europe, while the Ukrainian defence was quite outstanding during the qualifiers. They conceded just seven goals in 12 matches, which included a remarkable run of six clean sheets in a row.

Two of the Ukraine's best performances were away victories in Turkey and Greece. Their final crucial point came away in Tblisi despite an 89th-minute equaliser for the hosts. It denied Ukraine a victory but only put celebrations on ice until Turkey failed to win against Denmark in a 2-2 draw on the same day.

Oleg Blokhin's side could afford to relax with three games to go. They conceded four goals and let Turkey in for a win in the Ukraine.

FINAL QUALIFYING TABLE
EUROPE GROUP 2

	P	W	D	L	F	A	Pts
Ukraine	12	7	4	1	18	7	25
Turkey	12	6	5	1	23	9	23
Denmark	12	6	4	2	24	12	22
Greece	12	6	3	3	15	9	21
Albania	12	4	1	7	11	20	13
Georgia	12	2	4	6	14	25	10
Kazakhstan	12	0	1	11	6	29	1

	Date	Venue	Opponent	FIFA ranking	Result	Score		Scorers
1	04 Sep 04	Away	Denmark	15	D	1	1	Husin 56
2	08 Sep 04	Away	Kazakhstan	145	W	1	2	Byelyk 14, Ruslan Rotan 90
3	09 Oct 04	Home	Greece	15	D	1	1	Shevchenko 48
4	13 Oct 04	Home	Georgia	102	W	2	0	Byelyk 12, Shevchenko 79
5	17 Nov 04	Away	Turkey	12	W	0	3	Gusev 9, Shevchenko 17, 90
6	09 Feb 05	Away	Albania	86	W	0	2	Rusol 40, Husin 59
7	30 Mar 05	Home	Denmark	15	W	1	0	Voronin 67
8	04 Jun 05	Home	Kazakhstan	145	W	2	0	Shevchenko 18, Avdejev 83og
9	08 Jun 05	Away	Greece	15	W	0	1	Husin 81
10	03 Sep 05	Away	Georgia	102	D	1	1	Rotan 44
11	07 Sep 05	Home	Turkey	12	L	0	1	
12	08 Oct 05	Home	Albania	86	D	2	2	Shevchenko 45, Rotan 86
	Average FIFA ranking of opposition	86						

MAIN PLAYER PERFORMANCES IN QUALIFICATION

Match	1 2 3 4 5 6 7 8 9 10 11 12	Appearances	Started	Subbed on	Subbed off	Mins played	% played	Goals	Yellow	Red
Venue	A A H H A A H H A A H H									
Result	D W D W W W W W W D L D									
Goalkeepers										
Olekander Shovkovskyi		12	12	0	0	1080	100.0	0	1	0
Defenders										
Serhiy Fedorov		8	7	1	0	635	58.8	0	1	0
Andriy Nesmachny		11	11	0	0	990	91.7	0	2	0
Aleksandr Radchenko		3	1	2	1	137	12.7	0	0	0
Andrey Rusol		12	12	0	0	1080	100.0	1	1	0
Mykhailo Starostyak		2	2	0	1	138	12.8	0	0	0
Vyacheslav Sviderskyy		1	1	0	0	90	8.3	0	1	0
Vladyslav Vashchuk		1	1	0	0	90	8.3	0	0	0
Volodymyr Yezerskiy		10	10	0	2	850	78.7	0	2	0
Midfielders										
Oleg Gusev		8	8	0	1	704	65.2	1	0	0
Andriy Husin		9	8	1	2	697	64.5	3	1	0
Sergey Nazarenko		3	1	2	1	88	8.1	0	0	0
Ruslan Rotan		7	5	2	2	464	43.0	3	0	0
Rykun		2	0	2	0	39	3.6	0	0	0
Oleg Shelayev		9	6	3	3	550	50.9	0	2	0
Anatoli Timoshchyuk		7	7	0	0	630	58.3	0	1	0
Serhiy Zakarliuka		3	1	2	0	160	14.8	0	0	0
Forwards										
Oleksiy Byelyk		7	3	4	1	326	30.2	2	0	0
Sergei Rebrov		2	0	2	0	37	3.4	0	0	0
Andriy Shevchenko		9	9	0	3	775	71.8	6	0	0
Oleg Venglinski		1	0	1	0	23	2.1	0	0	0
Andrei Vorobey		7	5	2	3	417	38.6	0	1	0
Andrey Voronin		11	10	1	9	801	74.2	1	1	0

Key: ■ Played all 90 mins   ◄◄ Started but subbed off   ►► Subbed on   ☐ On the bench   ☐ Not in the squad

FINAL PROSPECTS

Ukraine showed during the qualifiers that they are a difficult side to break down.

They also have midfielders such as Dinamo Kiev's Ruslan Rotan, who are capable of scoring important goals.

However, despite having a solid defence and hard-working midfielders, AC Milan's striker Andriy Shevchenko remains Ukraine's jewel in the crown and most likely match winner.

Ukraine coach Oleg Blokhin has introduced some good young players in most positions, but he has yet to unearth another striker with the pace and clinical finishing skills of Shevchenko. Bayer Leverkusen's Andrey Voronin is likely to be the second striker but he only scored one from ten starts in qualifying.

Blokhin can be relied upon to get his tactics right and the Ukrainians will expect to reach the last 16.

THE MANAGER

Oleg Blokhin was appointed Ukraine's head coach in September 2003. He had a dazzling playing career and was regarded as one of the best strikers in Europe.

The 53-year-old Blokhin, who was born in Kiev when it was part of the old Soviet Union, won a record 112 caps for the USSR.

He spearheaded the Dynamo Kiev attack for 15 years and, apart from breaking most club and league records, was named European Player of the Year in 1975. Blokhin coached Greek clubs Olympiakos, PAOK and Ionikos before the Ukraine.

Oleg Blokhin

GROUP FIXTURES

SPAIN	Wed 14 June 1400 BST
SAUDI ARABIA	Mon 19 June 1700 BST
TUNISIA	Fri 23 June 1500 BST

ANDRIY SHEVCHENKO AC MILAN

A rumoured target for Chelsea billionaire Roman Abramovich, Andriy Shevchenko is the kind of player you break transfer records to get.

He won five Ukrainian league titles with Dinamo Kiev and came to the fore when he set the Champions League alight with his goals. AC Milan signed him for about £18m in 1999.

His first season in Serie A brought 24 goals and he hasn't stopped scoring since as Milan have won both the Italian League and the Champions League.

He captains the Ukraine and is part of a three-pronged Andriy strike force, with Andrei Vorobey of Shakhtar Donetsk and Andrey Voronin.

Shevchenko is a Top 12 Striker

| AGE 29 | STRIKER | WORLD RANKING 47 |

Zone	Europe
Population	46,847,877
Capital	Kiev
Language	Ukrainian, Russian
Top league	Premier League
Major clubs	**Capacities**
Dynamo Kiev	16,900
Shakhtar Donetsk	31,700
Dnipro Dnipropetrovsk	24,400
Where likely squad players play:	
In Ukraine	20
In Premiership	0
In other major five European Leagues	2
Outside major European Leagues	1
Number of Ukranian players playing:	
In Premiership	0
In other major five European Leagues	4

World Cup record

1930 -	Did not enter	1974 -	Did not enter
1934 -	Did not enter	1978 -	Did not enter
1938 -	Did not enter	1982 -	Did not enter
1950 -	Did not enter	1986 -	Did not enter
1954 -	Did not enter	1990 -	Did not enter
1958 -	Did not enter	1994 -	Did not enter
1962 -	Did not enter	1998 -	Did not qualify
1966 -	Did not enter	2002 -	Did not qualify
1970 -	Did not enter		

THE SQUAD

Goalkeepers	Club side	Age	QG
Olekander Shovkovskiy	Dinamo Kiev	31	12
Defenders			
Vyacheslav Checher	Metalurh Donetsk	25	1
Yurii Dmytrulin	Met Zaporizhzhja	31	1
Serhly Fedorov	Dynamo Kiev	31	8
Sergey Matiukhin	Dnipro	20	2
Andriy Nesmachniy	Dinamo Kiev	27	11
Oleksandr Radchenko	Dnipro	29	3
Andrey Husol	Dnipro	23	12
Vlylachesav Shevchuk	Shakhtar Donetsk	27	1
Mykhailo Starostyak	Shinnik Yaros]val	32	2
Vyacheslav Sviderskyy	Arsenal Kiev	27	1
Vladyslav Vashchuk	Dinamo Kiev	31	1
Volodymyr Yezerskiy	Dnipro	29	10
Serhiy Zadorozhny	Kryvbas Kryvyi Rhi	30	1
Midfielders			
Oleg Gusev	Dinamo Kiev	23	7
Oleg Husiev	Dinamo Kiev	23	2
Andriy Husin	Kryla Sovetov	33	9
Sergey Nazarenko	Dnipro	26	3
Ruslan Rotan	Dinamo Kiev	24	7
Rykun	Dnipro	28	2
Oleg Shelayev	Dnipro	29	9
Sermiy Shyshchenko	Metalurh Donetsk	30	1
Anatoli Timoshchyuk	Shakhtar Donetsk	27	9
Serhiy Zakarliuka	Metalurh Donetsk	29	3
Forwards			
Oleksiy Byelyk	Shahtar Donetsk	25	7
Aleksadr Kosyrin	Metalurh Donetsk	28	1
Sergei Rebrov	Dinamo Kiev	32	2
Andriy Shevchenko	AC Milan	29	9
Oleg Venglinski	AEK Athens	28	1
Andrei Vorobey	Shakhtar Donetsk	27	9
Andrey Voronin	B Leverkusen	26	11

■ Probable ■ Possible **QG** Qualification Games

ROUTE TO THE FINALS

Tunisia qualified for Germany after finishing top of African Group 5, beating Morocco into second place by a single point.

The Carthage Eagles won six, drew three and lost just one of their ten qualifiers. The only defeat came away to Guinea when they were beaten 1-0. Tunisia scored a healthy 30 goals in qualifying, with the Brazilian-born Francileundo Dos Santos finding the back of the net six times.

However, the Toulouse striker hit four of his six goals when they hammered Malawi 7-0 in Tunis.

Tunisia made certain of a place in the 2006 finals only after a nerve-wracking 2-2 home draw with Morocco in their very last qualifying match last October. Tunisia twice came from behind to snatch a point. Midfielder Adel Chadi, who plays his club football in Germany with Nuremberg, scored the second equaliser 20 minutes from time.

The luckless Moroccans (who also lost to Tunisia in the finals of the 2004 African Cup of Nations) ended their campaign unbeaten with five wins.

FINAL QUALIFYING TABLE
AFRICA GROUP 5

	P	W	D	L	F	A	Pts
Tunisia	10	6	3	1	25	9	21
Morocco	10	5	5	0	17	7	20
Guinea	10	5	2	3	15	10	17
Kenya	10	3	1	6	8	17	10
Botswana	10	3	0	7	10	18	9
Malawi	10	1	3	6	12	26	6

						FIFA ranking			
1	05 Jun 04	Home	Botswana	101	W	**4 1**	Ribabro 9, Hagui 35, 79, Zitouni 74
2	20 Jun 04	Away	Guinea	86	L	**2 1**	Braham 67
3	04 Sep 04	Away	Morocco	34	D	**1 1**	Dos Santos 11
4	09 Oct 04	Away	Malawi	108	D	**2 2**	Jaziri 82, Ghodhbane 89
5	26 Mar 05	Home	Malawi	108	W	**7 0**	Guemamdia 3, Dos Santos 12, 52, 75, 77, Clayton 60pen, Ghodhbane 80
6	04 Jun 05	Away	Botswana	101	W	**1 3**	Nafti 27, Dos Santos 43, Abdi 78
7	11 Jun 05	Home	Guinea	86	W	**2 0**	Clayton 36pen, Chedli 78
8	17 Aug 05	Home	Kenya	82	W	**1 0**	Guemamdia 2
9	03 Sep 05	Away	Kenya	82	W	**0 2**	Guemamdia 2, Jomma 85
10	08 Oct 05	Home	Morocco	34	D	**2 2**	Clayton 18, Chedli 69
	Average FIFA ranking of opposition			82			

MAIN PLAYER PERFORMANCES IN QUALIFICATION

Match Venue Result	1 2 3 4 5 6 7 8 9 10 H A A A H A H H A H W L D D W W W W W D	Appearances	Started	Subbed on	Subbed off	Mins played	% played	Goals	Yellow	Red
Goalkeepers										
Ali Boumnijel		8	8	0	0	720	80.0	0	0	0
Khaled Fadhel		2	2	0	0	180	20.0	0	0	0
Defenders										
Wissem Abdi		2	2	0	0	180	20.0	1	0	0
Anis Ayari		2	0	2	0	19	2.1	0	0	0
Khaled Badra		4	4	0	1	315	35.0	0	1	0
Jose Clayton		7	7	0	3	556	61.8	3	1	1
Kaies Ghodhbane		7	5	2	1	444	49.3	2	0	0
Karim Hagui		7	7	0	0	630	70.0	2	0	0
Radhi Jaidi		9	9	0	0	810	90.0	0	0	0
Karim Saidi		2	1	1	0	135	15.0	0	1	0
Hatem Trabelsi		6	6	0	0	540	60.0	0	0	0
Alaeddine Yahia		4	2	2	0	233	25.9	0	0	0
Midfielders										
Selim Ben Achour		6	5	1	3	434	48.2	0	2	0
Chaouki Ben Saada		4	3	1	3	213	23.7	0	2	0
Riadh Bouazizi		7	5	2	1	491	54.6	0	0	0
Adel Chedli		8	7	1	3	594	66.0	2	3	0
Jawhar Mnari		9	7	2	1	647	71.9	0	1	0
Mehdi Nafti		5	5	0	2	385	42.8	1	1	0
Hamed Namouchi		3	3	0	1	242	26.9	0	1	0
Forwards										
Najeh Braham		2	2	0	2	134	14.9	1	1	0
Francileudo Dos Santos		7	7	0	4	595	66.1	6	1	0
Haykel Guemamdia		4	3	1	3	232	25.8	3	1	0
Ziad Jaziri		5	5	0	2	417	46.3	1	1	0
Issam Jomma		4	1	3	0	183	20.3	1	0	0
Ali Zitouni		5	1	4	0	156	17.3	1	0	0

FINAL PROSPECTS

Germany 2006 will see Tunisia competing in their fourth World Cup finals, but they have yet to make it through to the second round.

Coach Roger Lemerre believes his team is well equipped to make a big impact at the tournament. His squad is packed with players who earn their living with top clubs across Europe. Bolton's Rahdi Jaidi, a sound defender with a useful knack of scoring set piece goals, will be familiar to English fans.

Lemerre will have his defence well organised around the captain and left back Hatem Trabelsi. Ali Boumnijel is still one of the best keepers in Africa, even though he will be 40 just days before the tournament starts.

Striker Dos Santos scored 50 goals in two seasons for Etoile in Tunisia. The naturalised Brazilian is small and nippy, nicknamed the Roadrunner, and scored on his Tunisia debut in 2003.

THE MANAGER

Roger Lemerre was appointed Tunisia head coach in 2002.

He became a national hero when he guided the Carthage Eagles to a historic win over Morocco in the final of the 2004 African Cup of Nations.

Lemerre was coach of the France side that won Euro 2000, but was also in charge of Le Bleus' shambolic performances at the 2002 World Cup.

The 64-year-old Frenchman has also managed Lens, Racing Paris and Racing Strasbourg. His understanding of Tunisian football stems from his time at top club side L'Esperance de Tunis.

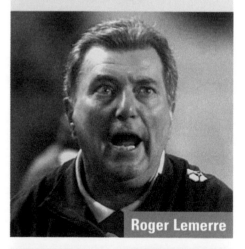

Roger Lemerre

GROUP FIXTURES

SAUDI ARABIA	Wed 14 June 1700 BST
SPAIN	Mon 19 June 2000 BST
UKRAINE	Fri 23 June 1500 BST

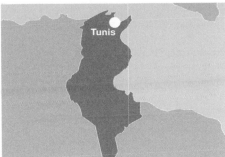

Zone	Africa
Population	10,145,329
Capital	Tunis
Language	Arabic
Top league	Ligue Professionnelle 1

Major clubs	**Capacities**
Esperance de Tunis	45,000
Etoile Sportive	25,000
Club Africain	45,000

Where likely squad players play:

In Tunisia	8
In Premiership	2
In other major five European Leagues	9
Outside major European Leagues	4

Number of Tunisian players playing:

In Premiership	2
In other major five European Leagues	11

World Cup record

1930 -	Did not enter	1974 -	Did not qualify
1934 -	Did not enter	1978 -	Group 3rd
1938 -	Did not enter	1982 -	Did not qualify
1950 -	Did not enter	1986 -	Did not qualify
1954 -	Did not enter	1990 -	Did not qualify
1958 -	Did not enter	1994 -	Did not qualify
1962 -	Did not qualify	1998 -	Group 4th
1966 -	Withdrew	2002 -	Group 4th
1970 -	Did not qualify		

KEY PLAYER

HATEM TRABELSI AJAX

Ajax's overlapping full back, Hatem Trabelsi leads the experienced and miserly Tunisian defence. Originally, a winger who has switched to right back, this will be his third World Cup.

He moved to Ajax in 2001 and has twice won the Dutch title with them. He was injured for the first quarter of 2004/5 finished the season strongly.

Playing record	12 mths lge	wcq
Appearances:	27	6
Minutes played:	2320	540
Percentage played:	61.4%	60.0%
Goals conceded:	29	3
Clean sheets:	12	4
Cards:	Y7, R0	Y0, R0
Defensive rating:	80mins	180mins
Defensive ranking:	69th	34th

AGE 27   **DEFENDER**   **WORLD RANKING** 624

THE SQUAD

Goalkeepers	Club side	Age	QG
Ali Boumnijel	Club Africain	40	8
Khaled Fadhel	Kayseri Erciyesspor	29	2
Defenders			
Wissem Abdi	CS Sfaxien	27	2
Anis Ayari	Samsunspor	24	2
Khaled Badra	Esperance	33	4
Anis Boussaidi	Metalurh Donetsk	25	1
Jose Clayton	Esperance	32	7
Kaies Ghodhbane	Samsunspor	30	7
Karim Hagui	Strasbourg	22	7
Radhi Jaidi	Bolton	30	9
Karim Saidi	Lecce	23	2
Hatem Trabelsi	Ajax	27	6
Alaeddine Yahia	St Etienne	24	4
Midfielders			
Selim Ben Achour	Guimaraes	24	6
Chaouki Ben Saada	Bastia	21	4
Riadh Bouazizi	Kayseri Erciyesspor	33	7
Adel Chedli	Nuremberg	29	8
Karim Essediri	Tromso	26	2
Jawhar Mnari	Nuremberg	29	9
Mehdi Nafti	Birmingham	27	5
Hamed Namouchi	Rangers	22	3
Wajih Sghaier	Esperance	27	2
Majdi Traoui	Etoile Du S Sousse	22	1
Forwards			
Radhouene Benwannes	Monastir	26	1
Najeh Braham	Eintracht Trier	29	2
Francileudo Dos Santos	Toulouse	27	7
Haykel Gumemdia	Strasbourg	24	4
Ziad Jaziri	Troyes	27	5
Mohamed Jedidi	Etoile	27	2
Issam Jomaa	Lens	22	4
Imed Mhadhebi	Nantes	30	1
Ali Zitouni	Troyes	25	5

■ Probable ■ Possible **QG** Qualification Games

SAUDI ARABIA

ROUTE TO THE FINALS

Saudi Arabia qualified for their fourth consecutive World Cup with ease topping the final Asian Group A table with four wins from six.

They also remained unbeaten in the six preliminary qualifiers. Veteran striker Sami Al Jaber scored on his international comeback in their opening Group A game in Uzbekistan, a match that finished 1-1. The Saudis secured their place in the 2006 finals with a 3-0 home win over Uzbekistan last June.

They ended their qualifying campaign in style, beating South Korea 1-0 in Seoul to record a double over the 2002 World Cup semi-finalists. They had already beaten them 2-0 in Dammam. However, the demands of the Saudi authorities resulted in two coaching casualties before the team could prepare for the finals.

Former Argentinian World Cup star Gabriel Calderon replaced Gerard van der Lem as coach, after the Dutchman led them in a disappointing 2004 Asian Cup. However, despite guiding Saudi Arabia safely through, Calderon himself was sacked in December and replaced by Brazilian Marcos Paqueta.

The challnges of the coach are shown in that the Saudi side used 60 players in the course of qualifying, including some 20 midfielders.

FINAL QUALIFYING TABLE
ASIA STAGE 3 - GROUP A

	P	W	D	L	F	A	Pts
Saudi Arabia	6	4	2	0	10	1	14
South Korea	6	3	1	2	9	5	10
Uzbekistan	6	1	2	3	7	11	5
Kuwait	6	1	1	4	4	13	4

				FIFA ranking				
1	18 Feb 04	Home	Indonesia	95	W	3	0	I.Al Shahrani 4, 39, Al Qahtani 45
2	31 Mar 04	Away	Sri Lanka	141	W	0	1	I.Al Shahrani 51
3	09 Jun 04	Home	Turkmenistan	105	W	3	0	Al Meshal 27, 45, Noor Hawsawi 32
4	08 Sep 04	Away	Turkmenistan	105	W	0	1	Al Qahtani 47
5	12 Oct 04	Away	Indonesia	95	W	1	3	Al Meshal 9, O.Sulaimani 13, Al Qahtani 80
6	17 Nov 04	Home	Sri Lanka	141	W	3	0	S.Al Harthi 6, Al Shlhoub 45pen, F.Fallatah 65
7	09 Feb 05	Away	Uzbekistan	54	D	1	1	Al Jaber 76
8	25 Mar 05	Home	South Korea	89	W	2	0	Khariri 29, Al Qahtani 74
9	30 Mar 05	Away	Kuwait	59	D	0	0	
10	03 Jun 05	Home	Kuwait	59	W	3	0	Al Shlhoub 19, 50, S.Al Harthi 82
11	08 Jun 05	Home	Uzbekistan	54	W	3	0	Al Jaber 8, 61, M.Al Harthi 88
12	17 Aug 05	Away	South Korea	89	W	0	1	Al Anbar 4
Average FIFA ranking of opposition		**73**						

MAIN PLAYER PERFORMANCES IN QUALIFICATION

Match	1 2 3 4 5 6 7 8 9 10 11 12	Appearances	Started	Subbed on	Subbed off	Mins played	% played	Goals	Yellow	Red
Venue	H A H A A H A H A H H A									
Result	W W W W W W D W D W W W									
Goalkeepers										
Mohammad Sharifi		1	1	0	0	90	8.3	0	0	0
Mbrouk Zaid		8	8	0	0	720	66.7	0	0	0
Defenders										
Ahmed Al Bahri		6	6	0	0	540	50.0	0	0	0
Ahmed Dukhi Al Dossari		5	5	0	0	450	41.7	0	2	0
Hamad Al Montashari		9	9	0	1	805	74.5	0	0	0
Naif Al Qadi		6	5	1	0	507	46.9	0	3	0
Mishal Al Saeed		2	2	0	1	154	14.3	0	0	0
Saleh Al Saqri		3	2	1	1	173	16.0	0	0	0
Redha Tukar Fallatah		7	7	0	0	630	58.3	0	1	0
Midfielders										
Manaf Abushgeer		5	5	0	4	389	36.0	0	2	0
Saheb Al Abdullah		6	4	2	1	398	36.9	0	1	0
Khamis Al Dossari		5	5	0	1	436	40.4	0	1	0
Taiseer Al Jassam		5	4	1	1	386	35.7	0	0	0
Ibrahim Al Shahrani		5	3	2	1	274	25.4	3	1	0
Mohammad Al Shlhoub		7	5	2	3	450	41.7	3	0	0
Khaled Al Thaker		6	6	0	1	534	49.4	0	0	0
Saud Khariri		7	7	0	2	597	55.3	1	4	0
Abdulaziz Khathran		4	4	0	0	360	33.3	0	1	0
Mohamed Noor Hawsawi		3	3	0	2	247	22.9	1	1	0
Forwards										
Mohammad Al Anbar		1	1	0	0	90	8.3	1	0	0
Sami Al Jaber		5	4	1	2	336	31.1	3	0	0
Talal Al Meshal		5	4	1	2	316	29.3	3	0	0
Yasser Al Qahtani		9	9	0	4	770	71.3	4	2	0

FINAL PROSPECTS

Saudi Arabia have been drawn in one of the easier groups, along with Spain, Tunisia and Ukraine.

They lost all three group games at the 2002 World Cup, failed to score a goal and were humiliated 8-0 by Germany, who took advantage of a disorganised defence.

However, the Saudis proved during the qualifiers that they now possess a well-disciplined back line and have a highly rated goalkeeper in the shape of Mbrouk Zaid.

The team all play domestic football in the wealthy Saudi Premier League and are primarily drawn from three top clubs Al-Shabab, Al-Hilal, Al-Ittihad.

It will be Al Jaber's fourth World Cup. The 33-year-old scored three goals in four starts in qualifying. Striker Yasser Al Qahtani (nine starts, four goals) and Mohammad Al Shlhoub (a skilful left-sided playmaker) will support him.

THE MANAGER

Brazilian Marcos Paqueta was appointed Saudi Arabia head coach on a two-year contract following the surprise dismissal of Argentinian Gabriel Calderon in December.

Calderon had received heavy criticism in the Saudi media about his training methods and tactics, despite having led the country to the finals. He was sacked after the side's poor showing at the West Asian Games in Qatar.

New coach Paqueta has extensive local knowledge of Saudi football, having guided the Riyadh-based club Al-Hilal to a league and cup double last season.

Marcos Paqueta

GROUP FIXTURES

TUNISIA	Wed 14 June 1700 BST
UKRAINE	Mon 19 June 1700 BST
SPAIN	Fri 23 June 1500 BST

Zone	Asia
Population	26,870,654
Capital	Riyadh
Language	Arabic
Top league	Premier League
Major clubs	**Capacities**
Al Shabab	27,000
Al Wadda	33,500
Al-Ittihad	35,000

Where likely squad players play:

In Saudi Arabia	23

Number of Saudi Arabian players playing:

In Premiership	0
In other major five European Leagues	0

World Cup record

1930 -	Did not enter	1974 -	Did not enter
1934 -	Did not enter	1978 -	Did not qualify
1938 -	Did not enter	1982 -	Did not qualify
1950 -	Did not enter	1986 -	Did not qualify
1954 -	Did not enter	1990 -	Did not qualify
1958 -	Did not enter	1994 -	Last 16
1962 -	Did not enter	1998 -	Group 4th
1966 -	Did not enter	2002 -	Group 4th
1970 -	Did not enter		

THE SQUAD

Goalkeepers	Club side	Age	QG
Rashed Al Mugren	Al-Shabab	29	1
Mohammed Babkr	Al-Nasr	33	1
Mohammad Sharifi	Al-Nasr	33	1
Mbrouk Zaid	Al-Ittihad Joddah	27	8
Defenders			
Ali Al Abdali	Al-Ahly Jeddah	26	1
Ahmed Al Bahri	Al-Ittifaq Dammam	25	6
A Dukhi Al Dossari	Al-Ittihad Jeddah	29	5
Saod A A Al Khaibari	Al-Ahly Jeddah	25	1
Hamad Al Montashari	Al-Ittihad Jeddah	23	9
Naif Al Qadi	Al-Ahly Jeddah	27	6
Mishal Al Saeed	Al-Ittihad Jeddah	22	2
Saleh Al Saqri	Al-Ittihad Jeddah	27	3
Redha H Tukar Fallatah	Al-Ittihad Jeddah	20	7
Walid Jahdali	Al-Ahly Jeddah	24	2
Hussein Sulimani	Al-Ahly Jeddah	29	2
Ridha Tukar	Al Shabab	31	2
Midfielders			
Manaf Abushgeer	Al-Ittihad Jeddah	26	5
Saheb Al Abdullah	Al-Ahly Jeddah	28	6
Khamis A Al Dossari	Al-Ittihad Jeddah	32	5
Abdullatif Al Ghannam	Al-Shabab	20	2
Taiseer Al Jassam	Al-Ahly Jeddah	21	5
Ibrahim Al Shahrani	Al-Ittihad Jeddah	31	5
Nassir Al Shamrani	Al-Wahda Mekka	23	3
Mohammad Al Shlhoub	Al-Hilal Riyadh	25	7
Khaled Al Thaker	-	24	6
Abdoh Autef	Al-Shabab	22	1
Saud Khariri	Al-Ittihad Jeddah	25	7
Abdulaziz Khathran	Al-Hilal Riyadh	22	4
Mohamed N Hawsawi	Al-Ittihad Jeddah	28	3
Forwards			
Saad Al Harthi	Al-Nasr	22	2
Sami Al Jaber	Al-Hilal Riyadh	33	5
Talal Al Meshal	Al-Ahly Jeddah	28	5
Yasser Al Qahtani	Al-Hilal Riyadh	23	9
Mohammed Haidar	Al-Ittihad Jeddah	26	2
Mohammad Khojah	Ohod Madina	24	1
Naji Majrashi	Al-Shabab	22	1

■ Probable ■ Possible **QG** Qualification Games

KEY PLAYER

YASSER AL QAHTANI AL HILAL

Yasser Al Qahtani is Saudi Arabia's most expensive player, following his $10m (approx £6m) transfer from Al-Qadissiyah to top side Al-Hilal.

He has pace and runs at defences and is also useful in the air. Amid managerial changes, Saudi Arabia used nearly 60 players in qualifying but Qahtani notched up the most time on the pitch, playing 770 minutes in nine appearances and scoring four goals.

During qualifying, he played a crucial role in the first game against South Korea. He notched an assist for the first goal and won a penalty, from which he scored, for the second.

His partner in attack is Saudi's top scorer Sami Al Jaber – 42 goals so far.

AGE 23   **STRIKER**   **WORLD RANKING –**

4th
VICTOR VALDES
BARCELONA

Barcelona's Victor Valdes is one of the best young goalkeepers around.

He replaced Turkey international Rustu Recber as first-choice at the Nou Camp. Valdes' imperious form last season helped Barcelona sweep to the Primera Liga title.

One of a current crop of brilliant young Spanish keepers – the others being Iker Casillas (Real Madrid) and Jose Reina (Liverpool) – Valdes has the form book on his side but is currently third in line for the Spanish goalkeeping jersey.

Playing record	12 mths lge	wcf
Appearances:	32	0
Minutes played:	2880	0
Percentage played:	86.5%	0
Goals conceded:	27	-
Clean sheets:	19	-
Cards:	Y3, R0	Y0, R0

(Valdes hasn't played for Spain in the qualifiers so doesn't have a Defensive rating.)

3rd
OLIVER KAHN
BAYERN MUNICH

Bayern Munich's Oliver Kahn may be reaching the end of an illustrious career but he remains one of the great goalkeepers in the world.

He captained Germany at the 2002 World Cup final and although Brazil claimed the title, Kahn was voted the tournament's most valuable player. Jens Lehmann of Arsenal is challenging Kahn for the position as No 1 keeper in the Germany side. The two players hate each other, so their rivalry is personal and acrimonious.

Playing record	12 mths lge	int
Appearances:	34	9
Minutes played:	2975	840
Percentage played:	87.0%	50.9%
Goals conceded:	24	15
Clean sheets:	16	3
Cards:	Y2, R0	Y0, R0
Defensive rating:	124mins	56mins
Defensive ranking:	3rd	19th

2nd
GREGORY COUPET
LYON

France goalkeeper Gregory Coupet is a dominating character on the field and a strong personality in the dressing room.

He is an excellent shot stopper and has good all-round skills, but it is his desire to win that makes him one of Europe's top players. Lyon signed him from Saint-Etienne in 1997 and despite rumours of big money transfers, Coupet remained where he was to become the club's longest-serving player. He's finally stepped out as first choice for France after years in Fabien Barthez's shadow.

Playing record	12 mths lge	wcq
Appearances:	41	6
Minutes played:	3690	540
Percentage played:	95.3%	60.0%
Goals conceded:	32	1
Clean sheets:	17	5
Cards:	Y1, R0	Y0, R0
Defensive rating:	115mins	540mins
Defensive ranking:	5th	1st

AGE 24	WORLD RANKING 32

AGE 36	WORLD RANKING 20

AGE 33	WORLD RANKING 18

THE TOP GOALKEEPER

CZECH REPUBLIC **PETR CECH**

Petr Cech has enough records to start his own book. His debut season in the Premiership saw Chelsea win their first league title for 50 years.

Cech played all bar three of the league games, keeping a record 24 clean sheets; Chelsea conceded only 15 goals – a record and Cech only let in a goal every 242 minutes on average.

Playing record	12 mths lge	wcq
Appearances:	36	13
Minutes played:	3240	1170
Percentage played:	85.7%	92.9%
Goals conceded:	21	11
Clean sheets:	19	7
Cards:	Y0, R0	Y0, R0
Defensive rating:	154mins	106mins
Defensive ranking:	1st	13th

AGE 24 **CHELSEA** **WORLD RANKING 7**

1st

THE TEAMS

EUROPE – UEFA

  CROATIA
Population 4.5m **Sq km** 57,000
WC finals 2 **winners** 0

 CZECH REPUBLIC*
Population 10m **Sq km** 79,000
WC finals 8 **winners** 0

  ENGLAND
Population 60.5m **Sq km** 245,000
WC finals 11 **winners** 1

 FRANCE
Population 60.8m **Sq km** 547,000
WC finals 11 **winners** 1

 GERMANY*
Population 82.3m **Sq km** 357,000
WC finals 15 **winners** 3

 HOLLAND
Population 16.4m **Sq km** 42,000
WC finals 7 **winners** 0

 ITALY
Population 58.1m **Sq km** 301,000
WC finals 15 **winners** 3

 POLAND
Population 38.6m **Sq km** 313,000
WC finals 6 **winners** 0

 PORTUGAL
Population 10.6m **Sq km** 92,000
WC finals 3 **winners** 0

 SERBIA & MONTENEGRO*
Population 10.8m **Sq km** 92,000
WC finals 7 **winners** 0

 SPAIN
Population 40m **Sq km** 505,000
WC finals 11 **winners** 0

   SWEDEN
Population 9m **Sq km** 450,000
WC finals 10 **winners** 0

SWITZERLAND
Population 7.5m **Sq km** 41,000
WC finals 7 **winners** 0

UKRAINE
Population 46.8m **Sq km** 604,000
WC finals 0 **winners** 0

* includes records for countries of Czechoslovakia, West Germany
and Yugoslavia

AMERICA – CONCACAF

 ARGENTINA
Population 39.8m **Sq km** 2.8m
WC finals 13 **winners** 2

 BRAZIL
Population 187m **Sq km** 8.5m
WC finals 17 **winners** 5

 COSTA RICA
Population 4m **Sq km** 51,000
WC finals 2 **winners** 0

 ECUADOR
Population 13.5m **Sq km** 284,000
WC finals 1 **winners** 0

 MEXICO
Population 107m **Sq km** 2m
WC finals 12 **winners** 0

 PARAGUAY
Population 6.4m **Sq km** 407,000
WC finals 6 **winners** 0

 TRINIDAD & TOBAGO
Population 1m **Sq km** 5,000
WC finals 0 **winners** 0

USA
Population 297m **Sq km** 9.6m
WC finals 7 **winners** 0

AFRICA – CAF

 ANGOLA
Population 12m **Sq km** 1.2m
WC finals 0 **winners** 0

 IVORY COAST
Population 17.5m **Sq km** 322,000
WC finals 0 **winners** 0

 GHANA
Population 22.2m **Sq km** 239,000
WC finals 0 **winners** 0

 TOGO
Population 5.5m **Sq km** 57,000
WC finals 0 **winners** 0

TUNISIA
Population 10.1m **Sq km** 164,000
WC finals 3 **winners** 0

ASIA – AFC

  IRAN
Population 68.5m **Sq km** 1.6m
WC finals 2 **winners** 0

 JAPAN
Population 127m **Sq km** 378,000
WC finals 2 **winners** 0

 KOREA REPUBLIC
Population 48.8m **Sq km** 98,000
WC finals 6 **winners** 0

 SAUDI ARABIA
Population 26.9m **Sq km** 2m
WC finals 3 **winners** 0

OCEANIA – OFC

 AUSTRALIA
Population 20.1m **Sq km** 7.7m
WC finals 1 **winners** 0

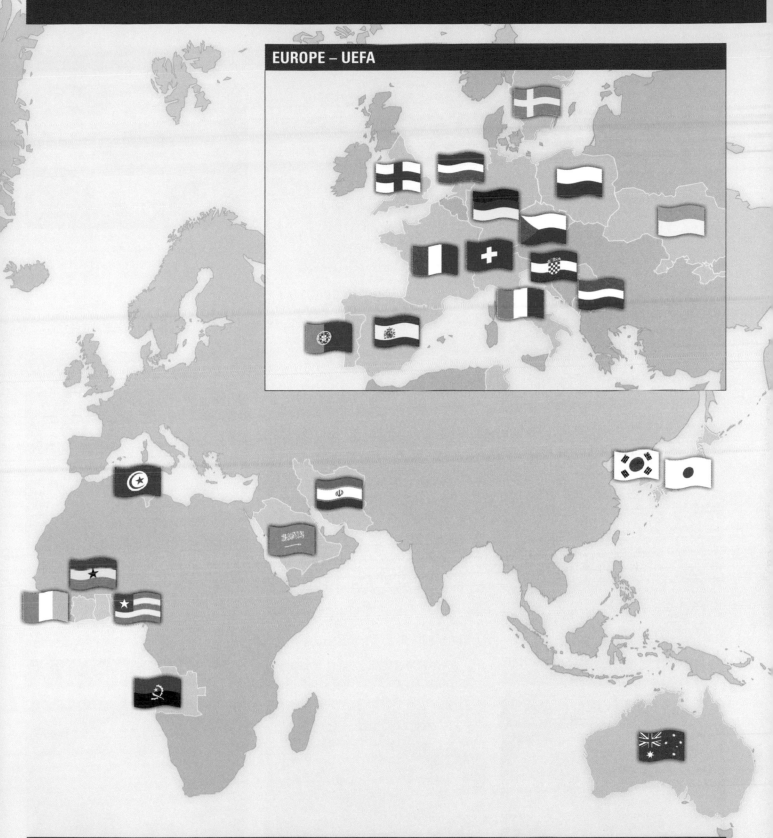

EUROPE – UEFA

PREVIOUS WINNERS & HOSTS

Year	Winners	Host	Year	Winners	Host	Year	Winners	Host
1930	Uruguay	Uruguay (South America)	1962	Brazil	Chile (South America)	1986	Argentina	Mexico (Central America)
1934	Italy	Italy (Europe)	1966	England	England (Europe)	1990	Germany	Italy (Europe)
1938	Italy	France (Europe)	1970	Brazil	Mexico (Central America)	1994	Brazil	US (North America)
1950	Uruguay	Brazil (S. America)	1974	Germany	Germany (Europe)	1998	France	France (Europe)
1954	Germany	Switzerland (Europe)	1978	Argentina	Argentina (South America)	2002	Brazil	Japan/S.Korea (Asia)
1958	Brazil	Sweden (Europe)	1982	Italy	Spain (Europe)	2006		Germany (Europe)

STADIUMS

3 DORTMUND

Stadium	Westfalenstadion
Capacity	66,981
Club team	Borussia Dortmund
City population	590,000

Matches

Trinidad & Tobago v Sweden, Germany v Poland, Togo v Switzerland, Japan v Brazil, 2nd round, Semi-final

4 FRANKFURT

Stadium	Waldstadion
Capacity	48,132
Club team	Eintracht Frankfurt
City population	650,000

Matches

England v Paraguay, South Korea v Togo. Portugal v Iran, Holland v Argentina, Quarter-final

1 BERLIN

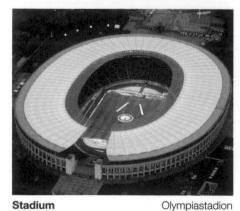

Stadium	Olympiastadion
Capacity	74,176
Club team	Hertha Berlin
City population	3.39m

Matches

Brazil v Croatia, Sweden v Paraguay, Ecuador v Germany, Ukraine v Tunisia, Quarter-final, Final

2 COLOGNE

Stadium	Volksparkstadion
Capacity	51,055
Club team	FC Cologne
City population	1m

Matches

Angola v Portugal, Czech Republic v Ghana, Sweden v England, Togo v France, 2nd round

5 GELSENKIRCHEN

Stadium	Arena AufSchalke
Capacity	53,804
Club team	FC Schalke
City population	278,000

Matches

Poland v Ecuador, USA v Czech Republic, Argentina v Serbia & Montenegro, Portugal v Mexico, Quarter-final

6 HAMBURG

Stadium	Hamburg Stadium
Capacity	51,055
Club team	Hamburg SV
City population	1.7m

Matches

Argentina v Ivory Coast, Ecuador v Costa Rica, Saudi Arabia v Ukraine, Czech Republic v Italy, Quarter-final

7 HANOVER

Stadium	Niedersachsenstadion
Capacity	44,652
Club team	Hannover 96
City population	525,000

Matches

Italy v Ghana, Mexico v Angola, Costa Rica v Poland, Switzerland v South Korea, 2nd round

8 KAISERSLAUTEN

Stadium	Fritz-Walter-Stadion
Capacity	41,170
Club team	FC Kaiserslauten
City population	100,000

Matches

Australia v Japan, Italy v USA, Paraguay v Trinidad & Tobago, Saudi Arabia v Spain, 2nd round

9 LEIPZIG

Stadium	Zentralstadion
Capacity	44,199
Club team	VfB Leipzig
City population	494,000

Matches

Serbia & Montenegro v Holland, Spain v Ukraine, France v South Korea, Iran v Angola, 2nd round

10 MUNICH

Stadium	Allianz Arena
Capacity	66,016
Club team	Bayern Munich & Munich 1860
City population	1.3m

Matches

Germany v Costa Rica, Tunisia v Saudi Arabia, Brazil v Australia, Ivory Coast v Serbia & Montenegro, 2nd round, Semi-final

11 NUREMBERG

Stadium	Franken-Stadion
Capacity	41,926
Club team	FC Nuremberg
City population	490,000

Matches

Mexico v Iran, England v Trinidad & Tobago, Japan v Croatia, Ghana v USA, 2nd round

12 STUTTGART

Stadium	Gottlieb-Dailmer-Stadion
Capacity	54,267
Club team	VfB Stuttgart
City population	590,000

Matches

France v Switzerland, Holland v Ivory Coast, Spain v Tunisia, Croatia v Australia, 2nd round, 3rd place.

OTHER BOOKS YOU MAY BE INTERESTED IN

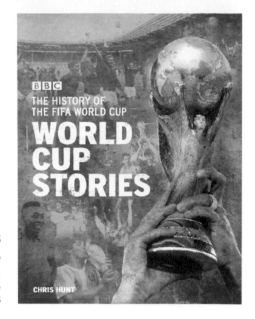

WORLD CUP STORIES

A HISTORY OF THE FIFA WORLD CUP
Based on the BBC Television series.
Price: £19.95
Publication date: 30 March 2006

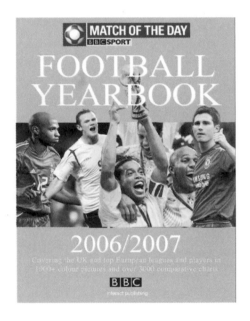

THE MATCH OF THE DAY
FOOTBALL YEARBOOK
2006-2007
The most comprehensive review of the football
season – and the first book out with all the
World Cup action.
Price: £19.99
Publication date: 28 July 2006

THE MATCH OF THE DAY
OFFICIAL ANNUAL
2006
The top 100 players in the world - revealed.
Price: £6.99
Publication date: 28 September 2006

Check out the Interact Publishing website
www.footballyearbook.co.uk